American Conservative Opinion Leaders

American Conservative Opinion Leaders

edited by Mark J. Rozell
and James F. Pontuso

Westview Press
Boulder • San Francisco • London

Epigraph on p. 233 from "Burnt Norton" in *Four Quartets,* copyright 1943 by T. S. Eliot and renewed 1971 by Esme Valerie Eliot, reprinted by permission of Harcourt Brace Jovanovich, Inc., and Faber and Faber Ltd.

Published in 1990 in the United States of America by Westview Press, Inc., 5500 Central Avenue, Boulder, Colorado 80301, and in the United Kingdom by Westview Press, Inc., 13 Brunswick Centre, London WC1N 1AF, England

Library of Congress Cataloging-in-Publication Data
American conservative opinion leaders/edited by Mark J. Rozell and
James F. Pontuso.
   p.   cm.
  ISBN 0-8133-0942-5
  1. Conservatism—United States—History—20th century. 2. United
States—Politics and government—1989–   . 3. Journalists—United
States—Attitudes—History—20th century. 4. Political scientists—
United States—Attitudes—History—20th century. 5. Public
opinion—United States—History—20th century. I. Rozell, Mark J.
II. Pontuso, James F.
E881.A44 1990
320.5′2—dc20   89-22609
                                                                                    CIP

Printed and bound in the United States of America

The paper used in this publication meets the requirements of the American National
Standard for Permanence of Paper for Printed Library Materials Z39.48-1984.

10   9   8   7   6   5   4   3   2   1

Contents

Preface

This book grew out of our discussions in 1988 about what would happen to American conservatism at the end of the Reagan era. We concluded that a study of the political ideas of America's leading conservative opinion leaders was in order. Only through such an examination could we understand the state of American conservative thought and the prospects for a political movement that was so influential during the Reagan years.

A second purpose of examining these opinion leaders is to display the rich diversity of thought present in modern American conservatism. For critics of the political Right who believe that the conservative coalition is monolithic and devoid of serious internal criticism, the chapters that follow should be eye-opening. The philosophical differences among conservatives are profound. Indeed, many conservatives devote more of their intellectual energies debating one another than they do criticizing the political Left.

Such internal debate is both a strength and a weakness. Political ideas must withstand scrutiny. Political thinkers often heed most seriously those criticisms leveled by their philosophical allies. Nonetheless, this kind of criticism from within can leave a political movement that is based on ideas splintered, leaderless and close to disarray. That appears to be the condition of the American conservative movement in the post-Reagan era.

Because the individuals studied in this book are well known and controversial, much of what is written about them is highly polemical and motivated by ideological considerations. Many of these analyses are found in such journals as *The Nation, National Review, The New Republic, Commentary, Partisan Review, American Spectator* and the *New York Review of Books*. Although the role that these and other leading journals play in the intellectual debate is important, our goal is significantly different: We seek to present original and balanced chapters.

A number of people helped this work come to fruition. We would like to take the unaccustomed step of thanking the contributors, whose diligence and insights made the book better than any we could have written on our own.

Sally Furgeson, our acquisitions editor at Westview Press, took a great deal of interest in this project from its inception and provided helpful insights throughout the important stages of manuscript development. Westview editors Jane Raese and Amy Eisenberg provided much-needed guidance through the book's completion. Jan Kristiansson did a most thorough job of copyediting the manuscript. Westview Press's two anonymous reviewers offered outstanding recommendations for revisions. Many of their suggestions were heeded by the contributors.

The following individuals read Chapters 2, 8 and 9 and offered helpful comments and criticisms: Kenneth W. Thompson, James Sterling Young (University of Virginia); John M. Kramer, Michele M. McClain (Mary Washington College); and Lynda M. Rozell (Hunton & Williams). Donna Packard provided much-needed and efficient typing assistance. Judy W. Singleton, Sherril O'Brien and Elizabeth Hoag thoroughly proofread the manuscript. Edythe Porpa produced the index.

The Mary Washington College Faculty Development Grant Committee, Hampden-Sydney College, the University of Virginia Raven Society Research Fellowship program and the White Burkett Miller Center of Public Affairs provided financial support for this book.

We would like to thank our wives. Lynda M. Rozell critically reviewed her husband's chapters and tolerated his constant queries on grammar. Anne M. Pontuso, R.N., C.C.R.N., shared her husband with his constant companion—a computer.

Mark J. Rozell
Vienna, Virginia

James F. Pontuso
Charlottesville, Virginia

1

Introduction:
Conservatism After Reagan

James F. Pontuso

As Ronald Reagan boarded the plane for his return to California on January 20, 1989, he left behind a triumphant political movement. Although some were pleased to see him depart, his conservative allies could take pride in the Reagan years. Under his presidency the nation had enjoyed a span of economic prosperity unprecedented in the post–World War II era. He had limited the expansion of the welfare state and reversed the trend toward a bigger and more intrusive national government. No new countries had fallen to Marxism-Leninism, and some had abandoned the doctrine altogether as Reagan had predicted they would in his 1981 speech before the British Parliament. Even the Soviet Union seemed to falter in its adherence to communism. During Reagan's tenure, a new leadership emerged in the Soviet Union that was far more willing to compromise with the West. Not only did the Soviets agree to pull their medium-range nuclear weapons out of Europe; they pledged to withdraw from Afghanistan and Angola. From the perspective of many conservatives, Reagan's military buildup and tough rhetoric had worked well. In order to keep up with American military spending, the Soviets were forced to choose a dynamic leader, Mikhail Gorbachev, who could reform their badly functioning economy. But even Gorbachev's charm could not transform the backwardness of the Soviet economic system without allowing greater political and social freedoms. Thus, a number of conservatives credited Reagan's policies with having brought about Gorbachev's reforms.

Reagan also had restored faith in the American system of government. His simple message proclaimed that the days of confusion, distrust and malaise were gone; "America was back." People responded to Reagan, for even when he bumbled, he was too affable to dislike. Confidence in government grew steadily during the 1980s, despite the setback of the Iran-contra controversy. The public perceived that Reagan's leadership produced successful government.

Whether or not Reagan's good fortune was due to luck, as his critics charged, his personal and political achievements had an effect on the nation's public agenda. For all his faults, some say because of them, Reagan led a reappraisal of America's political principles. So complete was his political achievement that the Democratic candidate for president in 1988 was reluctant to call himself a liberal, the political philosophy that had dominated the United States for more than fifty years.

Yet not everything that occurred during the Reagan years pleased conservatives. What galled them most was that having gained the nation's highest office, they were unable to fully carry through the social changes that had been so much a part of their credo. Although the Reagan Administration had some success in arresting the growth of the national government, there was no fundamental shift in public policy as occurred during the New Deal era. Legislation on the "moral issues," such as school prayer and abortion, was quickly abandoned, the military buildup came to a halt, and, in spite of the spending cuts, most government programs were kept in place.

What dashed the high hopes for major change that conservatives experienced in the heady days of 1980? A number of explanations come to mind. First, it could be that conservatives, so long in the political wilderness of American politics, became accustomed to their role as critics. Indeed, it is possible that conservative criticisms of the failures of the welfare state and of the weaknesses of America's military, rather than a positive vision of the future, were tactics designed to carry a conservative administration into office. Few people are likely to give up a tactic on which their past successes are based. And as it turned out, conservatives were better at criticizing than making the system work to their benefit.

Second, the much-heralded Republican realignment did not come about. Despite President Reagan's personal popularity, his party was not able to translate his charisma into broad-scale support for Republican candidates and principles. Whether this was because political parties were so weak that they could no longer reflect shifts in public opinion, or because the public was unwilling to follow Reagan down the conservative path, is presently unclear. What is beyond debate is that after some initial successes, the President had to scratch, twist and compromise for every legislative victory he won. The Administration's policy toward Nicaragua is a prime example. When the president, the cornerstone of whose foreign policy was to prevent the spread of Communist dictatorships, was unable to convince Congress to appropriate a paltry sum to aid opponents of a Communist dictatorship in this hemisphere, surely his clout with the legislative branch ought not to be overestimated.

Furthermore, for all his popularity, Reagan did not prove as effective as conservatives would have liked. Critics characterized him as an absentee president.[1] He delegated much of his authority to subordinates and almost never rebuked them. This made it nearly impossible to enforce discipline on the bureaucracy. Rather than through an orderly decisionmaking process, the Reagan Administration made policy through intense bureaucratic power struggles. The winner of that competition was not always the department with the best policy but the one with the most persistence and shrewdness in the ways of bureaucratic infighting. It was perhaps no surprise that the Administration was caught unaware of the arms-for-hostages scheme carried out in the National Security Council. Whether his inability to control the bureaucracy adequately stemmed from his leadership style—he was too nice a guy to fire anyone—or whether this inability was the result of his being too old to compel order within the executive branch made little difference to those who once expected Reagan to bring about a "revolution" in government.[2]

Nor did Reagan prove himself to be as conservative as many had initially hoped. After a halfhearted effort to put prayer back in public schools and to make abortion a matter of public rather than personal choice, he abandoned the field of "moral issues" to Senator Jesse Helms (R–N.C.) and such "New Right" leaders as the Evangelical ministers. For all the much-vaunted military buildup, Reagan was nearly as reluctant as President Jimmy Carter to exercise force as an instrument of foreign policy. Only once in eight years did he initiate a military strike against a terrorist state. The Intermediate-Range Nuclear Forces Treaty to reduce nuclear weapons in Europe showed that he was as willing to negotiate an arms deal with the Soviets as were his predecessors. And even with his success in cutting the rate of growth of the national government, he was not able to bring federal expenditures under control. Although criticisms of the President from the Right often were muted, Reagan's actions did not go unnoticed in the conservative camp.[3]

Beyond the problems of leadership, there were other unsettling difficulties facing the political Right. Conservatives were badly divided among themselves, which made a political consensus extremely difficult. The conservative coalition includes free marketeers, who want government intruding less into our private lives, and those interested in "moral issues," who would give the state more authority over our personal choices. There are fiscal conservatives, who favor a balanced budget, as opposed to supply-siders, who care less about spending than they do about stimulating the economy. There is, of course, the foreign policy debate. Is Soviet Russia the real threat to our security or is Marxism-Leninism? Those who see the Soviet Union as the challenge to American power call for tough, but not uncompromising measures to thwart Soviet power. Others see communism itself as an intractable ideological enemy of the West, one that must be fought and defeated wherever it exists if our way of life is to survive. Free-market conservatives, many of whom advocate trade with all nations, have been severely criticized by other conservatives who argue that open economic exchanges with the Soviet bloc undermine our national security.[4] There are even some neoconservatives, such as former U.N. Ambassador Jeane Kirkpatrick, who are on the Right in foreign policy issues but who part company with the movement on domestic affairs.

Any coalition, especially a ruling one, has disparate elements within it. The New Deal coalition, which included African-Americans as well as those from the solid segregationist South, demonstrated that politics makes strange bedfellows. But unlike the New Deal alliance, which was held together primarily on the basis of the (monetary) interests that its constituent groups gained by their party affiliation, the contemporary conservative partnership is mainly ideological. The members of the New Deal coalition had a common stake in submerging their ideological differences in the hope of gaining material benefits; the conservative alliance has no such binding interest.

In Great Britain it was once said that conservatives made up "the stupid party," for its members had held power so long that they thoughtlessly defended the status quo. In the United States this does not seem to be true. Conservatism was in such ill-repute for many years after the Great Depression that conservatives were forced to defend their views more vigorously than were liberals, who assumed that their ideas embodied the wave of the future. Conservatives became more original and innovative. Certainly they became more accustomed to the world of ideas, much as liberals (then called Progressives) had during the late nineteenth and early twentieth centuries when their principles were not held in high esteem.

Of course, one of the signs of the strength and vibrancy of the conservative movement is its rich variety and diversity of members. Yet, this diversity can cause political difficulties. Because conservatives hold their political views primarily on the basis of their principles, when those ideals are in conflict, the coalition is bound to be torn by bitter internal struggles. These battles did not emerge throughout most of the 1980s because of the eclectic personality of Ronald Reagan, who, as is true of many popular leaders, seemed to be all things to all people.

It is therefore a propitious time to investigate conservative principles. What is happening to the conservative movement after Reagan? Who are its leaders? What ideas are guiding its choice of actions? Where are the conflicts and where are the agreements among conservatives?

Before any of these issues can be addressed it is important to have a working definition of "conservative." Or, to put it as a Socratic question, what is conservatism? The answer to this question is not so simple as it may seem. For example, when Ronald Reagan came to power promising to cut the size of the government, decentralize administration, strengthen the free-market system, and limit the power of the bureaucracy, he was called a conservative. When Mikhail Gorbachev adopted many of the same policies, he was praised for his reforms and called a liberal.

One fairly common explanation of conservatism is that it wishes to support the status quo. All political action aims either at conservation—keeping things the way they are—or change—modifying them in hopes of making them better. But even here we cannot find a solid definition of conservatism. Reagan came to office as a visionary reformer. Far from wishing to conserve, he wanted to change the course of public policy. Moreover, free-market conservatives hardly consider stagnation a good thing. They favor innovation and change as a means of bringing about increased productivity. New technologies result in new ways of doing things, and this has the effect of making profound shifts in the structure of society and even can transform government.

The confusion over the meaning of conservatism is even more acute in the United States, where no conservative establishment has ever really held power. In fact, many Americans came to this country in order to escape the restrictive confines of conservative social structures.

In order to understand the older form of conservatism, we should turn to Europe prior to the Enlightenment. There, the governmental and religious authorities were not separated as they are today. The goal of the Church was to produce pious parishioners, and the aim of the state was to cultivate good citizens. The governmental, social and religious institutions used their united power and prestige to shape the character of individuals through the application of strict laws and codes of conduct to all aspects of human behavior. The government intruded into the everyday lives of people. Not only did it tell them what was lawful; it commanded the religion they should follow, the morals they should hold dear, the station in the social hierarchy they should keep, the professions they should pursue, and even the price they should charge for their goods (the fair-market price).

The Enlightenment was in many ways a reaction against the rigid framework of the "ancien regime." The philosophers of the Enlightenment called for the liberation of the human species, which would be possible if what was said to be higher than human—hence beyond human control—was rejected in favor of what humans could sense— that is, the material world that could be brought under human command. To accomplish their goals, these philosophers realized that mankind had to be emancipated from the authority of the Church. During the centuries of Christian rule, religious leaders had done little to oppose superstition, prejudice and ignorance among the people. On the contrary, the priests retained their position by keeping the flock backward and innocent. In a deeper sense, the position of the clergy rested on a belief that existence was governed by the laws of God. For the religious person, human beings were only objects of His creation, and their duty was to accept life as it was given to them.

The Enlightenment philosophers rebelled against the supine acceptance of human destiny. They proposed that the wretched surroundings in which most people existed could be surmounted once the power of the clergy was broken and all people learned to think for themselves. Further, the belief that human beings should not question divine laws had to be destroyed. Rather than understanding themselves as part of nature, people would see themselves as its lord. In this way, the laws of nature could be studied and then used to satisfy people's physical needs. The human race would be relieved of the constant struggle to provide for the necessities of life. Degradation, poverty and ignorance would be at an end.

The Enlightenment philosophers argued that intellectual pursuits had to be stripped of their normative content. In this view, science should show people how nature worked, not attempt to educate them as to the best use of this knowledge. The discoveries of science could be turned into technological inventions that, as Francis Bacon said, would relieve "man's estate." At the same time, a stable political foundation was to be constructed by turning people's attention away from matters that were likely to make them combative, such as theological disputes, and toward those matters that would make them peaceful, for example, commerce. Dedication to religion and morality was to be replaced by a rational calculation of self-interest, and concern over spiritual matters was to be kept a strictly private matter. Thus, the Enlightenment was based on the principle of giving people what they wanted: peace and material comforts.

The Enlightenment's principles found their political expression in the doctrine of Liberalism. The satisfaction of human desires could best be accomplished, according to Liberalism, if people were left alone to pursue their own interests in their own ways. All unnecessary hindrances to people's ambitions were to be removed. The government's major functions were to enforce contracts and to ensure that the contest for economic gain did not go so far as to upset the peace. The fundamental goal of such a state was to secure a realm of liberty, so that in their private lives people could live as they chose—hence, the name Liberalism.

The American Founders were devoted to the ideals of the Enlightenment. The Declaration of Independence was more than an instrument of separation from Great Britain; it was a symbol of the Enlightenment's aspirations and a clarion call for the liberation of the human race from the restrictive convenants of the past. The framers of the Constitution hoped that the "new political science," as Publius called it in *The Federalist,* would solve the problems of instability and turmoil that had haunted all free societies in the past. Making the Declaration a reality also meant allowing for something like a free economic system, one that left the individual unhampered to pursue his or her own interests and develop his or her own talents to the fullest.

From its very beginnings, then, the United States had a tradition of granting its citizens liberty. The tradition of America, therefore, has been Liberalism. Insofar as American conservatives pay allegiance to their political heritage, they are really liberals, as that term was originally understood.

The problem is that what it means to be a liberal has changed over time. Thomas Jefferson, perhaps the greatest "liberal" of his day, would certainly be shocked at the agenda of contemporary liberals. Although he warned against the growth of government, fearing its tendency to degenerate into tyranny, today's liberals seek a solution for many human problems by turning to the national government. At least in the economic arena, they are the ones who would have the government intrude on the liberty of the citizens.

Conservatism and the Difficulty of Defining the Common Good

All of this brings us to a consideration of the most difficult question facing conservatives: How do they define the common good? In an interesting article written prior to her conversion to the Republican Party, Jeane Kirkpatrick explained that the underlying flaw of the Republican Party, and by implication American conservatism, was that it had no notion of the common good.[5] The principle most strongly endorsed by conservatives has been personal freedom. But personal freedom can be, and often is, used to satisfy the most selfish desires. Although the love of freedom may elicit self-sacrifice, there is no compelling reason people will use their freedom to promote the good of the whole. The political manifestation of the weakness of conservatism has been its inability to overcome the liberal charge that it is a movement of the rich and selfish, that it is heartless, and that it does not care about the common people.[6]

Conservatives seem to realize that more is called for among the citizens of a nation than just the pursuit of self-interest. Although conservatism has been labeled a movement with no notion of the common good, conservatives attack liberals for having the wrong notion of the common good. Conservatives argue that liberals define the common good as the equitable distribution of material goods. There is nothing in that principle that elevates people to care for the nation or even to develop their own skills to the fullest.

Reagan's revival of old-fashioned patriotism and dedication to country was an example of conservatism's longing to bring a higher, spiritual or moral message into political life. For Reagan, patriotism was the means of overcoming private self-interest and of making duties to one's country and fellow citizens of greater worth than the concern for individual rights. Yet the principle used by Reagan to prompt patriotic feelings was a commitment to freedom. As we have seen, however, there is nothing in the principle of freedom that necessarily leads to dedication to the common good. Indeed, Reagan was the most successful at promoting patriotism when he could show that the American way of life was threatened by a hostile power, Soviet communism, and ironically when he praised the American people for their ingenuity and industriousness. Evidently, Americans are most dedicated to their country when they are afraid or when they are pursuing their own material gain.

Only on the "moral issues" was there any hint of the old conservatism in which the state dictated moral behavior. Such restrictions have never been true to the spirit of America's political principles. Perhaps this was why Reagan was able to carry through many of his economic reforms, which returned some autonomy to the individual, and build up the military, which was essential for protecting people from foreign threats to the American way of life, but was unable to enact restrictions on freedom of choice, such as laws banning abortion or requiring school prayer.

In many ways, Reagan's successes and failures are indicative of the foremost tension within American conservatism—the desire to preserve liberty, on the one hand, and the urge to ensure moral order, on the other. In one way or another, conservatives of whatever ilk seem to have confronted this dilemma. As the chapters in this book show, the solutions to this difficulty have not always been easy.

Obviously, these problems are not the only matters that unite conservatives. What do they have in common? First, it is not true to say, as many do, that American conservatives fear government. It is more accurate to say that they fear the vices of human beings. Both government and citizens must be restrained, according to conservatives, because if given the opportunity, nearly every person will be tempted to abuse his or her position. Conservatives tend to subscribe to the principle that there is a certain constancy of human nature—including its darker aspects. Therefore, there is both a need for government in order to restrain people and a fear of government because leaders, too, are people and therefore need to be restrained.

Conservatives take as a given that human beings are self-interested; thus, they do not subscribe to the indefinite progress of the human race. They do not believe that all social reforms, no matter how well intended, will usher in better conditions. In fact, many reforms are so impractical that they are likely to lead to worse conditions than would have occurred if matters were just left alone. Nevertheless, conservatives do tend to believe in individual responsibility. People can use their talents and wills to improve themselves and even develop a certain excellence of character. The reform of society may be impossible, but the development of the individual is not.

Conservatives seem more aware of the fragility of decent political communities than do other groups within the political spectrum. To flourish, decent governments need to be protected from outside threats and internal dissension. Conservatives are willing to pay allegiance to unsophisticated notions, such as patriotism, because these impulses act as counterweights to the all-too-human desire to seek nothing but self-interest.

The chapters in this book present the ideas of many of America's leading conservative thinkers. Limitations of space make it impossible to introduce every shade of conservative thought or every important conservative thinker, but the ideas of some of the most consequential conservative opinion leaders are reflected in these pages. The authors have made no effort to build up or tear down the conservative movement. They have attempted to offer a balanced and critical look at the strengths and weaknesses of one of the most important intellectual movements of our time.

Notes

1. See, for example, Thomas P. O'Neill, *Man of the House: The Life and Political Memoirs of Speaker Tip O'Neill* (New York: St. Martin's Press, 1987), pp. 401–402.

2. In his *The Triumph of Politics: Why the Reagan Revolution Failed* (New York: Harper & Row, 1986), former Office of Management and Budget director David A. Stockman details the basis for his admittedly naive expectation that Reagan's 1980 election would initiate a "revolution."

3. For an appraisal of the Reagan years, see Charles O. Jones, ed., *The Reagan Legacy: Promise and Performance* (Chatham, N.J.: Chatham House, 1988), especially pp. 172–192; John L. Palmer, ed., *Perspectives on the Reagan Years* (Washington, D.C.: Urban Institute Press, 1988); B. B. Kymlicka and Jean V. Matthews, *The Reagan Revolution?* (Chicago: Dorsey Press, 1988).

4. The free-trade versus national security debate was particularly intense during the controversy over whether the Reagan Administration should lift the grain embargo imposed on the Soviet Union by President Carter.

5. Jeane Kirkpatrick, "Why We Don't Become Republicans," *Commonsense* 2, no. 3 (Fall 1979): 27–35.

6. Michael Kinsley argued that "Reagan's cutbacks of government aid reflect an abandonment of notions of social obligation, if the words 'social' and 'obligation' have any nuance at all" (quoted in William A. Shambra, "From Self-Interest to Local Social Obligation: Local Communities v. National Community," in Mary P. Nichols, ed., *Readings in American Government* [Dubuque, Iowa: Kendall/Hunt, 1983], p. 83).

PART ONE

Conservatism and Tradition

American conservative thought is characterized by a profound dilemma: the desire to pass on certain conservative principles and the need to make those principles relevant to the modern era. Inherent in this dilemma is a conservative debate over the principles themselves. Lest there remain any doubt about the degree of internal dissension within American conservatism, Mark J. Rozell's chapter on George F. Will shows that conservatives cannot even agree on the role that government should play in society. When Will argued that true conservatism is characterized by big government and welfare-state programs, he was lambasted by other self-styled conservatives who no longer considered Will one of their own.

As James F. Pontuso demonstrates, Russell Kirk may have laid, in the 1950s, the foundation for today's successful conservative movement. Kirk did not consciously spearhead a political movement; he instead developed a core of appealing American conservative ideas by taking his cues from the eighteenth-century English thinker Edmund Burke. Pontuso's chapter raises fundamental questions about the implications of following Kirk's reliance on tradition as a source of wisdom.

William F. Buckley, Jr., is the most familiar proponent of American conservative thought. John Wesley Young attributes Buckley's success in part to the *National Review* founder's marketable personality. But Young also makes clear that Buckley understood early that ideas rule the world and worked prodigiously to popularize conservative ideas. Buckley's ideas may lack "theoretical depth" and his philosophy may be characterized by inconsistencies. Nonetheless, Buckley has achieved his goal of playing a leading part in making conservatism fashionable.

Edward Banfield is primarily an academic theorist. Yet Banfield's writings have influenced numerous conservative opinion leaders. He

11

has been the teacher of many conservative scholars, including James Q. Wilson. David E. Marion focuses on a major theme of four decades of Banfield's scholarship—the inherent problems arising out of progressive thought and democratic utopianism. Like Russell Kirk, Edward Banfield is an admirer of Burke. Marion questions whether Banfield's reliance upon circumstances and good fortune, combined with a conviction that depreciates what can be achieved through human invention, leads to nihilism or cynicism.

The clash of traditionalist conservative values with the modern era is highlighted by the current controversies over abortion and AIDS policy. Roger M. Barrus points out that the former Surgeon General of the United States, C. Everett Koop, has been a central opinion leader in these two policy areas since the Reagan-Bush era began. Koop's efforts as a policymaker–opinion leader to be pragmatic in his responses to the abortion and AIDS controversies have opened him up to conservative criticisms of inconsistency. Yet Koop has been consistent in his altruism and selfless devotion to the welfare of all who suffer. Barrus's chapter reveals that to adequately confront complex social and medical issues in the modern era, traditionalist values are essential. Modernism therefore needs traditionalism, and traditionalists need to be pragmatic in their approaches to modern society's problems.

2

George F. Will's
"Tory" Conservatism

Mark J. Rozell

Political commentator George F. Will is one of America's most respected opinion leaders. His biweekly syndicated columns and bimonthly *Newsweek* articles won him the Pulitzer Prize for commentary in 1977. In addition, the members of the U.S. Congress and their staffs voted Will their most admired journalist in a 1983 *Washington Journalism Review* poll.

Will's credentials as a political commentator are impressive. By his twenty-sixth year Will had completed two bachelor's degrees, a master's degree in philosophy at Magdalene College of Oxford University, and a Ph.D. in political science at Princeton University, where he wrote what he calls a "sprawling, undisciplined, garrulous" dissertation on political tolerance.[1] Will later taught political science for a few years at Michigan State University and at the University of Toronto. He became "exasperated with the academic climate" and left teaching to work as an aide to Senator Gordon Allott (R–Colo.).[2] From 1970 to 1972 Will wrote speeches and did research for the senator, who in 1972 lost a bid for a fourth term. Will then joined *National Review*'s editorial staff and outraged the magazine's loyal Republican audience by attacking President Richard Nixon's Watergate statements as "mental whiplash" and an "indigestible mess."[3] Will proudly recalls that on July 5, 1973, as a commentator on "Agronsky and Company" he called for Nixon's impeachment, thereby becoming the nation's first political columnist to state that position.[4] At that time Will was already writing a weekly column for the *Washington Post*. A year later he began a bimonthly column for *Newsweek*. Will's syndicated column now reaches hundreds of newspapers nationwide. He also appears regularly as a discussant on ABC's "This Week with David Brinkley."

For many conservatives who believe that the nation's news media project a liberal bias, George F. Will's success as a political commentator makes him suspect. Will, in fact, is a self-styled political and cultural conservative. Yet much of the criticism of Will's thought comes from other self-professed "conservatives." For example, *National Review*'s Joseph Sobran accuses Will of shrewdly positioning himself for favorable treatment by the "liberal press." In Sobran's view, "Will is on the side of the liberal angels."[5] In a review of Will's *Statecraft as Soulcraft,* Sobran objects strongly to Will's brand of conservatism:

> This is conservatism properly understood? I call it toothless, coffee-table Toryism, nicely calculated for liberal consumption. . . . The enemies of conservatism will be only too glad to grant its author diplomatic recognition as the representative of a cause they hate, as "spokesman," for people they prefer not to hear from. The worst of it is, he seems to be auditioning for the role.[6]

In another article featured in *National Review,* M. J. Sobran, Jr. proclaims that Will, "an almost unabashed sourpuss," is "openly disdainful" of the concerns of most conservatives.[7] *Human Events* writer Allan H. Ryskind claims that Will "sails under false colors." Political commentator Kevin P. Phillips calls Will a "creature" of the *Washington Post.*[8] James Neuchterlein writes in *Commentary* that Will often "sound[s] like a closet liberal."[9] Finally, *Modern Age* writer Samuel T. Francis argues that Will rejects classical conservatism's skepticism of administrative centralization because such a position "would defeat [Will's] pragmatic purpose by alienating and frightening the liberal and establishment elites he is trying to impress."[10]

It must seem peculiar that a number of philosophical conservatives often harshly criticize America's most widely recognized conservative commentator. An examination of Will's brand of conservatism clarifies the sources of these criticisms. I disagree with critics who argue that Will adopts positions only to gain favor with "establishment elites." Such accusations trivialize Will's ideas. In what follows, I ignore the issue of Will's motivations and instead clarify the controversy over Will's conservatism by identifying the major tenets of his political philosophy. I assess how well Will's philosophy fits within the tradition of American conservative thought and discuss whether his political alternatives are viable.

The argument presented here is twofold. First, Will's project is noble in that he seeks to elevate the American political experience beyond notions of pure self-interest. In Will's view, public policymaking should be more than just an aggregation of self-interested groups pursuing narrow agendas. Will rejects the alternatives posed by modern-day liberals and conservatives because both glorify selfishness and fail to articulate a coherent vision of the public good.

Second, despite the virtue of his project, Will fails to advance a viable prescription for the ills that he identifies. Will's conception of citizenship, which requires a vigilant attention to the public good, is not consistent with the American temper and political tradition. That temper and that tradition are more closely aligned with the notion that state protection of private interests and property enhances the citizen's affection for the political community. Citizens, in this sense, can be trusted to protect the public interest as a means of ensuring the free pursuit of individual interests and material gain. In extraordinary circumstances citizens can be counted upon to forego selfish gain temporarily to protect the society that provides them both personal and economic freedom.

Will's major contribution to political thought is that he challenges conservatives to define a conception of the public good based upon more than love of free markets. Although his alternative may not suit the American temperament, he identifies problems in contemporary conservative thought that serious thinkers must address.

Will's Conservatism

Will's critics complain that his writings carry a touch of arrogance concerning the correctness of his own views and how these views reflect a coherent public philosophy. There may be some justification for this complaint. For example, Will states, "Everything I write, especially some of the so-called lighter pieces, reflects a carefully protractedly developed view of the world."[11] Will has a tendency to preface comments concerning his conservative philosophy with the statement "conservatism, properly understood," implying that forms of conservatism other than his own are something different. Many conservatives object to the notion that proper conservatism entails vigorous support for "big government," higher taxes, welfare-state programs, and government regulations such as restrictions on handgun ownership and requirements that drivers fasten seat belts—all positions Will perceives as necessary elements of a "true" conservative philosophy. Consequently, Will's disagreements with other conservatives illuminate his own brand of conservatism.

Will's project is ambitious. He asserts that his "aim is to recast conservatism in a form compatible with the broad popular imperatives of the day."[12] Will also believes that "the cluster of ideas that is commonly thought to constitute conservatism should be pried apart and reconstituted."[13] Yet to many of his critics Will appears to be redefining "conservatism" to fit more closely with his own political philosophy.

According to Will, two values are essential to any conservative philosophy: equality of opportunity and justice. In his view free markets deny equal opportunity and undermine social justice. Will notes that whereas true conservatism is based on an inclusive vision of the common good, free markets reduce the "public good" to the arbitrary outcome of voluntary arrangements.

Will rejects the libertarian strain within much of modern conservatism. The libertarian belief that the social good is defined as the aggregate of individually made decisions "is often not an empirical conclusion, but a philosophical premise."[14] Modern conservatives and libertarians allegedly lack a philosophy of the common good and do not understand the importance of fostering citizen virtues, community values and patriotism. In Will's words, "Just as the nation is said to be saturated with 'conservatives,' I am arguing that there are almost no conservatives, properly understood."[15] Will contends that we need a "new conservatism" that fosters and cultivates citizen virtues.

Tory conservatism, the philosophy of those who believe in the preservation of traditional practices and institutions and of the core values of civilization, is Will's alternative to contemporary conservatism. He correctly perceives a contradiction in much of modern conservatism. Many conservatives speak of the importance of traditional institutions such as family, church and community but simultaneously exalt the marketplace as though they were wholly unaware of its effects on traditional institutions:

> Capitalism undermines traditional social structures and values; it is a relentless engine of change, a revolutionary inflamer of appetites, enlarger of expectations, diminisher of patience. Republicans see no connection between the cultural phenomena they deplore and the capitalist culture they promise to intensify; no connection between the multiplying evidence of self-indulgence and national decadence (such as pornography, promiscuity, abortion, divorce, and other forms of indiscipline) and the unsleeping pursuits of ever more immediate, intense and grand material gratifications.[16]

A major flaw in modern conservative thought, according to Will, is that it adopts economic doctrine as political philosophy. Will proclaims that "it is odd" that individuals who believe in the need to cultivate citizenship against momentary passions defend an economic doctrine that has the opposite effect:

> Economics is about contemporary calculations of short-term interests; it is about the immediate and the quantifiable, to the exclusion of the venerable and sentimental.[17]
> Traditional conservatism has not been, and proper conservatism cannot be, merely a defense of individualism and individualist "free-market" economics. Conservatism is about the cultivation and conservation of certain values, or it is nothing.[18]

Several objections to Will's analysis are germane. Many analysts are uncomfortable with his Tory conservatism. Ronald Dworkin argues that the preservation of civilization is not the first of all public aspirations. He maintains that although it is possible to have "civilization" without "justice," any civilization worth preserving must be founded on some correct notion of justice. Otherwise, "like slaves at Monticello," it is a disgrace and an embarrassment.[19] Nelson W. Polsby argues similarly that Tory conservatism is acceptable as long as the society being preserved is based on "some minimal level of decency and justice."[20] A Tory in the Third Reich is hardly a worthy representative of proper conservatism.

Will's conservatism is not a project to conserve all traditions and values in established societies, only "worthy" ones. Will is not a reactionary seeking blindly to preserve practices simply because they are "traditional." Dworkin's criticism that Will's Toryism lacks any conception of justice is incorrect. Polsby more correctly argues that Will is preoccupied with injustice. Will in fact argues that a conservatism that wishes to preserve traditional institutions must be based on a just social order. Here he largely agrees with many modern welfare-state liberals who believe that free markets undermine justice and that government must actively foster a more just society. In an interview with *Christianity Today* Will tells of his own children living in an affluent community only ten miles from poverty-stricken Anacostia where many children are also being raised: "That's worrisome, and it ought to be especially worrisome to a conservative because conservatives are nationalists. They say we all ought to be Americans, to share certain values, and to feel positive about the community."[21]

Unlike many welfare-state liberals, Will does not believe that government should actively promote a more egalitarian society. In our society, he contends, social status and wealth are largely related to persons receiving their just deserts. In that sense, differences in social classes are "just." Will does not seek to promote equal outcomes in our society; rather, he seeks to enhance opportunities. He believes that government must adopt a vigorous role in enhancing the opportunities of young people from poverty-stricken locations.

It is fair to ask whether Will's critique of capitalism is balanced or accurate. Will's argument that markets do not effectively regulate destructive appetites such as pornography, drug use and prostitution is undoubtedly true. But these appetites are regulated to some extent by nonmarket mechanisms in our society. Thoughtful defenders of capitalism recognize that markets are imperfect regulators of human appetites and that government has the moral authority to legally proscribe certain activities. Although Will is correct to argue that government is not vigorous enough in its efforts to regulate base appetites, he should not ascribe to all conservatives a belief in the absolute virtue of the marketplace.

Also, is it fair to accuse advocates of free enterprise of pursuing unabashed self-interest with no concern for or conception of the common good? Many advocates of the marketplace argue that enlightened self-interest is often more conducive to the pursuit of happiness, virtue and the common good than is a society regulated by temporary public leaders. Politics also involves self-interested behavior, and free markets are important correctives against possible coercion by a political elite that seeks to impose its own conception of the public good on society. In this sense, public officials pursuing their notions of the public good may end up destroying many of the core values of our civilization, including economic freedoms and liberty. Thus, the regulator of voluntary transactions in society may be destructive of the traditional order.

The problem with Will's argument is that he portrays the choice between big government and free markets as a choice between justice and injustice. Actually the choice is between degrees of injustice. Whether we rely upon government regulation or upon the marketplace, there are "winners" and "losers" in society. In an environment of scarce resources, some individuals pursuing their own interests "win" in the marketplace, and some individuals pursuing their own interests "win" in the policy arena. The question is not simply whether we want justice or injustice, but rather, whom we want to regulate the distribution of society's scarce resources.

Another problem is Will's assertion that modern conservatism's faith in the marketplace is based on philosophical dogma, not empirical evidence. This claim may be correct for some conservatives, but certainly Will should not generalize without providing his own evidence. In fact, Will fails to provide evidence for his own claims of big government's beneficial effects. Will asserts that welfare-state programs enhance justice and equal opportunity, but he is short on specifics as to how government can contribute to the common good and which programs are best suited to that objective.

For example, to foster a sense of community, patriotism and civic virtue, Will advocates national service for all young citizens. A peacetime military conscription, he argues, provides citizens with a sense of national pride and obligation.[22] Will also believes that busing for racial integration is an unacceptable violation of individual freedom: "Busing is a kind of conscription. Any conscription is a significant excision from American freedom and can be justified only rarely, and for clear, urgent goals."[23]

These two positions on conscription seem contradictory. But at the same time, under Will's conception of big government, busing for racial integration seems as defensible as national service for the enhancement of community, patriotism and civic virtue. Advocates of busing assert that they seek to improve the citizenry's sense of community through racial integration. Given the abstract nature of Will's big-government conservatism, numerous policies can be defended as contributing to "community values." Will provides no consistent guidelines to identify specific policies that are conducive to the achievement of community values.

Many conservatives today raise important questions concerning the social and psychological effects of welfare-state programs on recipients and argue persuasively that an overly paternalistic government can be damaging to individual self-esteem and reliance. As a self-styled big-government conservative and friend of the modern welfare state, Will does not seriously address this argument. There is, therefore, a legitimate basis for many conservatives' disagreements with Will. He is able to chastise modern conservatives for their alleged overreliance on the marketplace because he fails to take seriously their more trenchant critiques of government regulation. In Will's view, modern conservatives who wish to shrink government's domestic responsibilities are only interested in not paying for benefits received by others:

What is called "conservatism" might better be called infantilism. Those of us blessed with small children recognize childishness when we see it. Increasingly, the nation, like a child, wills the end without willing the means to the end. The end is a full platter of government services. The means to that end is the energetic government that does the inevitable regulating and taxing. Today's "conservatism?" The average voter has looked into his heart of hearts, prayed long and hard, and come to the conclusion that it is high time the government cut his *neighbor's* benefits.[24]

Will's Statecraft

Will's alternative of big-government conservatism is more than just a critique of contemporary conservative thought. He provides a serious argument that government is a positive force in society, not a necessary evil. Many conservatives, he notes, argue that the federal government is incompetent and cannot solve problems of inner-city decay and poverty; simultaneously, these conservatives ask citizens to give up their sons and daughters and billions of tax dollars to achieve global objectives such as reuniting Lebanon.

This alleged contradiction is less evident than Will believes. Many conservatives argue that the federal government is better at providing some services (national defense and security) than it is at providing others (programs to overcome poverty and inner-city decay). Will fails to understand the fundamental difference between government pursuit of nondiscretionary security objectives and government provision of highly discretionary domestic spending programs. Defense is a "public good" that only the federal government can adequately supply. There are alternative suppliers of domestic services, including traditional intermediary powers such as businesses, civic associations, church groups and neighborhood organizations.

Yet Will insists that a strong federal government is necessary to achieve conservative objectives. Will traces his own conservatism to the ideas of Aristotle, Edmund Burke, John Newman and Benjamin Disraeli. He argues that contemporary conservatives, fond of quoting Burke, fail to recognize that Burke was "the author of a celebration of the state."[25] Will claims that today's "*soi-disant* conservatives" have probably never taken the time to read Burke and are more familiar with Barry Goldwater's *Conscience of a Conservative* than they are with *Reflections on the Revolution in France.*[26]

Will also believes that modern conservatism's animus toward big government is traceable to America's founding. Will argues that the United States is an "ill-founded" regime based upon "the stale, false notion that government is always and only an instrument of coercion, making disagreeable excisions from freedom."[27] According to Will, James Madison, our chief constitutional architect, was "exclusively" concerned with the problem of controlling passions. By trying to control passions with countervailing passions, Madison apparently neglected the more noble objective of overcoming or reforming passions. For Madison, "The political problem is seen entirely in terms of controlling the passions that nature gives, not nurturing the kind of character that the polity might need."[28]

Unlike the ancient philosophers, the American Founders focused on a "sociology of the factions" rather than on a "sociology of virtue or the husbandry of exemplary elites."[29] The ancients considered self-interestedness a defect. The American Founders, contrarily, built a political regime around the notion that self-interested behavior must be understood and encouraged rather than discouraged. Under the Founders' scheme, politics is "defined negatively." That is, politics focuses on protecting individuals from one another rather than on cultivating citizen virtue. Will argues that no sense of social cohesion can exist within a political community founded on the glorification of self-interest.[30]

Here Will advances a common thesis. It is central to the arguments of diverse groups of theorists including adherents to Leo Strauss's political thought and certain writers on civil religion. Will makes an important contribution by bringing this argument to an audience outside the scholarly community. In his *Statecraft as Soulcraft* Will combines his training as a political theorist with an elegant, accessible writing style. Yet the elegant simplicity of Will's thesis should not obscure the fact that this issue is more complex than he reveals. For instance, his belief that the American Founders ignored the necessity of fostering "exemplary elites" neglects the many writings of both Thomas Jefferson and Alexander Hamilton on the importance of fostering an aristocracy of talent in the United States. To substantiate this criticism of the founders, Will needs to extend his analysis beyond Madison's writings.

It is also an overstatement to maintain that Madison was "exclusively" concerned with controlling passions. While it is correct to say that Madison's *Federalist* essays contain little discussion of virtue, Will's assertion that the "Madisonian model" represents the Founders' vision is overstated. In a *Modern Age* review George W. Carey observes that "the maintenance and cultivation of virtue" were "major concerns" of the founding era. In fact, "the institutions of society were looked upon as a vehicle for the transmission of virtues necessary for self-government."[31]

Government and Good Citizenship

In Will's view, good citizenship implies "moderation, social sympathy and a willingness to sacrifice private desires for public ends."[32] America's rhetoric of individualism apparently disinclines citizens to think in terms of national interests. Will contends that government has important duties that extend beyond satisfying citizens' desires. He argues that even in a free society, government is obligated to censor consumer preferences as a means to pursue long-term national objectives:

> Government exists not merely to serve individuals' immediate preferences, but to achieve collective purposes for an ongoing nation. Government, unlike the free market, has a duty to look far down the road and consider the interests of citizens yet unborn. The market has remarkable ability to satisfy the desires of the day. But government has other, graver responsibilities, which include planning for the energy needs, military and economic, of the future.
>
> Unfortunately, many citizens today think of themselves primarily as consumers, and think government's primary duty is to facilitate enjoyable consumption.[33]

Will notes that both liberals and conservatives look at government negatively. In Will's view, political liberals at least are willing to advocate government regulation as a means of enhancing the public good. He contends that conservatives must come to grips with the modern welfare state.[34] Charles Krauthammer therefore praises Will for defending "many welfare state reforms against the ravages of Reaganism."[35] Will points out that any healthy polity needs to "incorporate altruistic motives. . . . It does so in domestic policies associated with the phrase 'welfare state.' These are policies that express the community's acceptance of an ethic of common provision."[36]

Will praises many accomplishments of the "old liberalism," including social security, the Tennessee Valley Authority project and the 1960s civil rights laws. These programs helped citizens to better lead their own lives. Will offers the highest praise for the civil rights laws, which, he believes, are examples of government's ability to foster values conducive to the common good. Will wants to expand upon the accomplishments of "old liberalism" with increased government support for education, school lunch programs and aid to the handicapped. Regarding school lunch programs Will notes that "we should spend more money on nutrition programs, because it is simply a fact that nutrition bears on the development of the mind."[37]

Will's policy views are criticized by both self-professed conservatives and liberals. Many conservatives reject his defenses of the modern welfare state and big government. Some political liberals criticize Will for not going far enough in his support of welfare-state programs. Two liberal-centrists, Charles Krauthammer and James Fallows, for example, argue that Will's defense of "old liberalism" is persuasive. Yet, they note that "new liberalism" also seeks to enhance the goals of equal opportunity, community values and civic virtue through such initiatives as affirmative action programs, racial quotas and busing, all of which Will opposes. If big-government conservatism justifies civil rights legislation, they ask, why is it opposed to affirmative action programs?[38]

These objections raise important questions concerning Will's philosophy. What is the basis for the distinctions that Will draws? How is he able to support certain welfare-state programs on conservative principles while opposing others? The major problem is that Will's philosophy tends to be overly abstract. His general principles concerning the need for compassion, "social sympathy," virtue and moderation do not always help us determine which policy prescriptions are appropriate for a modern philosophy of conservatism.

Will is most persuasive when arguing that government should act to improve the inner lives of its citizens. To improve the inner lives of its citizens, government must "legislate morality." To legislate morality effectively, however, government makes substantial excisions from personal freedoms: "The truly conservative critique of contemporary American society is that there is too much freedom—for abortionists, pornographers, businessmen trading with the Soviet Union, young men exempt from conscription, to cite just four examples."[39]

In Will's view, our government is not sufficiently vigorous in its efforts to regulate some destructive appetites such as pornography. He believes that there is too much tolerance in our society for certain base appetites. But more dangerous than excessive tolerance of pornography are "the reasons given for tolerating it,"[40] particularly the rationale that "one man's Shakespeare is another man's trash." Will observes that people subscribing to this rationale are arguing, in effect, that democratic citizens are "idiots" incapable of self-governance. Cannot a reasonable person tell the difference between Shakespeare and smut? In Will's formulation, a danger to our disciplined liberties emanates from individuals such as former Supreme Court justice William O. Douglas who believed "that we must . . . tolerate *Hustler* (magazine) because if we censor *Hustler,* we will not know where or how to stop."[41] Will continues, "Well I know where and how to stop. People more discriminating than Justice Douglas do. They understand that life is not quite that random and standards are not as capricious."[42]

Will opposes liberalized drug use in our society for many of the same reasons that he despises pornography. He notes that it is unfortunate that the arguments concerning marijuana decriminalization and legalization focus primarily on the medical evidence of damage to individual physiologies. Will believes that it is necessary to legislate against the use of recreational drugs, even if medical evidence is inconclusive, because the major issue is the effect of recreational drugs on the "community's character."[43]

Will's analysis exposes an important problem inherent in contemporary libertarian thought. Many libertarians support legalized recreational drugs on the basis of these principles: (1) citizens generally understand the personal risks involved with privately arrived at decisions and should be free to determine for themselves which consequences they are willing to bear in return for the "right" to partake in certain pleasurable activities; and (2) unregulated drug use has the added benefit of satisfying a public demand where a profit can be made in the marketplace.

Will asserts that the libertarian defense of drug use is a shallow argument. The libertarian defense of legalized recreational drugs ignores these problems: (1) individually arrived at decisions have consequences beyond their immediate effects upon the individual—the evidence of deformed and retarded children born of a previous generation's recreational drug users is too compelling to ignore; and (2) many libertarians ignore the effects on third parties of legalized drug transactions between "consenting adults." It is fair to ask what happens to the moral fabric of a society in which recreational drug use is provided legal sanction. Because young citizens take their moral bearings from their surroundings, a society in which the laws teach that harmful behavior is acceptable to the community may not produce citizens of high moral character. Therefore, Will's assertion that government must be concerned with the moral character of its citizens is convincing.

The most controversial aspects of Will's views concern the issues of political tolerance and First Amendment freedoms. He contends that freedom of speech is not an absolute right in our society. Will's views came to light in a lively exchange with members of the American Civil Liberties Union (ACLU) over the "right" of free speech and assembly for the American Nazi party. At the time of this debate the American Nazi party was organizing a march in Skokie, Illinois, 60 percent of whose residents were Jewish. Will notes that if the right to compete in the free market of ideas implies the right to win, then the logic of the position of ACLU members defending the Nazis' "rights" is "that it is better to be ruled by Nazis than to restrict them."[44] Will's argument is reasonable. The First Amendment is intended to promote certain political ends, such as republican government. The American Founders understood the distinction between license and liberty and between permissible and proscribable speech.[45]

The strength of Will's position becomes clear when we consider what happens to the moral fabric of a society in which the "rights" of Nazis are protected. It is fair to inquire what happens to the character of citizens taught from a young age that obnoxious groups such as the

American Nazis deserve equal protection under the law and are entitled to compete for public sentiments with mainstream groups in the free market of ideas.

Government may also advance the goal of good citizenship by encouraging nationalist sentiments. For example, the Soviet threat is the focus of many of Will's foreign policy writings. This emphasis is consistent with Will's views on the need for a sense of community, patriotism and citizen virtues. The existence of a common enemy provides a basis for developing a sense of national community and spirit. Will argues that in foreign affairs a sense of national purpose and identity must transcend parochial loyalties. While many critics condemned former president Ronald Reagan's anti-Soviet rhetoric as inflammatory and undiplomatic, Will praised Reagan's denunciations of Soviet leaders as "liars" and "cheats" on the basis that such rhetoric correctly established the target of danger in the minds of generally complacent democratic citizens.

Modern conservatism's skepticism of government competence is, according to Will, largely ruinous to the process of trying to deal with large-scale problems in the international environment. Will believes that in addition to awakening citizens to the Soviet threat, national leaders must alert the public to the personal sacrifices needed to deal adequately with this problem. National leaders "must enlist the public's support for strenuous, complex exertions regarding the larger world. This will involve not only procuring complex, expensive military assets, such as the MX missile, but also attempting to change the policies, and perhaps governments, of nations like Cuba and Libya."[46]

Will is most critical of free-trade advocates who apparently are willing to compromise national security by selling technology to hostile foreign regimes. He believes that the government provides too much freedom to businessmen to trade with the Soviets. Will contends that government-imposed restrictions on free commerce are necessary to combat the Soviet threat. On this point Will frequently cites Aleksandr Solzhenitsyn's criticisms of Western-based capitalists for selling advanced technology to the Soviet government.[47]

Will appears to have a clear conception of the role of big-government conservatism in foreign policy. Public leaders must speak candidly to citizens about the kind of society we wish to live in and why vigorous government action is necessary to protect the community. These leaders must also identify the nature of the threats to the community. Government, therefore, has a legitimate role to play in restricting the personal and economic freedoms of citizens when their actions are perceived as harmful to the national security.

Conclusion

George F. Will's views form an unusual brand of political conservatism. Will simultaneously is staunchly anti-Soviet and very critical of capitalism. His domestic policy views are often compatible with the arguments of welfare-state liberals. His views on the necessity of government to actively cultivate the moral character of its citizens envision an expansive role for government in a regime characterized by ordered liberty.

Will's views do not always appear to fit neatly into any delimiting category such as "conservative" or "liberal." Yet Will does appropriate the title "conservative" to describe his public philosophy. In Will's view, the alleged contradictions in his philosophy are simply reflections on the confused state of modern conservatism.

Will challenges modern conservative defenders of capitalism to realize the potentially destructive effects of free markets on the social order. He compels conservative defenders of commercialism to consider whether unrestricted free trade may place Western democracies at a disadvantage in competing with totalitarian regimes. In essence, Will is asking modern-day conservatives to think carefully about the major assumptions of their public philosophy. Additionally, as a national political journalist Will may be using his position of influence to create virtue in a regime in which people are free to be almost anything, including virtuous.

But Will's alternative is problematic. He argues that modern conservatives should appropriate a conception of the public good that demands citizens be constantly watchful of community interests. He comes close to expecting citizens to subordinate personal interests to an imprecisely defined general good. In practical terms, Will advocates a variety of governmental interventions into the economy to achieve such purposes. In addition to an expanded welfare state, Will advocates increased funding for foreign policy objectives such as undermining hostile totalitarian regimes. Increased taxes represents his one means of providing for such domestic and foreign policies.

Will's proposals are undoubtedly very demanding of the citizenry. America has not shown by example that Will's project of redefining the philosophy of individual freedom and liberty is realistic. His conception of big-government conservatism appears largely incompatible with traditional American notions of freedom and self-government. These notions, although under attack from the political Left, are still fundamentally rooted in the American temperament. Will makes an important contribution to political thought by exposing tensions in contemporary conservatism and by demanding that contemporary conservatives elaborate a coherent vision of the public good. Will's expectation that conservatives elevate their conceptions of politics above notions of self-interest is persuasive. His alternative of providing a massive expansion to the liberal welfare state, however, hardly qualifies as "conservatism, properly understood."

Notes

1. Quoted in Neil A. Grauer, *Wits and Sages* (Baltimore, Md.: Johns Hopkins University Press, 1984), p. 243.

2. Ibid.

3. Ibid., pp. 244–245.

4. Ibid., p. 244.

5. Joseph Sobran, "The One True Conservative," *National Review,* June 10, 1983, p. 696.

6. Ibid., p. 698.

7. M. J. Sobran, Jr., "The Joy of Puritanism," *National Review,* June 9, 1978, p. 726.

8. Ryskind and Phillips are quoted in Grauer, *Wits and Sages,* p. 247.

9. James Neuchterlein, "George Will and American Conservatism," *Commentary* (October 1983): 39.

10. Samuel T. Francis, "The Case of George Will," *Modern Age* (Spring 1986): 143.

11. Quoted in Grauer, *Wits and Sages,* p. 241.

12. George F. Will, *Statecraft as Soulcraft: What Government Does* (New York: Simon & Schuster, 1983), p. 12.

13. Ibid.

14. Ibid., p. 22.

15. Ibid., p. 23.

16. George F. Will, *The Pursuit of Virtue and Other Tory Notions* (New York: Simon & Schuster, 1982), pp. 36–37.

17. Will, *Statecraft as Soulcraft,* p. 118.

18. Ibid., pp. 119–120; also see George F. Will, *The Morning After: American Successes, 1981–1986* (New York: Free Press, 1986), p. 366.

19. Ronald Dworkin, "Review of *The Pursuit of Happiness,*" *New York Review of Books,* October 12, 1978, p. 20.

20. Nelson W. Polsby, "A Special Kind of Conservative," *Fortune,* July 25, 1983, p. 106.

21. George F. Will, quoted in Rodney Clapp and Beth Spring, "The Convictions of America's Most Respected Newspaper Columnist," *Christianity Today,* July 13, 1984, p. 26.

22. Will, *The Pursuit of Virtue,* p. 45.

23. George F. Will, *The Pursuit of Happiness and Other Sobering Thoughts,* (New York: Harper & Row, 1978), pp. 65–66.

24. Ibid., p. 186.

25. Will, *Statecraft as Soulcraft,* p. 28.

26. George F. Will, "The Presidency in the American Political System," *Presidential Studies Quarterly* 14 (Summer 1984): 332.

27. Will, *Statecraft as Soulcraft,* p. 22.

28. Ibid., p. 39.

29. Ibid., p. 40.

30. Ibid., pp. 43, 45.

31. George W. Carey, "Moral and Political Foundations of Order," *Modern Age* (Winter 1985): 74.

32. Will, *Statecraft as Soulcraft,* p. 134.

33. Will, *The Pursuit of Happiness,* p. 72.

34. Will, "The Presidency," p. 330.

35. Charles Krauthammer, "The Two Conservatisms," *The New Republic,* June 16, 1981, p. 27.

36. Will, *Statecraft as Soulcraft,* p. 120.

37. Quoted in Dinesh D'Souza, "Op Artists," *Policy Review* 31 (Winter 1985): 50.

38. Krauthammer, "The Two Conservatisms," pp. 26–30; and James Fallows, "The Foundation of Liberalism," *Atlantic* (May 1983): 98–101.

39. Will, *The Pursuit of Virtue,* p. 45.

40. Quoted in Grauer, *Wits and Sages,* p. 243.

41. Ibid.; also see Clapp and Spring, "The Convictions," p. 26.

42. Grauer, *Wits and Sages,* p. 243.

43. Will, *The Pursuit of Happiness,* pp. 69–70.

44. George F. Will, "Nazis: Outside the Constitution," in R. E. DiClerico and A. S. Hammock, eds., *Points of View* (Reading, Mass.: Addison-Wesley, 1980), p. 278.

45. Ibid.

46. Will, *The Pursuit of Virtue,* p. 48.

47. Ibid., pp. 30–32, 156–157, 160–167.

3

Russell Kirk:
The Conservatism of Tradition

James F. Pontuso

The conservative movement in the United States achieved a startling political success with the elections of Ronald Reagan in 1980 and 1984. Few could have foreseen twenty or thirty years ago that what seemed to be a discredited or largely ignored set of principles would become the dominant public philosophy. Yet during the high tide of liberalism, one writer struggled against the "progressive" temper of the time, forcing his readers to question whether the massive changes then taking place in the social structure might not do more harm than good. It can be said that the publication of Russell Kirk's widely read *The Conservative Mind* in 1953 laid the foundation for the current conservative movement and therefore that Kirk may be the intellectual father of modern-day American conservatism.[1]

In many ways the intellectual acceptance of conservatism mirrored its political success. Both rode a wave of resentment against the prevailing liberal agenda, just as both found it easier to attack the foibles of their opponents than to present a cogent formulation of their own doctrines. Therefore, to best understand Kirk's importance we must turn to his criticisms of liberalism.

Kirk's Critique of Liberalism

Kirk's rebuke of liberalism begins with his attack on the principles of the Enlightenment. He argues that the Enlightenment attempted to replace the complex structure of human relations with simple and universal formulas about the natural rights of all people. These new rights did not grow out of the long tradition of the West; they derived instead from ideas based solely on abstract notions, such as equality, liberty and fraternity.

But why does Kirk oppose natural rights? Here Kirk takes his convictions primarily from his philosophic mentor, Edmund Burke. Burke reacted against the ravages of the French Revolution, which, he believed, were caused by the endeavor to apply abstract doctrines of natural rights to the practical affairs of government and society. I will not rehearse the entire argument of *Reflections on the French Revolution;* instead, I will briefly point out some of the reasons Kirk, following Burke, maintains that abstract ideas cannot be used to guide human behavior.

According to Kirk abstract ideas give people expectations that are impossible to fulfill. Such ideas cause civil unrest by stirring up desires for social transformation that can never be realized. People become deluded by the hope that social and political relations can imitate the simple and universal formulas of natural rights. But human relations are never so simple, and in order for people to accept natural rights, they must ignore all the hard lessons learned from the experience of past civilizations.

Moreover, speculative visions of social reform have never been known or seen to exist; that is, they are impractical. The abstract ideas of the Enlightenment are particularly onerous for Kirk because they do not acknowledge the evil in humans. Adherents of these principles are either naive, and thus politically ineffective, or they are cruel in the quest to make imperfect human beings live up to their expectation of human perfectibility. Hence, the leaders of the French and Bolshevik revolutions, although driven by the most idealistic motives, committed some of the greatest crimes against humanity.[2]

The political and social movements founded on theoretical claims aim at destroying past civilization and culture in order to create a world consistent with ideals of natural rights. But to overturn the order of society is to destroy the work of past generations whose people also labored to be decent and civilized. Culture does not grow overnight, and its destruction is a supreme act of hubris. Radical social transformation implies that the contemporary generation is so far superior to its fathers and grandfathers that it need pay no attention to the mores on which these ancestors based their lives.

In addition, natural rights are founded on the notion that the individual's desires are supreme and that society ought to satisfy those yearnings. Liberalism has always preached that a concern for self-interest would free people from the shackles of ignorance and stupidity while at the same time liberating them from social, governmental and religious authority. Liberalism's hope was that people would use this newly won autonomy to enrich their existence. Part of liberalism's success rests on its promise that progress and human betterment can be achieved without all the duties associated with custom and religion.[3] Kirk explains: "From its beginnings, the liberal movement . . . had within it a fatuous yearning for the destruction of all authority. The early liberals were convinced that once they should overthrow established governments and churches, supplanting them by rational and egalitarian and purely secular institutions, the principal difficulties of the human condition would nearly terminate. Poverty, ignorance, disease, and war might then cease."[4]

Kirk argues that the constraints of culture that liberals so abhor, in truth, serve to civilize humans. When all customary boundaries are cast aside, humans have only their own imperfect reason to oversee their behavior. They become confused and alienated from their lives. In such a condition the individual comes to be "the solitary human atom, above all authority, tradition, and conscience."[5] More important, lacking guidance, human reason is too easily influenced by "lust and whim." For Kirk human beings are not naturally good; in fact, quite the reverse holds true. It is culture that teaches people right from wrong and restrains their baser motivations. To overthrow the old ways is to suspend those restrictions that raise humans above their merely physical or animal natures.[6]

Along with the notion of human perfectibility and a contempt for tradition, liberalism also is sustained by a belief in progress. It is ironic, Kirk claims, that liberals are contemptuous of all myth but are committed to the myth of progress and democracy, as if providence assured the success of the liberal agenda.[7] Furthermore, he points out, ours is an age that has seen greater atrocities committed than in any other. A person would have to be blind or incurably naive to have overlooked the vicious corners of the human soul exhibited in the Nazi death camps or the Communist Gulag. In fact, he contends, it was exactly because so much trust was put in the goodness of man and the progress of history that adequate political safeguards were not taken to protect mankind from the infamous deeds of the twentieth century.[8]

Kirk also criticizes liberalism for its overemphasis on the principle of equality, a tendency that has become more pronounced over time. While he does not dispute the tenet of giving equal things to equal people, he argues that there are very few instances in which people are actually equal. Surely, he reasons, not everyone has an equal claim to rule. Some are better trained, are more educated and have superior talent. Nor is equality of wealth a choice-worthy goal. "The just man knows that men differ in strength, in intelligence, in energy, in beauty, in dexterity, in discipline, in inheritance, in particular talents; and he sets his face, therefore, against any scheme of pretended 'social justice' which would treat all men alike."[9] Even attempts to equalize opportunity are unsound because "in nine cases out of ten . . . differences of intelligence, strength, swiftness" are the causes of inequality of wealth. Moreover, the attempt to equalize conditions could decrease initiative and so injure the economic system as to make the situation much worse for all people, most especially the poor. Finally, Kirk maintains, there are different ways of life, and the rewards of those various pursuits can never be made commensurable. For example, those who cultivate a life of the mind receive a far different reward than those who pursue a life of money-making.[10]

Clearly Kirk's views on equality raise serious difficulties for anyone interested in equity. As C. Wright Mills pointed out, Kirk tends to confuse natural and conventional kinds of inequality. To say that some people are born with greater talent than others is not the same as saying that those who inherit their families' wealth deserve their privileged positions.[11] Yet this is exactly what Kirk asserts when he writes, "That some men are richer than others, and that some have more leisure than others, and that some travel more than others, and that some inherit more than others, is no more unjust, in the great scheme of things, than that some undeniably are handsomer or stronger or quicker or healthier than others."[12] But is it truly just that those with minimal talent who inherit great riches are able to use their affluence to gain greater rewards than those with much capability but none of the advantages of wealth?

Kirk's reproach of equality should not be taken as a wholehearted endorsement of a policy of free-market economics. He does rely on the market to provide a fairly equitable distribution of material rewards, but he understands that there are enormous shortcomings if market considerations are the only guidelines used for making decisions about the common good. Kirk reminds us that today's economic conservatives hold the same principles as classical Liberals do. Both groups share the view that self-interest and the pursuit of money are the predominant motivations of human behavior and that all political associations must reflect this fact by affording individuals the greatest possible liberty to pursue their own creature comforts.

Kirk faults this position on a number of grounds. First, the view that human beings seek only their own self-interest is too simplistic; no single factor can explain the motions of the human soul. Second, because humans are more than the sum total of their bodily desires, acquisition and consumption of material goods can never be wholly satisfying. Third, there must be order before there can be liberty, both in the moral and political realms. Without political order there is only anarchy, or "as in the French Revolution, one ends with unlimited despotism."[13] Without order in the moral sphere mankind falls prey to "a deadly sin, pride of spirit, the arrogant rationality of the man who believes he has the right to judge all things in heaven and earth according to his petty private taste."[14] Such people often are not constrained by the probity of economic rationality, and eventually turn to crime as a means of gratifying their pleasures. Fourth, Kirk reproaches those who measure worth solely in terms of economic growth. He laments the fact that the thirst for profit has destroyed so much of what is useful and elegant in the past. For example, he warns civil libertarians against selling out national parks to private developers. Finally, he contends that the state is not merely an instrument of oppression. It serves to protect the nation from outside threats and domestic violence. Therefore, it is a precondition to a peaceful and free society. It also may serve positive ends, such as the protection of the environment or the fulfillment of the Christian duty of providing for the needs of the poorest citizens in a way that will not encourage them to become profligate at the nation's expense.

Despite Kirk's position as the philosophic father of the conservative movement, an important political difference exists between Kirk and former president Ronald Reagan. Reagan successfully employed the politics of optimism, arguing that the greater part of the nation's ills could be solved if only the government would get off the backs of the people and allow them to apply their energies and talents to the problems at hand. In this venture, private interest would serve the public good, for the profit motive would spur people's ingenuity. Kirk, on the other hand, fears that unplanned change of whatever kind, even that generated by the movements of the free market, could be destructive to the harmony and stability of society. Kirk goes so far as to claim that true conservatism resists change because it has a tragic view of existence, implying that most change is likely to have adverse consequences.[15]

Kirk summarizes his differences with free-market conservatives in the following way. Conservatives, as opposed to libertarians and free marketeers, believe (1) in a transcendent moral order; (2) in an ordered liberty; (3) in bonds to society that run deeper than mere self-interest; (4) in the reality that human beings are not essentially good; (5) in the notion that the state is not merely the great oppressor but also is an instrument of human action; (6) and in a world in which the ego does not dominate all activity.[16]

One of the most onerous consequences of liberalism's optimistic appraisal of historical progress, according to Kirk, is that it stirred the hope that perfect social equality and harmony were practical goals. But when these aspirations did not materialize, as they could not, they sparked more radical philosophies of social transformation. In other words, he claims, communism is a natural outgrowth of the failure of the principles originally laid down by Liberalism. It is clearly beyond the scope of this chapter to include Kirk's criticism of communism. Suffice to say that he adds his voice to other conservatives, who, relying on the evidence presented by dissidents from the various Communist nations, brand Karl Marx's doctrine as the most barbaric and inhuman political movement in the history of the human race.[17]

According to Kirk even at their best, regimes founded on natural rights principles result in the centralization of government. "Enlightened reformers" inevitably come to rely on centralized and authoritarian governmental structures in order to foster social improvement among the less advanced populace. Ironically, the natural rights doctrine results in the atrophy of the habits of self-government. It prepares the way, as Alexis de Tocqueville claimed, for a loss of citizen virtue.[18] It fosters an unseemly regard for physical gratification by putting too great an emphasis on material well-being. Therefore, it deprecates all those extraordinary achievements of humanity in art, culture and learning that have little to do with bodily comfort. If the goals of liberals were actually achieved—that is, if there were universal peace, equality, and plenty—what would mankind have left to achieve? Does not the human race need some challenge to spur it on? Will not we become what Nietzsche called "last men" if the central government instantly satisfies our every whim? Kirk "join[s] in the resistance to the destruction of old patterns of life, damage to the footings of the civil social order, and reduction of human striving to material production and consumption."[19]

Perhaps the most far-reaching philosophic repercussion of liberalism is its rejection of any permanent or transcendent principles. The consequence of such a view is that nothing is deemed intrinsically good or evil. Without such guidelines, the most savage human passions may be unleashed on the world. It is little wonder that our age has descended to such inhumanity. Kirk is fond of ridiculing this position by retelling the story of Samuel Johnson, who "on being told of a neighbor who maintained that there exists no distinction between virtue and vice, said only, 'Why, then, let us count our spoons when he leaves.'"[20]

The Problem of Abstract Natural Rights

But if the liberal ideas of abstract natural rights lead human beings astray in their quest to find ordering principles for their lives, where should they turn for such knowledge? Here again Kirk turns to Burke to provide an answer. Although Burke did not reject the concept of rights altogether, he argued that seeking to apply such simple and universal concepts to the affairs of everyday life ignores the complexity of social existence. Change for the better is possible, but it must be conducted slowly, cautiously and prudently. General ideas such as peace, justice, equality, freedom and brotherhood may all be choice-worthy goals, but when attempting to apply such theories to actual circumstances, one must take into account the particulars. Thus, whatever speculative rights exist need to be expressed through specific institutions and customary ways of doing things. There may be abstract rights, but it takes concrete habits, customs and laws—in short, a culture—for people to enjoy these privileges.[21]

For Kirk a nation's culture is wiser than any individual or generation. A culture is the accumulated wisdom of the ages. Through a long process of trial and error, a culture adopts those mores and habits that "work" and rejects those that are found wanting. Although it may be impossible for any individual to understand why a particular practice is salutary to society, still it should be recognized that traditional ways of doing things would not survive the test of time unless they had some social advantage. Kirk quotes Burke with approval on this point:

> As the ends of such a partnership cannot be obtained in many generations, it becomes a partnership not only between those who are living, but those who are dead, and those who are to be born. Each contract of each particular state is but a clause in the great primeval contract of eternal society, linking the lower with the higher nature, connecting the visible and invisible world, according to a fixed compact sanctioned by the inviolable oath which holds all physical and moral natures, each in their appointed place.[22]

Another source of social cohesion, according to Kirk, is that provided by the "divine origin of social disposition."[23] What Kirk means by this appeal to the divine is not exactly clear. Sometimes he argues, along with Aristotle, that man is a social being and that social organization is natural to the human condition. At other times, however, he seems to claim that certain social institutions are actually ordained by God. The hand of God is manifest in the long-standing practices of social and political integration. As an example of this Kirk attempts to show how Judeo-Christian principles are at the core of Western philosophy, politics and morals.

The confusion is made even more serious by Kirk's reliance on the work of Eric Voegelin. Although Voegelin does maintain that a divine plan is manifest in history, he does not claim, as does Kirk, that the longevity of a custom is necessarily a measure of sacred consent. Quite the contrary, Voegelin argues that over time social customs actually obscure the meaning of revelatory events. The major intent of Voegelin's work is to recapture the original meaning of mortal glimpses into the eternal, a feat made more difficult by the accumulation of doctrines and interpretations that surround those events. Moreover, Voegelin holds that it is quite impossible for human beings to distinguish between sacred and mundane historical events. Surely he does not agree with Kirk, who holds traditional mores in such high esteem as to avow that they are prescriptions from God.

Although time and space preclude a full consideration of the implications of Kirk's assertion that social activities are ordained by God, it is proper to ask which institutions are looked upon favorably by the Deity. Are those preferred only by conservatives suitable to the Almighty, or was the New Deal, as some insisted at the time, an example of God's grace? Perhaps God was working his will through the Civilian Conservation Corps (CCC)? My father-in-law, who was unemployed before finding work at a CCC camp, certainly thought the job was a godsend.[24]

The Importance of Tradition

For Kirk, tradition is the most important source of human conduct. To best understand Kirk's views on this subject, we must turn to his description of the American political system, which in many ways represents his ideal. "Not abstractions," he writes, "but prudence, prescription, custom, tradition, and constitution have governed the American people."[25] In his book *The Roots of the American Order,* Kirk details how an "informal constitution," consisting of the acquired wisdom of Western culture, informed those who actually wrote our fundamental documents. The informal constitution existed as a complex body of ideas and practices America had inherited from past civilizations, from religion and from the ideas of great thinkers. It was, and is, more important in furnishing Americans with mores than is the Declaration of Independence or our written Constitution.

It is beyond the scope of this chapter to fully detail how each of the traditions of the past contributed to our founding. Here, I can only catalog some of what Kirk presents as the origins of our political and cultural heritage. From ancient Israel the Founders "inherited an understanding of the sanction of law," especially the principles of moral order supplied by the Ten Commandments. From ancient Greece they took an awareness of the virtues of political participation and of the need for a mixed regime in order to moderate government. Plato and

Aristotle gave them a deeper understanding of the human condition. From Rome they learned that decent political orders rest on the virtue of the citizens and that when virtue falters, even the most powerful and far-reaching political organization is doomed to fail. From Christianity, which Kirk argues is the most important source of order for American society, the Founders learned that one ought to hope for the best from human beings but that one ought to prepare for the worst. Kirk claims that the notions of human equality and the worth of the individual were derived from the Christian conviction of the "equality of all men before the judgment-seat of God." And the Founders' dedication to limited government and the institutions necessary to maintain those limits arose out of an awareness that it is prudent to have reservations toward all earthly authority, for humans are sinful. From Great Britain the Founders inherited a respect for the rights of citizens (the Magna Carta and trial by jury), a system of law resting on the accumulated wisdom of the ages (common law), and a long tradition of the habits of self-government.[26]

What, if anything, is wrong with Kirk's interpretation of the founding? For one thing it is not accurate. One need only consider the Declaration of Independence to realize that our nation is based on natural rights and the universal principles of the Enlightenment. Kirk recognizes that at least in part, the Declaration is a statement of abstract ideals. Insofar as that is true, Kirk opposes the Declaration. But he also attempts to show that the Declaration grew out of the rights of Englishmen. That is, it was not just an abstract theory but incorporated the practices that the colonists inherited from Great Britain. This argument cannot bear up under close scrutiny, however. Although it is true that the American Revolution began as a defense of the rights of Englishmen against the arbitrary use of power by the King, it culminated in a general theory of consent found nowhere in the British constitution. John Adams, one of Kirk's conservative models, explained in *Novanglus:* "[Great Britain] has, after one hundred and fifty years [of colonial rule], discovered a defect in her government, which ought to be supplied by some just and reasonable means, that is, by the consent of the colonies; for metaphysicians and politicians may dispute forever, but they will never find any other moral principle or foundation of rule of obedience, than the consent of the governed."[27]

Kirk's interpretation of the Declaration and its relationship to the Constitution is strikingly similar to the position of Charles Beard in his *An Economic Interpretation of the Constitution.* Both agree that the Constitution was a reaction against the abstract and democratic ideals of the Declaration. Both maintain that the Constitution was an effort by the "better sorts of men" to quell the democratic disorder that occurred, in part, as a result of the Declaration's egalitarian goals. Of course, Kirk's conclusion about which document is praiseworthy is just the opposite of Beard's. Kirk holds that the Constitution was the sober integration of the social wisdom of past ages into our institutions of government and a rejection of the wild radicalism of the Declaration.[28]

Here, too, I believe it is safe to say that Kirk's views on the founding are off the mark. It is true that the Declaration was a bold and novel statement of human rights, but it is no less true that the Constitution was a bold and novel political mechanism for maintaining those rights. For example, of the authors of *The Federalist,* only John Jay, in *The Federalist,* No. 2, reasoned that the proposed Constitution would succeed because it was based on the common traditions and customs of the people of the United States. Both Hamilton and Madison argued persuasively that the Constitution was a radical deviation from the existing practices of Americans. The foundations of America were not to be based on English common law or even on the traditions of the West—rather, they would rest on the "new political science." For example, after complaining about the instability that destroyed all previous free governments, Hamilton explained that Americans need not be anxious because "the science of politics, however, like most other sciences, has received great improvement."[29] Consider, too, the following remarks by Publius:

It has been frequently remarked that it seems to have been reserved to the people of this country, by their conduct and example, to decide the important question, whether societies of men are really capable or not of establishing good government from reflection and choice, or whether they are forever destined to depend for their political constitutions on accident and force.[30]

Harken not to the voice which petulantly tells you that the form of government recommended for your adoption is a novelty in the political world; that it has never yet had a place in the theories of the wildest projectors; that it rashly attempts what it is impossible to accomplish.

But why is the experiment of an extended republic to be rejected, merely because it may comprise what is new? Is it not the glory of the people of America, that whilst they have paid a decent regard to the opinions of former times and other nations, they have not suffered a blind veneration for antiquity, for custom, or for names, to over-rule the suggestions of their own good sense, the knowledge of their own situation, and the lessons of their own experience?

Happily for America, we trust for the whole human race, they [the American revolutionaries] pursued a new and more noble course. They accomplished a revolution which has no parallel in the annals of human society. They reared the fabrics of governments which have no models on the face of the globe.[31]

The novelty of the undertaking [the constitutional convention] immediately strikes us. . . . The most that the convention could do in such a situation [the likely demise of the Articles of Confederation], was to avoid the errors suggested by the past experience of other countries, as well as of our own; and to provide a convenient mode of rectifying their own errors, as future experience may unfold to them.[32]

What difference does it make if Kirk got his history wrong? There are important implications to Kirk's analysis of the founding.

First, rather than elevating the work of the Founders by connecting their creation to tradition, Kirk actually diminished their achievement by failing to understand how original and revolutionary the new form of government established by the Constitution was. If the "informal constitution" was really the basis of the American political system, why did the Articles of Confederation, which after all came out of the republican tradition, fail so miserably? The real question facing the Founders was this: Could human beings use their reason to control their own future and destiny? All human history up to that time gave a clear and unequivocal answer—no. In large groups people could not govern themselves. To say that the government of the United States was merely a culmination of ideas, customs and institutions borrowed from past ages is to miss the important change in the history of the human race that the American Constitution brought about.

A second issue raised by Kirk's analysis of the founding can best be stated as a question: What is the basis of our political community? If, as Kirk maintains, the Declaration is merely a rationale for American separation from the British Crown, does he take the same position as Stephen Douglas? Douglas held that the Declaration was not meant to apply to "all Men," but only to the white inhabitants of North America who separated from Great Britain over the price of tea. Does Kirk then agree with Justice Taney in *Dred Scott* that African-Americans were not and could never become citizens of the United States?

In truth, the great appeal of America has been that it accepts human beings regardless of their culture, religion or race. That is, America is based on the universal and abstract doctrine of the rights of man, a creed so simple in its message that it has been possible for immigrants to become Americans virtually in one day. This principle, although often breached in practice, has remained the polestar of our political existence.

The question of race and slavery is used as an example here quite intentionally, for Kirk's views raise an even more disturbing possibility.

If the old, tried and true practices are the good, and slavery is an old, tried and true practice, does that make slavery good? Kirk goes so far as to justify the position of John Randolph, a slaveholder, whose defense of the peculiar institution led him to reject the Declaration and along with it the "principle . . . that all men are created free and equal . . . because it is not true."[33] Perhaps Kirk does not intend to condone slavery by his assertion that the old is synonymous with the good. Yet, accepting Kirk's doctrine of veneration of antiquity might lead one to tolerate a social practice nearly as ancient as civilization itself.

Some of the Founders, including Adams, thought that one of the great advantages of our republic over those of former ages was that ours was based on natural rights and therefore considered slavery wrong. According to Adams: "If Americans had no more discretion than the Greeks, no more humanity, no more consideration for the benign and peaceful religion they profess, they would still have to consider, that the Greeks had in many places forty slaves, and in all places, ten to one free citizen; that the slaves did all the labour, and the free citizens had nothing to do but cut one another's throats."[34]

Racism is also an old practice in America. Does that make Jim Crow laws and the disenfranchisement of African-Americans justifiable? In the end, Kirk's reliance on custom as the source of wisdom leaves conservatism open to the charge that always has been effectively leveled against it: Conservatism is little more than a disguise for racism. Kirk's political ideas do little to combat this accusation, for he praises prejudice: "Conformity to custom—call it prejudice, if you will—makes a man's virtue his habit, as Burke expresses this idea."[35] Although Kirk is considered the father of contemporary conservatism, his preference for prejudice over reason actually does more to discredit conservatism than to nurture its strength.

The Difficulties of Reliance on Tradition

Now Kirk might respond that there is an important distinction to be made between principles and abstractions. Abstractions cause people to plunge rashly into schemes of social transformation in hopes of attaining the kind of perfection only possible in theory. When under the spell of such speculative ideas, people do not accord proper regard to the needs and limitations of particular circumstances.

Principles are those perennial aspirations of human achievement and conduct learned from a serious study of the past and of the reflections of wise people. Indeed, Kirk lambasts reforms in education that would abandon the traditional liberal arts curriculum, insisting that to cut people off from the body of Western knowledge makes them unprepared to meet even the challenges presented by everyday life. In particular, he complains that liberal intellectuals, who champion many of the academic reforms, seem more interested in molding "society nearer to their heart's desire" than in discovering the truth.[36]

Principles act as the prudently applied standards of human behavior. But from where do principles arise? Occasionally in his writings, Kirk states that they derive from the insight of the wise thinkers. More often, however, he repeats his assertion that all knowledge is acquired from tradition, which in turn can trace its origin to religion because "philosophy, art, law and all the more important elements of civilization developed out of religious principle and faith."[37] Such an assertion causes the reader of Kirk to wonder whether he is really more interested in understanding the truth or in inculcating traditional morality. Does he support a liberal arts education because it gives a glimpse into the nature of things—meaning that one must test the tradition against the phenomena—or does he think that the tradition is the source of all wisdom? (To put it in the terms of an aphorism of the Middle Ages: "If you have an opinion different than Aristotle's, change your opinion.") Yet, is there not a kind of wisdom that can be gained only if thinking people go beyond all conventions, doubt all truths, and divorce themselves from all certainties? Such, in fact, may be what it means to live a life of the mind.

Another way of looking at the problem is to speculate on what Kirk would have done if he were an Athenian asked to decide the fate of Socrates. Clearly Socrates' philosophy upset the customs of Athens and challenged the long-held beliefs of the political community. Moreover, Socrates was theoretical. His "what is?" questions (What is justice? What is courage? What is beauty?) were intended to investigate the true nature of things as opposed to their particular expressions (Courage is what Achilles does). One cannot help but conclude that Kirk's opposition to abstract reasoning and his devotion to tradition might have led him to vote with the majority of Athenians to condemn Socrates.

Thus, in addition to the political and polemical problems caused by Kirk's ideas, there are serious theoretic shortcomings to his views. For example, if wisdom is found in social practices maintained for a long period, to be conservative one surely ought to support the New Deal and its goals, for the New Deal is more than fifty years old. Does this mean, too, that a Soviet citizen must embrace the rule of a one-party state because that party has held power for seventy years? The Enlightenment, with all its stress on abstract rights, has gained a complete victory over the hierarchical structure of former times, and it is nearly four hundred years old. If conservatives learn what is proper from the social practices of culture carried out for a long period, they should accept these doctrines. But Kirk rejects these principles, perhaps because he thinks more abstractly than he realizes.

The difficulty raised by Kirk's reliance on tradition as a source of wisdom can be put as follows. If the old is the good, how do we know when to change? If social practices are the sources of one's ideas about what is proper, just and good, and social practices change into corrupt forms and those changes are adopted by a culture during an extended time, what grounds can one have for criticizing those practices?[38] The paramount ideas of the era that Kirk looks back so fondly upon were predominantly Christian. Those mores have long since been displaced by the philosophic principles of the Enlightenment. Today, people look more to scientists and engineers to solve their problems than they do to priests. As Allan Bloom points out, the current popular culture even reflects an awareness of the relativism proclaimed in the philosophy of Friedrich Nietzsche.[39] If Kirk's theory is followed to its logical conclusion, Western culture was justified in jettisoning Christian mores for German relativism because part of Christianity's ethical code did not work well enough to stand the test of time.

The source of Kirk's dilemma on this matter is his depreciation of the human faculty of reason. In his attempt to counter the simple-minded application of theory to practical affairs, Kirk abandons theory altogether. He thus puts himself in the position of having to judge the worth of practices by their longevity and continuity, that is, by how well they work. But when that continuity is broken, as in the case of Christianity's weakening hold on the West, Kirk's theory leaves us little choice but to throw ourselves into the arms of historical inevitability. In other words, Kirk is a historicist.

Conclusion

There is much to recommend the ideas of Kirk—most of all his practical good sense. He reminds us to take life as it comes, with all its variety, complexity and uncertainty. He warns us against adopting the delusion that an abstract theory of social reform will resolve all human dilemmas. He tells us to act prudently in politics, for to shake the foundations of society may raze the entire edifice. He points out that self-control and virtue make one master of one's destiny and therefore lead to happiness.[40] But in the deepest sense, I must conclude that Kirk's views are dangerous because they close people's minds. They give people a "moral" justification for prejudice and for doing things the way they have always been done. For example, imagine the effect on a college student imbued with Kirk's doctrines. Such a person might conclude: My ideas are quite as respectable as any I encounter here in academia; because they are my prejudices and they reflect long-standing ideas passed down to me by my family and social class, I will not feel any compunction to ponder the great political alternatives to the American way of life as presented by Jean-Jacques Rousseau and Karl Marx and, perhaps most importantly, by Plato and Aristotle.[41]

Notes

1. Harry Jaffa, "Defenders of the Constitution: Calhoun Versus Madison, A Bicentennial Celebration" (Irving, Tex.: University of Dallas, 1987), p. 1.

2. They become what Kirk calls "terrible simplifiers." Russell Kirk, *The Roots of the American Order* (Malibu, Calif.: Pepperdine University Press, 1978), p. 9; and Russell Kirk, "Edmund Burke and the Constitution," *The Intercollegiate Review* 21, no. 2 (Winter 1985-86): 3–11.

3. Russell Kirk, *Beyond the Dreams of Avarice* (Chicago: Henry Regnery, 1956), p. 34.

4. Russell Kirk, *The Enemies of Permanent Things* (LaSalle, Ill.: Sherwood Sugden, 1984), p. 284.

5. Kirk, *Beyond the Dreams of Avarice,* p. 13.

6. Kirk, *Enemies of Permanent Things,* p. 283.

7. Kirk, *Beyond the Dreams of Avarice,* p. 33.

8. For example, Kirk is very critical of "liberation theology." He argues that it ignores all the patterns of human behavior we have known and experienced for uncounted time in hopes of ushering in a new age of peace and social harmony. Therefore, it is silly because it is impractical and dangerous because its adherents are unprepared to meet the challenges of evil that exist in the core of the human soul. The leaders of movements to transform society are not the tender souls one meets at liberation theology gatherings but the hard-hearted men who are willing to take whatever steps are necessary to carry out their dreams of destruction and rebirth. See Russell Kirk, "Promises and Perils of 'Christian Politics,'" *The Intercollegiate Review* 18, no. 1 (Fall-Winter 1982); 18, 20–23.

9. Russell Kirk, "The Problem of the New Order," in William F. Buckley, Jr., ed., *American Conservative Thought in the Twentieth Century* (Indianapolis: Bobbs-Merrill, 1970), p. 361.

10. Ibid., pp. 361, 375–376.

11. C. Wright Mills, *The Power Elite* (New York: Oxford University Press, 1959), pp. 326–327.

12. Kirk, "The Problem of the New Order," p. 367.

13. Russell Kirk, *Reclaiming a Patrimony* (Washington, D.C.: Heritage Foundation, 1982), p. 8.

14. Kirk, *Beyond the Dreams of Avarice,* p. 35.

15. Ibid., pp. 31, 35, 38; Kirk, *Reclaiming a Patrimony,* pp. 7–8, 26, 33; Kirk, *The Enemies of Permanent Things,* pp. 256–257; and Kirk, "The Problem of the New Order," pp. 379–380. Compare Russell Kirk, "Enlivening the

Conservative Mind," *Intercollegiate Review* 21, no. 3 (Spring 1986): 25–28, in which he insists that conservatism must present new ideas if it is to remain politically viable.

16. Kirk, *Reclaiming a Patrimony,* pp. 31–32. Elsewhere he gives the following six attributes to conservatism: (1) belief in transcendent order; (2) affection for the variety and mystery of human existence; (3) conviction that civilized society requires orders and classes and thus that a "classless society" is neither possible nor desirable; (4) persuasion that freedom and private property are linked; (5) faith in prescription and distrust of those who want to remake society according to some conjectural ideal; (6) recognition that not all change leads to progress—change must occur, but only under the guidance of prudence (Russell Kirk, *The Conservative Mind* [Chicago: Henry Regnery, 1953], pp. 8–9.

17. Kirk, *The Enemies of Permanent Things,* pp. 128–131, 139, 145–146, 151–181; and Kirk, "The Problem of the New Order," pp. 371, 378.

18. Kirk, *The Conservative Mind,* pp. 10–61; Kirk, *The Enemies of Permanent Things,* pp. 60–68, 71, 85, 95, 195, 241–249; and Russell Kirk, "The Prospects for a Territorial Democracy in America," in Robert A. Goldwin, ed., *A Nation of States* (Chicago: Rand McNally, 1963), pp. 42–64.

19. Kirk, *The Conservative Mind,* p. iii.

20. Russell Kirk, *The Intemperate Professor* (Baton Rouge: Louisiana State University Press, 1965), p. 124.

21. Kirk, *The Conservative Mind,* pp. 1–70; and Russell Kirk, *Randolph of Roanoke* (Chicago: University of Chicago Press, 1951), p. 38.

22. Kirk, *The Conservative Mind,* p. 17. Kirk explains that "[we] moderns, Burke continued, tend to be puffed up with a little petty private rationality, thinking ourselves wiser than the prophets and law-givers, and are disposed to trade upon the trifling bank and capital of our private intelligence. That way lies ruin. But though the individual is foolish, the species is wise; and given time, the species judges rightly" (Kirk, *The Enemies of Permanent Things,* p. 29).

23. Kirk, *The Conservative Mind,* p. 17.

24. Kirk, *The Enemies of Permanent Things,* pp. 30–31, 251–281. Compare Eric Voegelin, *The Ecumenic Age* (Baton Rouge: Louisiana State University Press, 1974), pp. 1–58. Also see Russell Kirk, "I Must See the Things; I Must See the Men; One Historian's Recollections of the 1930's and 1940's," *Imprimis* 16, no. 10 (October 1987). Here Kirk seems to argue in favor of the initial changes instituted by the New Deal.

25. Kirk, *The Enemies of Permanent Things,* p. 166.

26. Kirk, *The Roots of the American Order,* pp. 27, 29, 51–96, 175, 368–374.

27. John Adams, *Works of John Adams* (Boston: Little, Brown & Co., 1851), vol. 4, p. 106.

28. Kirk, *The Roots of the American Order,* pp. 393–440.

29. Alexander Hamilton, John Jay, and James Madison, *The Federalist Papers,* No. 9 (New York: Modern Library, n.d.), p. 48.

30. *The Federalist,* no. 1, p. 3.

31. *The Federalist,* no. 14, pp. 84–85.

32. *The Federalist,* no. 37, p. 266.

33. Kirk, *Randolph of Roanoke,* p. 35. Kirk writes that Randolph appealed "to human nature, to the ways of God toward man and civilized man toward man, and not to the romantic or historical concepts of irrevocable 'human rights!'" (p. 19).

34. John Adams, *Defence of the Constitution of the United States* (New York: AMS Press, 1971), vol. 1, pp. 303–304; also see pp. 20, 159–160, 256. For a discussion of Adams's rejection of the ancient tradition of republicanism because of that tradition's reliance on slavery, see John W. Danford, "Commerce and the Constitution: What Does the Constitution Constitute?" (Paper presented at the Annual Meeting of the American Political Science Association, in affiliation with the Center for the Study of the Constitution, Chicago, Illinois, September 3–7, 1987).

35. Kirk, *The Enemies of Permanent Things,* p. 36.

36. Kirk, *Beyond the Dreams of Avarice,* p. 7; Kirk, *The Intemperate Professor,* pp. 120–130; and Kirk, *The Roots of the American Order,* p. 36.

37. Kirk, *The Enemies of Permanent Things,* pp. 37–38; and Kirk, *Beyond the Dreams of Avarice,* p. 3. He writes that "'intellectual' is a pejorative term meant to imply reason divorced from religion, tradition, honor, and duties" (Kirk, *Beyond the Dreams of Avarice,* pp. 8–9.

38. See the battle between the "Just Speech" and "Unjust Speech" in Aristophanes' *Clouds* for a witty treatment of this problem.

39. Allan Bloom, *The Closing of the American Mind* (New York: Simon and Schuster, 1987).

40. Kirk, *Beyond the Dreams of Avarice,* 51, 55; and Kirk, *Reclaiming a Patrimony,* p. 7.

41. See, for example, Kirk's attack on the philosophy of Rousseau, "The Problem of the New Order," p. 360. Yet Rousseau presents perhaps the strongest defense of tradition, custom and virtue ever given in his *Letter to D'Alambert.*

4

William F. Buckley, Jr.: Conservatism with Class

John Wesley Young

Of all the conservatives whose views are examined in this book, perhaps none is better known than William F. Buckley, Jr., self-conscious conservatism's most flamboyant spokesman in the popular press and on television. For the past thirty-five years, Buckley has succeeded more than anyone else in changing the public image of conservatives. Before him, more than a few Americans accepted the stereotype of the conservative as a Stone Age relic, a dull, dreary opponent of enlightenment and progress. Buckley presented a different picture. Bright and audacious, an amusing mix of the patrician and the vulgarian in his speech and manner, he gave conservatism something it had been sorely lacking before his arrival on the intellectual scene: a sense of humor.[1] Here for once was a marketable conservative commodity, not only a brilliant debater but an admirer of Bach, an enthusiast for harpsichords and Honda motorbikes, a graduate of Yale capable of quoting St. Thomas in the original Latin, and, best of all, an entertainingly compulsive tweaker of liberal noses. If this was Neanderthal Man, the anthropologists, it seemed, would have to revise their textbooks.

Buckley's contribution to the postwar American conservative movement as a polemicist and founder-editor of *National Review* is well known and widely acknowledged. But has he contributed anything original to conservative thought, or has he been merely a popularizer of other conservatives' ideas? For that matter, what sort of conservative is he—a traditionalist, a libertarian or some other variety uniquely his own?

To answer these questions we need to look beyond the image of the teeth-baring controversialist with a penchant for hyperbole and consider the substance underlying Buckley's rhetoric. This will be difficult to do, for although he has long proclaimed the benefits to America of a vigorously programmatic conservatism, Buckley has never attempted to set forth in a systematic fashion his conception of such a conservatism. That conception emerges only piecemeal from ephemeral newspaper columns, articles and occasional speeches. Moreover, in three decades of almost daily polemical combat Buckley has sometimes changed his views or failed to give them perfectly consistent expression. Nevertheless, there are certain lines of continuity in his thought, certain themes that recur through the years. From his first book, *God and Man at Yale,* which won him national notoriety, to his most recent compilation of articles and essays, *Right Reason,* his fundamental outlook has hardly altered.

Buckley's brand of conservatism contains four essential elements: a belief in the critical importance of religion for the civil social order; advocacy of limited government and a free-market economy; militant anticommunism; and unremitting opposition to liberalism as the ideology of Western decline. In what follows I will briefly consider each of these elements in turn, after which I will try to determine whether they form a coherent and logically consistent whole. Lastly, I will assess the nature of Buckley's contribution to American conservatism.

The Role of Religion

When the author of *Atlas Shrugged,* the Russian-born radical libertarian Ayn Rand, met William F. Buckley for the first time, she gave him a curt lecture on religious superstition: "You ahrr too intelligent to believe in Gott."[2] Buckley's reply is not recorded, but one can well imagine that he took exception. Far from coming about by chance, the order and life of the universe, he once quipped, are the products of "Central Planning."[3] Furthermore—and here Buckley is merely echoing the much-admired Edmund Burke—men and women are by their nature religious animals. Whether or not "intelligent" conservatives must believe in a central planner, they will not ignore the importance of that fact for civilization.[4]

As a devout Catholic, Buckley professes to believe, among other things, in the incarnation of Christ, original sin, heaven and hell and the possibility of redemption for a fallen humanity.[5] But the particular religious doctrines he embraces are in themselves less significant for conservative philosophy than are their implications for society and government. For example, even though men are "capable of sweetness," the existence of evil and the fact of human corruption, Buckley would argue, preclude the attainment of utopia. On the contrary, any attempt by fallible human beings to set up on earth a secular version of the

Kingdom of God—to "immanentize the eschaton," in Eric Voegelin's famous phrase—is doomed to frustration and will likely culminate in a vicious struggle for power and the imposition of tyranny on the masses. Given the frailty of the flesh and the imperfection of human understanding, the best we can reasonably hope for from government is that it will safeguard our rights and maintain the necessary minimum of order and equity.[6]

But it seems that even this much—a relatively free and orderly commonwealth—is precarious. For it presupposes a citizenry among whom religious sentiments are strong. What holds societies together and makes a people a people, Buckley suggests, is their common recognition that as children of the same Father they must respect and care for one another. When this belief has decayed, the bonds of community dissolve and society becomes little more than an aggregation of self-interested and self-worshipping individuals. In an interview in 1970 with—of all publications—*Playboy* magazine, Buckley expressed his concern that the American people have reached precisely this stage of "moral disintegration": "The most conspicuous attribute of the twentieth-century American is his self-indulgence. . . . I think that ours is an egocentric society. The popular notion is that there is no reciprocal obligation by the individual to the society, that one can accept whatever the patrimony gives us without any sense of obligation to replenish the common patrimony—that is, without doing what we can to advance the common good. This, I think, is what makes not only Americans but most Western peoples weak."[7] The anomie prevailing in American life, Buckley went on to assert, has resulted in part from people's suspension "from any relationship to the supernatural." Of this religious uprootedness the rise of the drug culture is only one of the more sordid symptoms.[8]

As Buckley sees it, the decline of religious piety in America and the West in general has had several deplorable consequences. First, it has spawned the "rabid secularism" exemplified by recent U.S. Supreme Court rulings on prayer in public schools. Moreover, the movement toward extreme separation of church and state that these rulings have accelerated has played its part in eroding civic loyalty. "If church and state are to be separated to that extent," Buckley has written regarding a Supreme Court decision invalidating a voucher system in California as a violation of the First Amendment, "then the society that asks us for patriotic attachment to it has singularly less appeal than once it had."[9]

Second, the spiritual impoverishment of life has given rise to the spread of moral and ethical relativism. In the *Playboy* interview, Buckley decried "the successful intellectual offensive against epistemological optimism—against the notion that some things are better than others and that we can know what those things are."[10] Unfortunately, said Buckley, the philosophical relativism to which Oliver Wendell Holmes and John Dewey gave such influential expression has filtered down to ordinary people, in whose growing aimlessness and immorality it finds reflection. One of its worst effects, however, has been to weaken the will of the Western nations, and the United States in particular, to resist their enemies. For, Buckley asked, if we accept that truth and moral codes are not absolute, how can we assert that one society and its values are superior to another society and its values? More concretely, how can we claim that Western society, with its recognition of what used to be called the rights of man, is one whit better than a Communist society that denies to its people as a matter of course the most basic civil liberties? And if we are no longer convinced that Western society is in some sense better than Communist society—convinced, in other words, that truth and right are absolute and are on our side—Western nations have nothing left for which to fight and sacrifice. Instead they are reduced to pursuing amoral policy objectives. Lacking moral imperatives, a foreign policy grounded in relativism will be inadequate to deal with the threat from the East or to generate "the energy to resist the sovietization" of life.[11]

Third, the loss of a belief in a transcendent moral order leaves people with no reliable standards against which to judge the actions of government and individuals. If we deny the existence of a higher law than that of the state, racial toleration, for example, "becomes a mere matter of social convenience" dependent entirely upon the pleasure of the state or the favorable disposition of public opinion at any given moment.[12] Should relativism triumph completely, then America, founded upon a belief in natural law and natural right, could no longer provide the kind of climate in which liberty, justice and decency could be secure.

It is not clear whether Buckley agrees with his late friend, the world-weary ex-Communist Whittaker Chambers, that Western civilization, the members of whose intellectual elite have cast aside its religious traditions in favor of secular rationalism, is so far gone in moral corruption as to be "a wreck from within."[13] Still less is it clear whether Buckley believes the West can recover from its moral corrosion. But it is worth noting that on more than one occasion he has quoted Chambers's melancholy observation that the West has reached its "great nightfall."[14]

Limited Government

Buckley began his career in the early 1950s as an ardent libertarian completely convinced of the virtues of capitalism and the vices of collectivism. A sharp critic of the New Deal, he denounced even the mildest version of a planned economy as "the way station on the road to 1984."[15] Affordable or not, the welfare state, he contended, would lead to the erosion of individual freedom as the masses traded their liberties one by one for the false security that an overpowerful government provided.

Since those early days, Buckley has moderated his antistatist rhetoric and even appears at times to have made his peace with the welfare state. With some reservations he accepts the idea of a social safety net, for example, although he would not cast that net as widely as most would. And although he enthusiastically supported former president Ronald Reagan's efforts to reverse the flow of power from the states to Washington, he concedes there are some tasks besides national defense, such as protecting the environment, that the federal government may sometimes better perform than states, localities or private individuals.[16]

But while he has reconciled himself to some extent with the welfare state and the positive role of government as a problem-solver, Buckley retains a visceral distrust of "the genus state."[17] For all the good it may do, it remains a fearful master, far more apt to work mischief than to rule benevolently. As "the prime historical oppressor," government requires "constant domestication."[18] For Buckley the best government—that is, the least oppressive—is one that confines itself, or is confined, to largely Lockean dimensions. More or less in accordance with the principles of the Declaration of Independence, it will concern itself mainly with protecting life, liberty and property. In addition, because economic freedom is inseparable from political freedom, it will interfere as little as possible with the economy, leaving in that sphere as wide latitude as possible for individual initiative and decisionmaking.[19]

Such a government will, of course, be hedged about with constitutional restraints such as checks and balances and a bill of rights. Although it will be in some sense of the word a "popular" government, it will not necessarily be fully democratic. On the contrary, Buckley holds no brief for democracy. Far from being the antithesis of tyranny, rule by the people, he warns, can itself lead to enslavement of the individual. As in Perón's Argentina or Allende's Chile, the multitude, seized by a "passion for redistribution" and dangerously susceptible to demagogic appeals, may sanction the plundering of private property or the deprivation of minority rights by the state.[20] It is therefore a mistake to make democracy, as liberal ideologues have done, an end in itself, appropriate even to newly emerging nations with no experience in self-government. The proper end of a civilized people, according to Buckley, is not a democratic society but a "virtuous" one in which "the people must be free, and should live together peaceably, in order, justice and harmony, guided by prescriptive and traditional norms." Between this sort of society and a democratic one, there can be "no fixed correlation."[21]

Admittedly, democracy can be made to work well, given a favorable set of circumstances and, as in the United States, a politically mature people. But even under optimal conditions, Buckley advises, democracy needs to be tempered by constitutional checks against the potential tyranny of a self-interested majority. Indeed, he would go further than does the Constitution in its present form in frustrating the will of the majority. For example, he supports the proposed constitutional amendment limiting the president—that prime expression of plebiscitary democracy in America—to a single six-year term.[22] More controversially, he has often advocated withholding the right to vote from the illiterate, the ignorant and the politically irresponsible. In the early 1970s, for instance, he opposed extending the franchise by constitutional amendment to eighteen-year-olds, and a decade earlier he earnestly defended suffrage restrictions in the southern states.[23]

It is only fair to add that in recent years Buckley has softened his critique of democracy, sometimes even choosing to accentuate its virtues above its vices. The reason for this shift of emphasis probably has nothing to do with a newfound faith in the masses; gratifying as it must be to him that Americans have moved in a rightward political direction since 1968, Buckley will probably never fully share the populist enthusiasm of New Right activists such as Richard Viguerie and Jack Kemp. Rather, the source of his more amicable treatment of democracy seems to be his irritation with American liberals for having cravenly declined to defend the nation's institutions against the assault of radical students and professors in the late 1960s. Precisely at the moment when they should have been meeting the challenge from Communists abroad and the New Left at home, progressive-minded people suddenly developed doubts about the system that had served so well for so many years their projects for reform. Many of them even indulged in the irrational anti-Americanism of the time. The upshot of all this, as Buckley pointed out in 1969, is that conservatives, long accustomed to criticizing American culture from outside the generally liberal mainstream, now find themselves by default in the role of defending "what is best in America"—including the democracy some of them had once maligned with an almost aristocratic disdain.[24]

Anticommunism

Until the early 1950s Buckley, like many other conservatives of that day, favored a foreign policy of isolationism. A Taft Republican by family tradition, he believed America's place was to mind its own business and set a good example for the rest of the world. As cold war rivalries flared into hot war hostilities on the Korean peninsula, however, Buckley veered increasingly toward an internationalist posture—not because of any conversion to Wilsonian principles but because of a deep conviction that world communism had to be confronted and defeated if Western civilization was to survive. Joseph Stalin's ill-gotten empire loomed ominously in Buckley's thinking, the gravest of all threats, as he saw it, to religion, freedom and humane values. Further, it appeared that one nation alone—the United States—possessed the strength to stand up to the Soviet Union and thwart its plans for imposing on the rest of the world its atheistic ideology. Given the grim geopolitical realities, America could no longer afford the luxury of high-minded isolation.[25]

Reasonably or not, Buckley has always tended to view U.S.-Soviet relations through a Manichaean pair of spectacles. Years before an American president popularized the term, he was denouncing the Soviet Union as an evil empire bent on world conquest and ruled by "the most unmitigated liars in the history of the world."[26] By contrast, the United States, in his view, harbors no aggressive designs whatsoever. Indeed, America has accepted only with utmost reluctance its "unfortunate historical duty . . . to do something about the bad guys."[27] All too half-heartedly at times, it has had to mount a "great cosmic effort, however disheveled, to give freedom and democracy and decency a chance against the communist monolith."[28]

A "great cosmic effort" against so formidable a foe as Buckley conceives world communism to be would seem to entail a nearly total mobilization of the nation's resources and energy, and Buckley has never been shy about saying what drastic measures he thinks are needed if we are to prevail in the struggle. To begin with, we must recognize that communism is a worldwide conspiratorial movement and that therefore the Soviets and their allies are actively engaging in subversive activities inside the United States and other democracies. From this it follows that we must attempt to identify and root out the traitors in our midst, the Alger Hisses and Harry Dexter Whites who, from positions of public trust or from within the peace and labor movements, secretly aid and abet the enemy in its bid for global supremacy.[29] This course of action Buckley urged most eloquently during the heyday of Senator Joseph McCarthy, of whom he was one of the most vocal (although by no means entirely uncritical) defenders.

But Buckley did not stop at suppressing the clandestine agents of communism within America's borders. In the 1950s and 1960s, at any rate, he was calling for the suppression of subversive *ideas* as well. To that end he not only supported the Smith Act—which made it a crime to advocate the overthrow of the U.S. government by force or violence or to conspire to that end—but also upheld the right of schools and colleges to discharge Communists and Communist sympathizers from their faculties. Totalitarian modes of thought such as communism and fascism, spurious although they be, regrettably do appeal to some people, Buckley argued, and thus no democratic society determined to preserve itself and the Western heritage should allow these alien ideologies an equal hearing in the "market of ideas." If a democratic society cares about freedom it must, when the circumstances warrant, impose legal or social sanctions against ideas inimical to freedom—must, in other words, limit the right of expression for those who do not believe in and actively seek the end of freedom. "Freedom is not served by extending to the enemies of freedom, freedom to mine the city and whistle while they work."[30]

Besides combatting communism domestically, a vigorous anti-Communist policy, Buckley believes, would aim at rolling back the tide of Communist conquest abroad. It would, for instance, sponsor liberation movements in countries dominated directly or indirectly by the Soviets, such as Angola and Nicaragua. As long ago as the early 1960s, in fact, Buckley was enunciating a kind of prototype of the Reagan Doctrine. The way to ensure peace and freedom for the world, he wrote in *Rumbles Left and Right,* would be to "neutralize" the expansionist Communist powers; and one means of neutralizing them would be to give militant encouragement to "those rare spirits" in Communist-dominated areas "who are willing to risk their lives in order to bring freedom to themselves and their families."[31]

In addition to sustaining freedom fighters with American arms and cash, we must, Buckley insists, be ready and able to intervene with military force in countries threatened with Communist takeover and unable to do the job alone. Accordingly, Buckley has approved of every American anti-Communist military undertaking from the Korean War to the invasion of Grenada. But a policy of military intervention, he would hasten to say, makes sense only if we maintain both conventional and nuclear superiority over our rivals, who respect nothing so much as they respect strength.[32] For this reason Buckley has consistently championed larger Pentagon budgets and given his blessing to the B-1 bomber, the MX missile, the Strategic Defense Initiative and virtually every other program intended to strengthen America's strategic position. At the same time, convinced that the Soviets are treacherously seeking a first-strike capability against the United States,[33] he has opposed as disadvantageous to the West every major Soviet-U.S. arms agreement from the Partial Test Ban Treaty to the recent treaty eliminating intermediate-range nuclear missiles in Europe.

Not surprisingly, Buckley has tended to view détente and "peaceful coexistence" as a trap the Soviets have set in order to lull the West into a false sense of security while they proceed apace with an enormous arms buildup and the subjugation of Central Africa, Indochina and the Americas. Détente, he wrote shortly before the fall of South Vietnam, "is impacted diplomatic hypocrisy. We're not spending any less on defense on account of détente, and in fact we should be spending more. We have not achieved freedom for Eastern Europe. We have not brought peace with honor to South Vietnam. What has détente done for us except provide a backdrop for the exchange of toasts between American Presidents and Communist tyrants?"[34] Better a return to cold war tensions than the continuation of such a self-deluded policy.

Buckley has always given the impression that he prefers confrontation with the Soviets to accommodation, even at the risk of nuclear war, and he has never been particularly receptive to the argument that all-out war might make an end of the Western civilization whose values he cherishes. "If it is right that a single man is prepared to die for a just cause," he wrote a quarter of a century ago, "it is right that an entire civilization be prepared to die for a just cause."[35] No doubt the attainment since then of strategic parity, if not superiority, by the Soviet Union has made nuclear conflict a less thinkable alternative for Buckley. But in any case he continues to press for decisive action to counter the "world epidemic" of communism, from "total ostracism" of the Soviet Union in retaliation for martial law in Poland to a naval blockade of Central America to impede the passage of arms to the Sandinistas and the Salvadoran rebels.[36]

Liberalism and Western Weakness

For all of Buckley's efforts to push American foreign policy in a more "hawkish" direction, he has long seemed convinced that the West is losing its war-that-is-not-a-war with communism. This state of affairs he attributes not to a lack of military might but to a lack of will in America's "disintegrated ruling elite."[37] If the nation's leaders lack the will to wage war to the finish against the Soviet empire, Buckley has argued, it is because—and this goes for members of both political parties—in their intellectually formative years they have been steeped in the doctrines of modern egalitarian liberalism, "the reigning secular ideology of the West."[38] "I happen to believe," Buckley wrote in 1963, "that if there were not a single Communist spy in America, we'd still be losing the cold war—because the classrooms of Harvard are simply no substitute for the playing fields of Eton. And where our statesmen go to school, they drink deeply in liberalism, and liberalism makes for

the worst and most ineffective foreign policy in the history of diplomacy."[39] The "loss" of China and Vietnam, the "betrayal" of Eastern
Europe, the establishment in the Western hemisphere of Soviet bridge-
heads in Cuba and Nicaragua—Buckley recites a lengthy catalog of
policy failures for which he blames "the Liberal Establishment."[40]

But why should the liberals, who stood fast and carried the day
against fascism in an earlier era, have failed so abysmally against the
equally totalitarian adversary of the Left? Buckley suggests several
explanations. One is that many liberals have a paralyzing obsession
with peace. More precisely, they fear that direct confrontation with the
Soviet Union would erupt in nuclear war, and they can imagine nothing
worse than that, not even slavery. Hence, in their view, we should do
nothing to provoke the Soviets, least of all attempt to set free their
captives in Eastern Europe and elsewhere. Rather than risk war, the
liberals prefer "constructive dialogue" and negotiation with the enemy.
But because, as Buckley contends, the enemy merely uses dialogue and
negotiation to win through duplicity what it cannot acquire through
outright conquest, the policy of settling fundamental disputes with the
Communists through talk and written agreements is tantamount to
surrender.[41]

But it seems that fear of war does not by itself account for the
timidity of American—and by extension, Western—policy toward the
Communist world. The liberals' resolve is further weakened, according
to Buckley, by their awareness that Communists profess to be seeking
many of the same goals as liberals do. Indeed, in the Communists'
faith in progress and rationality, in their contempt for tradition, and
in their ruthless use of state power supposedly to achieve social justice,
liberals tend to see only a more militant version of their own ideology.
This partial identity of aims and ideals explains the selective indig-
nation of those liberals who, to the detriment of American foreign
policy, prefer to harp on the sins of comparatively harmless and pro-
American right-wing dictators such as Anastasio Somoza than to lift
so much as an accusing finger against far more dangerous and vehe-
mently anti-American left-wing dictators such as Daniel Ortega. Among
the more extreme liberals, indeed, the unspoken rule, as James Burnham
used to say, is *il n'y a pas d'ennemi a gauche*—there is no enemy to
the Left. Wherefore the feebleness of liberalism's response to the obvious
threat posed by communism.[42]

Even if liberals do recognize the Communist threat for what it is,
Buckley regards liberal ideology as a poor match for Marxism-Leninism.
For all its terrors, the latter at least holds forth to the masses the
promise, however deceptive, of a classless millenium. By contrast,
liberalism, thoroughly secular in outlook, offers no such redemptive

vision. Apart from a vapid faith in democracy, it gives people nothing to believe in—nothing, at any rate, for which they would be willing to die.[43]

And this is because in a certain sense liberals do not themselves believe in anything. That is to say, as philosophical pragmatists they reject the notion of ultimate truth. In its place they substitute a commitment to an "open society" in which any and all opinions are tolerated and truth is treated as tentative and instrumental. Under the influence of the relativistic open-society doctrine, many of America's institutions of higher learning, Buckley has charged, have ceased to foster in their students an "allegiance to the great certitudes of the West."[44] But without this allegiance, where do we find the fortitude to give battle to those who would destroy the West and its way of life? Who, after all, would make the supreme sacrifice for anything so uninspiring—and in practice unattainable—as an "open society"?

It is an altogether somber picture Buckley sketches, one of a great civilization caught in the grip of an ideology that saps its confidence in itself. Whether the picture is accurate is another question. One might object, for instance, that it was a liberal administration that ordered the Berlin airlift and fought a war of containment in Korea. For that matter, it was a liberal president who faced down a Communist dictator over missiles in Cuba and a liberal president who committed nearly 1 million troops to the defense of South Vietnam.

Buckley denies none of this. What he does deny is that America's postwar containment policy, essentially the creation of liberals, is proof of their resolve. On the contrary, containment (as opposed to liberation) is for Buckley a fundamentally defeatist policy, for it sends the enemy the message: What's yours is yours, and what's mine is up for grabs. As a status quo policy, moreover, it is morally bankrupt, for by implication it abandons those already suffering under Communist oppression. In any case, Buckley would add, many liberals have long since traded containment and Wilsonian ideals for an "international egalitarianism" that sees no moral difference between the superpowers.[45]

Even if Buckley's characterization of liberals and liberalism is a misrepresentation, there is a certain plausibility to his argument that ultimately the retreat or decline of a great nation—if in this case decline is what it is—is traceable to the university and to a change of thinking within the governing elite. This line of reasoning makes at least as much sense as blaming the alleged decline on "imperial overstretch." Buckley's conviction that ideas have consequences, and that nowadays many of the ideas being circulated in American universities are nothing short of pernicious, is reflected in his much-quoted remark that he

would rather be governed by the first two thousand names in the Boston
directory than by the faculty of Harvard:

> Not, heaven knows, because I hold lightly the brainpower or knowledge
> or generosity or even the affability of the Harvard faculty: but because
> I greatly fear intellectual arrogance, and that is a distinguishing charac-
> teristic of the university which refuses to accept any common premise.
> In the deliberations of two thousand citizens of Boston I think one would
> discern a respect for the laws of God and for the wisdom of our ancestors
> which does not characterize the thought of Harvard professors—who, to
> the extent that they believe in God at all, tend to believe He made some
> terrible mistakes which they would undertake to rectify; and, when they
> are paying homage to the wisdom of our ancestors, tend to do so with
> a kind of condescension toward those whose accomplishments we long
> since surpassed.[46]

Conclusion

This necessarily brief summary of Buckley's conservative philosophy
has omitted many of its interesting and sometimes surprising nuances,
such as his early advocacy of affirmative action and his plea for
decriminalizing the use of cocaine. Enough has been said, however, to
confirm George Nash's portrayal of Buckley as an "ecumenical" conservative.[47] In his thinking, as in the pages of the periodical he brought
into being, all the major strands of contemporary conservatism—the
libertarian, the traditionalist, the anti-Communist—are represented in
an eclectic whole. In Buckley's thunderings against statism we see the
libertarian; in his praises of religion and public virtue, the traditionalist;
in his call for a crusade against the Soviet nemesis, the militant anti-
Communist.

As Buckley himself admits, there is nothing particularly original in
any of these stances. The antistatist views he derives from his father's
famous libertarian friend Albert Jay Nock, as well as from associates
such as Frank Chodorov and Milton Friedman. The traditionalist views,
so evident in his comments on the Harvard faculty, are reminiscent of
Russell Kirk, a longtime contributor to *National Review.* Buckley's
challenge to liberalism and the open-society doctrine probably owes a
great deal to Willmoore Kendall, his political science professor at Yale.
And his anticommunism is little more than a restatement of the views
of such disillusioned men of the Left as Whittaker Chambers, Frank
Meyer and James Burnham, all of whom worked with Buckley at one
time or another as senior editors of *National Review.* Buckley, indeed,
has been profoundly influenced by the group of conservatives and ex-

radicals who gathered about him in the early years of the journal. If there is any originality in his conservatism, it is not in his ideas but in his inimitable manner of expressing them.[48]

If it is true, as some have said, that Buckley personifies the postwar American conservative movement, it is also true that he personifies some of the contradictions and tensions within that movement. Take, for instance, the tension between conservatism's traditional antimajoritarian outlook and the conservative populism that emerged in the 1960s.[49] At times, Buckley, like the conservative movement, seems torn between the patrician's distrust of the rabble and the stalwart republican's reliance on the virtue and good sense of a free citizenry. For example, as we have seen, he fears the power of the majority to oppress the minority. At the same time, however, he would trust society—that is, the majority—to proscribe or inhibit the expression of opinions it deems dangerous to public order and safety.

Or, again, take the tension between the libertarian and traditionalist concerns of conservatism, between the pursuit of maximum personal freedom and the pursuit of order and civic virtue. This tension is reflected in Buckley's ambivalence about the nature of civil society. On the one hand, especially in his early work in which approval of laissez-faire individualism and antipathy toward government are most pronounced, he sometimes appears to regard society as nothing more than a contractual arrangement, a rational mechanism for maximizing private self-interest.[50] In fact, many of his early Catholic critics made a point of contrasting what they called Buckley's atomistic "Manchester liberalism" with the communitarian theology of various papal encyclicals.[51] On the other hand, as noted earlier, Buckley does recognize the duty of citizens to put aside self-interest and help "replenish the common patrimony." In condemning egoistic individualism and extolling "the wisdom of our ancestors," Buckley sides with the traditionalists who affirm that society is an organic growth greater than the sum of its separate parts.

Consider, finally, the tension between a thoroughgoing libertarianism and militant anticommunism. Like all good libertarians, Buckley wants to reduce the power and scope of government and expand the liberty of the individual. Like all fervent anti-Communists, moreover, he wants to rid the world of the Communist curse. But a nearly total war such as he wishes us to wage against the Soviet empire would likely require, as he himself concedes, a vast and probably oppressive national security apparatus.[52]

Clearly, the garment of Buckley's conservatism is not a seamless one. Of course, there is nothing unusual in anyone's adhering simultaneously to potentially conflicting beliefs. Most of the time it may be possible to reconcile them. The important question, the answer to which will tell us much about the person who holds them, is which beliefs take precedence in case of unavoidable conflict. If forced to decide among his libertarian, traditionalist and anti-Communist allegiances, which would Buckley choose? The answer to that depends upon the particular issue that forces him to make such a choice. A good rule of thumb is that Buckley will never favor a libertarian position over the others if it means ignoring what he considers to be the legitimate claims of the community.

The best illustration of this is his attitude toward U.S.-Soviet rivalry. Expecting a major war to break out shortly between the superpowers, he warned in 1952 that a full-scale conflict would make necessary "the instrument of a totalitarian bureaucracy within our shores." This centralization of power would almost certainly put an end to individual liberty, perhaps permanently. Should conservatives then support such a war? He, for one, was prepared to do so, however sorrowfully. For the sake of national survival and the defeat of an enemy even more deadly to personal liberty than an American dictatorship would be, he would "accept Big Government for the duration." Perhaps after the war freedom could be resuscitated.[53] Thus, for the war issue at least, the anti-Communist and nationalist in Buckley eclipse the libertarian.

For the same reasons as he would accept gargantuan government in wartime—national defense and survival—Buckley has supported military conscription "in extraordinary situations" as well as a government-sponsored "crash program" to find alternative sources of energy.[54] Furthermore, this staunch proponent of free-market capitalism has painted a most unflattering portrait of shortsighted capitalists who engage in profitable trade with the nation's great enemy, the Soviet Union.[55] None of these positions has endeared him to dogmatic libertarians such as Murray Rothbard and Karl Hess. Neither has his support for sedition laws and a national identity card—positions he likewise takes in the interest of national security.[56]

Although Buckley is aware of the tensions in a fusionist conservatism such as his own, he has never bothered to give them close scrutiny. Yet it would be of great interest if he did, and for that reason, perhaps, friends such as John Kenneth Galbraith have urged him to quit journalism and concentrate on writing books that "give a theoretical depth" to his views.[57] But one suspects that Buckley is temperamentally incapable of making the effort to systematize his thought. By nature he is much more attuned to the thrust and parry of public debate than to the sedate life of a scholar.

Aside from being its popular symbol, what has Buckley contributed to the conservative movement? Without question, his contribution has been to recognize that ideas rule the world. If American presidents now speak darkly of evil empires and swear by the principle of limited government, and if candidates of all parties now dread to have the label "liberal" pinned upon them, it is partly because thirty years ago Buckley was able to get a hearing for articulate conservatism. This he did by providing it with a twice-monthly forum through which its leading spokesmen could reach the nation's opinion-molders. Among the earliest and most devout readers of *National Review* was a Democrat named Reagan.[58]

"If I have not myself dug deeper the foundations of American conservatism," Buckley reflects, "at least I have advertised their profundity."[59] And he has done so with a charm and wit[60] that have won him admirers even on the Left. Dick Gregory, of all people, called him a "beautiful cat," and during his unsuccessful but lively campaign for mayor of New York City in 1965, Groucho Marx said that if he lived in New York he would vote for Buckley.

Some who remember Buckley as a younger man say that his rhetoric has lost its cutting edge, that the fire that once raged in his belly and devoured so many liberals in its day has dwindled to an ember. If they mean he has mellowed, they are undoubtedly right. Ever since the Democratic Convention of 1968, when he blew up at Gore Vidal on nationwide television, Buckley has been far less likely to question an opponent's virility or to suggest, in a moment of vexation, summary execution for political enemies such as Martin Luther King, Jr. This mellowing is a mark of maturity more than a sign of creative power depleted. And even if it were true that Buckley has seen better days as a polemicist, his place in American intellectual history is already assured.

Notes

1. For this observation I am indebted to Lewis S. Feuer.
2. William F. Buckley, Jr., *Right Reason* (Boston: Little, Brown, 1985), p. 410.
3. William F. Buckley, Jr., *Execution Eve—and Other Contemporary Ballads* (New York: G. P. Putnam's Sons, 1975), p. 461.
4. See William F. Buckley, Jr., *The Governor Listeth* (New York: G. P. Putnam's Sons, 1971), p. 302; William F. Buckley, Jr., *The Jeweler's Eye* (New York: G. P. Putnam's Sons, 1969), p. 23; and William F. Buckley, Jr., *Inveighing We Will Go* (New York: G. P. Putnam's Sons, 1972), pp. 53–54.
5. On Buckley's Catholicism see his comments in Robert Campbell, ed., *Spectrum of Catholic Attitudes* (Milwaukee: Bruce Publishing, 1969), esp. pp. 1, 35, 41–42, 45–46; and William F. Buckley, Jr., *Rumbles Left and Right* (New York: G. P. Putnam's Sons, 1963), p. 146.

6. For Buckley's condemnations of "gnostic utopianism" and the "ideological vanity" responsible for it, see Buckley, *The Governor Listeth,* p. 316; William F. Buckley, Jr., "The Road to Serfdom: The Intellectuals and Socialism," in Fritz Machlup, ed., *Essays on Hayek* (Hillsdale, Mich.: Hillsdale College Press, 1976), pp. 104–105; William F. Buckley, Jr., *The Unmaking of a Mayor* (New Rochelle, N.Y.: Arlington House, 1977), p. 173; William F. Buckley, Jr., *A Hymnal: The Controversial Arts* (New York: G. P. Putnam's Sons, 1978), p. 425; and Buckley, *Inveighing We Will Go,* p. 274. Also see Campbell, ed., *Spectrum of Catholic Attitudes,* pp. 41–42. For Buckley's succinct explanation of the phrase "immanentize the eschaton," see Buckley, *Execution Eve,* p. 311.

7. Buckley, *Inveighing We Will Go,* pp. 52–53. Also see Buckley, *Right Reason,* p. 44. Compare William F. Buckley, Jr., *Cruising Speed—A Documentary* (New York: G. P. Putnam's Sons, 1971), p. 179; Buckley, *Execution Eve,* pp. 270–272; and Buckley, *The Jeweler's Eye,* pp. 252–253.

8. Buckley, *Inveighing We Will Go,* p. 53.

9. Buckley, *Execution Eve,* pp. 271–272. For Buckley's view that the Supreme Court has become "a presumptuous ethical-political tribunal" whose pronouncements have undermined self-government, see pp. 455–457. Also see Buckley, *Inveighing We Will Go,* p. 325.

10. Buckley, *Inveighing We Will Go,* p. 53.

11. See Buckley, *Cruising Speed,* p. 248; and William F. Buckley, Jr., *United Nations Journal: A Delegate's Odyssey* (New York: G. P. Putnam's Sons, 1974), p. 257.

12. Buckley, *Right Reason,* p. 44.

13. William F. Buckley, Jr., ed., *Odyssey of a Friend* (New York: G. P. Putnam's Sons, 1969), pp. 67–68.

14. Ibid., p. 68.

15. Buckley, *Rumbles Left and Right,* p. 41. Also see William F. Buckley, Jr., *Up from Liberalism* (New York: Hillman Books, 1959), pp. 201–205.

16. But he insists that for the conservative, "the presumption remains against state involvement" or else in favor of local, "organic" solutions to problems in preference to federal solutions. See Buckley, *The Unmaking of a Mayor,* pp. 97, 211; and Buckley, *Up from Liberalism,* pp. 218–219. For Buckley's views on government welfare programs, see William F. Buckley, Jr., *Four Reforms* (New York: G. P. Putnam's Sons, 1973), pp. 19–45; Buckley, *The Unmaking of a Mayor,* p. 176; and Buckley, *Right Reason,* p. 93.

17. William F. Buckley, Jr., "The Party and the Deep Blue Sea," *Commonweal* 25 (January 1952): 391.

18. Buckley, *The Unmaking of a Mayor,* p. 172.

19. See ibid., p. 107; Buckley, *Inveighing We Will Go,* pp. 46, 292; and Buckley, *Up from Liberalism,* p. 197.

20. See Buckley, *Inveighing We Will Go,* pp. 169–170, 188. Also see Buckley, *Up from Liberalism,* pp. 130, 137–138, 141–144, 149; Buckley, *A Hymnal,* p. 27; and Buckley, *The Governor Listeth,* p. 40.

21. *Up from Liberalism,* p. 143.

22. Buckley, *Four Reforms,* pp. 12–14. Compare Buckley, *Up from Liberalism,* p. 67. For Buckley's view that democracy is "right for America" but

not necessarily for other countries, see "An Interview with William F. Buckley, Jr.," *Mademoiselle* (June 1961): 120.

23. Buckley, *The Governor Listeth,* pp. 396–398; and Buckley, *Up from Liberalism,* pp. 145–149. "The problem of the South," Buckley wrote in 1959, "is not how to get the vote for the Negro, but how to train the Negro—and a great many whites—to cast a thoughtful vote" (*Up from Liberalism,* p. 148). Also see Buckley, *The Jeweler's Eye,* pp. 65–67; Buckley, *Inveighing We Will Go,* p. 42; and William F. Buckley, Jr., "Going Against the Liberal Grain," *Maclean's,* January 18, 1982, p. 20.

24. See Buckley, *The Governor Listeth,* pp. 151–156. Compare George H. Nash, *The Conservative Intellectual Movement in America: Since 1945* (New York: Basic Books, 1976), pp. 249–251.

25. Nash, ibid., pp. 123, 125; Buckley, *Inveighing We Will Go,* pp. 72–73; and William F. Buckley, Jr. and L. Brent Bozell, *McCarthy and His Enemies* (Chicago: Henry Regnery, 1961), p. 245.

26. Buckley, *The Governor Listeth,* p. 238. Also see Buckley, *Right Reason,* pp. 96–97, 228–230.

27. Buckley, *United Nations Journal,* pp. 34–35. Also see Buckley, *Inveighing We Will Go,* p. 292; and Buckley, *Right Reason,* p. 238.

28. Buckley, *Right Reason,* p. 307. Buckley wrote these words in 1984. Note his insistence even at that late date that world communism, in spite of occasional squabbles and schisms in the Marxist-Leninist camp, presents an essentially united front against the bourgeois West. For Buckley's view that world communism remains an anti-Western monolith even though the West might exploit the feud between Russia and China, see p. 215; Buckley, *The Governor Listeth,* p. 108; and Buckley, *Inveighing We Will Go,* p. 32.

29. On these points see especially Buckley's chapter, "The Committee and Its Critics," in William F. Buckley, Jr. and the editors of *National Review, The Committee and Its Critics* (Chicago: Henry Regnery, 1963), pp. 13–33. Also see Buckley, *The Unmaking of a Mayor,* p. 244.

30. Buckley, "The Committee and Its Critics," p. 33. Also see Buckley, *Inveighing We Will Go,* pp. 49–51; William F. Buckley, Jr., *God and Man at Yale* (Chicago: Henry Regnery, 1951), pp. 145–161, 172–190; Buckley and Bozell, *McCarthy and His Enemies,* pp. 310–335; and Buckley, *Rumbles Left and Right,* pp. 136–137.

31. Buckley, *Rumbles Left and Right,* pp. 58–59.

32. See "An Interview with William F. Buckley, Jr.," p. 124.

33. Buckley, *Inveighing We Will Go,* p. 20.

34. Buckley, *Execution Eve,* pp. 57–58. Also see pp. 201–202; and Buckley, *Inveighing We Will Go,* pp. 19, 95.

35. William F. Buckley, Jr., "On Dead-Red," *National Review,* December 4, 1962, p. 424.

36. Buckley, *A Hymnal,* p. 240; and Buckley, *Right Reason,* pp. 99, 121–125, 257.

37. Buckley, *McCarthy and His Enemies,* p. 4. Also see Buckley, *Execution Eve,* pp. 55, 242.

38. Buckley, *Up from Liberalism,* p. 168. Buckley made this statement in the 1950s, when the Republican party could still with plausibility be said to be controlled by "Eastern Seaboard Liberals" such as Nelson Rockefeller and Thomas Dewey. See Buckley, *Execution Eve,* pp. 261–262.

39. Buckley, *The Jeweler's Eye,* p. 53.

40. "A loose and spontaneous association of the people who occupy most of the command posts in our society, who tend to react the same way to certain kinds of stimuli, and who—because they are the style setters of the age—pretty well succeed in planting their axioms on the public thought process" (*The Jeweler's Eye,* p. 38).

41. See, especially, Buckley, *Rumbles Left and Right,* pp. 54, 57–58.

42. Buckley, *The Jeweler's Eye,* pp. 41–42; and Buckley, *Inveighing We Will Go,* pp. 79–80. Also see James Burnham, *Suicide of the West* (New Rochelle, N.Y.: Arlington House, 1964), pp. 205–220. For Buckley's views on American policy toward repressive right-wing governments, see Buckley, *Inveighing We Will Go,* p. 293; Buckley, *A Hymnal,* p. 62; Buckley, *Execution Eve,* p. 44; and Buckley, *Right Reason,* p. 256.

43. Buckley, *Up from Liberalism,* pp. 133–134.

44. Buckley, *Rumbles Left and Right,* p. 139. Also see pp. 81, 137–138, 141; Buckley, *Up from Liberalism,* pp. 172–173; and Buckley, *God and Man at Yale,* pp. 157, 193. Buckley's most detailed critique of the open-society doctrine, written jointly with his brother-in-law, is in Buckley and Bozell, *McCarthy and His Enemies,* pp. 308–335.

45. See Buckley's comments in Steve Allen, Willmoore Kendall, William F. Buckley, Jr., L. Brent Bozell, Robert Hutchins, and James MacGregor Burns, *Dialogues in Americanism* (Chicago: Henry Regnery, 1964), pp. 18–19; Buckley, *Rumbles Left and Right,* p. 151; Buckley, *Inveighing We Will Go,* p. 73; and Buckley, *Execution Eve,* pp. 35–38. Compare Buckley, *The Jeweler's Eye,* pp. 104–107.

46. Buckley, *Rumbles Left and Right,* pp. 134–135.

47. Nash, *Conservative Intellectual Movement,* p. 184.

48. On the sources of Buckley's conservatism, see ibid., pp. 15, 18, 120, 340, 376n; and Charles Lam Markmann, *The Buckleys* (New York: William Morrow, 1973), pp. 56–57, 99, 183. Also see Buckley, *The Jeweler's Eye,* p. 10; Buckley, *Cruising Speed,* p. 73; and Buckley, *A Hymnal,* pp. 415–416.

49. Nash, *Conservative Intellectual Movement,* p. 338.

50. This, at least, seems to be the implication of such passages as Buckley, *God and Man at Yale,* p. 79; and Buckley, "The Party and the Deep Blue Sea," p. 391.

51. Markmann, *The Buckleys,* pp. 102–103; also see pp. 190–192. For Buckley's reply to these critics, see William F. Buckley, Jr., "Father Fullman's Assault," *Catholic World* 175 (August 1952): 328–333; and William F. Buckley, Jr., "A Very Personal Answer to My Critics," *Catholic World* 192 (March 1961): 360–365. Compare Buckley, *Inveighing We Will Go,* p. 56.

52. See Buckley, "The Party and the Deep Blue Sea," pp. 392–393.

53. Ibid.; and William F. Buckley, Jr., "Letter to the Editor," *Freeman* 5 (January 1955): 244. Also see Buckley, "The Committee and Its Critics," pp. 15–16.

54. Buckley, *Up from Liberalism,* p. 194; Buckley, "The Committee and Its Critics," p. 15; and Buckley, *Right Reason,* p. 143.

55. Buckley, "The Road to Serfdom," pp. 101–102; and Buckley, *A Hymnal,* pp. 53–57.

56. Buckley, *The Governor Listeth,* pp. 310–312; and Buckley, *A Hymnal,* pp. 216–218. For Buckley's criticism of Rothbard and other "fanatical" anti-statists, see Buckley, *The Jeweler's Eye,* pp. 16–17; Buckley, *Inveighing We Will Go,* pp. 294–296; and Buckley, *The Governor Listeth,* pp. 145–150.

57. Buckley, *Cruising Speed,* pp. 249–250.

58. On Buckley's purpose in founding *National Review* and his faith in "the power of ideas," see Nash, *Conservative Intellectual Movement,* pp. 146–149; William F. Buckley, Jr., "Publisher's Statement," *National Review,* November 19, 1955, p. 5; William F. Buckley, Jr., *Overdrive* (Garden City, N.Y.: Doubleday, 1983), p. 29; and Buckley, *Rumbles Left and Right,* p. 155. Also see Janice Castro, "All the President's Magazines," *Time,* December 15, 1980, p. 78.

59. Buckley, *Cruising Speed,* p. 250.

60. A small but revealing sample: In the early days of his public television show "Firing Line," Buckley was asked why Bobby Kennedy turned down repeated invitations to appear on the program to face questioning from Buckley. "Why does baloney reject the grinder?" he replied (Markmann, *The Buckleys,* p. 252).

5

Edward Banfield:
Taming the Spirit
of Modern Progressivism

David E. Marion

The fragile character of decent political orders and the temptations of democratic utopianism are not unfamiliar themes to students of the history of political philosophy. These themes guided reflections and discourse on political life from pre-Socratic to relatively recent times. They are not, however, the staples out of which contemporary political analysis has been forged during much of this century. Claims arising out of common underlying convictions about the unlimited possibilities and perfectibility of political life have come to dominate writing and teaching in the social sciences. Not surprisingly, such thoughts have migrated from academic halls to exercise considerable influence over the political process in general and policymaking in particular. It is with a view to responding to such reasoning and its political conse-quences that Edward Banfield has devoted his scholarship for more than four decades. As there is such a close link between contemporary reformist thinking and his writings, an initial review of the dominant thrust of modern political discourse is an essential preface to an examination of Banfield's political teaching.

Contextual Observations

The commitment to unlimited progress through social reform is visible in classic form in the political thought of progressives such as Woodrow Wilson who sought desperately to bring democratic principles to perfection in the United States and abroad. In turn, progressive thought facilitated and received formal expression in the substantive reforms of the New Deal. Although often treated as a discrete period in American history, the New Deal is best understood as an extension of the work of progressives who believed that the political community was open to manipulation to the end of perfecting the way of life of the people. What this meant in practice for adherents of progressive thought was that society had a moral obligation to make every effort to assure full participation for all citizens in the enjoyment of the fruits of a vibrant community of rights, with the beginning point being the purification of the democratic bona fides of the political process. The effect over time of this thinking has been to produce a collective amnesia regarding not simply the limited ends of the American constitutional order but the fragility of decent even if not perfect communities, as well as the related dangers of political idealism. Serving as a powerful reminder of these considerations are the writings and teaching of Edward Banfield.

The New Deal, in fact, forms an interesting backdrop for an assessment of Banfield's political thought and writing. New Deal thinking drew sustenance from the conviction arising in modernity that science enables man to conquer chance itself and hence solve the beguiling problems of human existence. This faith in the unlimited beneficence of science complements the altered goal of political life in modernity. No longer is classical or medieval moral or civic virtue the principal end; now the achievement of commodious self-preservation in a society dedicated to the advancement of rights and interests through both individual and group action is the goal.

New Deal thinking can be traced to the insistence of progressive period figures such as Oliver Wendell Holmes that the Constitution establishes processes of governance that freely stand apart from endorsements of particular economic or social practices or policies. To take one example, Holmes protested in his famous dissent in *Lochner* v. *New York*[1] that the Constitution did not enact Herbert Spencer's theory of social statics or mandate a single legitimate economic arrangement. Rather, according to Holmes, the people are free to embrace paternalism, capitalism or socialism depending on their expressed preferences. The only constitutional concern is that the people are given the opportunity to choose freely. In effect, Holmes argued for the deconstitutionalization of opinion on economic and social issues. Without pausing here to consider whether his thinking permits a convincing defense of a cohesive community, the practical consequence of this argument is significant. With the eventual widespread acceptance of Holmes's position, it became permissible to build a coalition around any set of preferences, an opportunity that the New Dealers used to full advantage by the mid-1930s. Electoral power replaces reflections on permanent constitutional principles that are presumed to shape the way of life of the people. For example, whether to regulate production becomes an electoral question, not an issue to be decided in terms of what the Constitution stipulates.

The open-endedness of the Holmesian approach contrasts sharply with the reasoning of John Marshall, who treated the Constitution as the proper touchstone for deciding important regime issues. Such, for example, was Marshall's reasoning in *Fletcher* v. *Peck,*[2] a decision that overturned a seemingly defensible action by the Georgia legislature in response to a tainted transaction involving the sale of state land. For Marshall, constitutional protection for vested property rights superceded the immediate concerns of the state. Where Marshall looked for guidance in such matters from the architectonic principles of the republic, Holmes and the Progressives looked to the will of transitory majorities.

The result of the Progressives' approach to political activity is that attention shifts from a concern for preserving the way of life underwritten by the Constitution, or even understanding the meaning of the Constitution as a guiding document, to finding out how best to mobilize public opinion and interest group support behind a set of preferences. The obvious consequence is that the satisfaction of preferences ends up driving governmental action and rhetoric. The general good is defined in terms of the aggregation of satisfied individuals or interest groups. The advancement of individual rights and personal or group interests is the engine that moves the entire order in keeping with a radicalized view of the rights-oriented nature of the system.

Although the American founding grew out of the modern natural rights tradition, Banfield and other scholars of his persuasion understood that the framers retained a healthy premodern suspicion of utopianism and innovation in matters of political affairs. Witness James Madison's caution to Thomas Jefferson regarding the desirability of inviting regular alterations in the laws and institutions of the country.[3] The absence of just such caution and moderation contributed to the excesses of the French Revolution. By contrast with its continental counterpart, the American Revolution was informed by what Martin Diamond termed "sober expectations" about the proper objects of government and thus avoided the factious violence that the French continued to endure long after 1789.

Unlike Madison, the Progressives and their progeny wedded the communitarian idealism of Jean-Jacques Rousseau and the moralistic idealism of Immanuel Kant with the modern faith in science in a fashion that overwhelmed any remnants of the cautionary thinking of the Founders. The effect of this Progressive thought was magnified in turn by the desire of the people for solutions to extraordinary social and economic problems to the end of promoting comfortable preservation. As a consequence, reformist thought and rhetoric that would expand the role of government and promote democratic egalitarianism have come to dominate political life in the twentieth century.

Significantly, the democratic spirit or temperament together with the elevation of interest group competition to a central place in politics in turn lends strength to value-neutral behavioralism. Toleration is the great virtue of behavioralists and of democratic times—hence, the disposition to avoid value judgments except in the case of intolerance that threatens coalitional politics or restrictions on individual freedom. The winner in the democratic arena deserves to prevail in the end. The object of politics is to create a winning coalition in which toleration of diversity provides not only an advantage but constitutes a virtue. An insistence on narrowly defined ideological purity or on parochialism of any stripe emerges as a handicap to success and an outright vice. Beyond the glorification of equality and the democratic process, even principle-based appeals become problematical in this scheme. These considerations were important ingredients in New Deal politics. What is missing in contemporary political thought, however, are the checks on personal politics and on public opinion itself that received special emphasis in the writings and labors of the founding generation. Here at a minimum is what is restored in the writings of Edward Banfield.

So strong is the hold of reformist thinking on society that any questioning of its virtues appears heretical. Edward Banfield has dared to raise the heretical question, and the price has not been small. Charges of ideological conservatism and even racism have been leveled against his work. Drawing on what might be characterized as a partial or incomplete version of the political thought found in *The Federalist Papers* and in Alexis de Tocqueville's *Democracy in America*,[4] Banfield confronts the new-style positivistic-democratic politics of the twentieth century. It is to the character of his teaching as a response and alternative to modern social science (including policy science) thinking regarding the proper ends and arrangement of political communities that this chapter now turns.

Celebrating Common Sense

The task to which Banfield has committed his efforts can be usefully highlighted by the recognition that the study of politics has to a large extent been reduced to an examination of the minutiae of everyday life: polls revealing momentary public preferences, bloc alignments on courts, and roll-call votes in legislative chambers. Attitudes and behavior are typically treated as independent variables in political affairs that have a life of their own. The short designation for this approach to political study is behavioral reductionism. Among other things, this approach is a response to the insistence that political study ought to be a value-neutral exercise in the positivistic tradition. In turn, the moral relativism of behavioralism reinforces the conviction that the political process ought to be open to citizens to freely advance both personal and group interests—hence, the connection between progressive thinking and contemporary behavioralism that was forged by the time Banfield began to reflect on political affairs in the 1950s.

There is an older analytical and philosophical tradition that surfaces in works of Banfield's such as *The Unheavenly City Revisited* that holds that the real stuff of politics has to do with the way of life of a people in the broadest and grandest sense of that phrase.[5] In the older tradition, the minutiae of politics turn out not to be interesting in themselves but only as they bear on the life of the people. According to this tradition, the shaping of a community's way of life, along with judgments about its moral and political health, properly deserves consideration by all serious students of politics.

Banfield recognizes that the thoughtful study of political matters must begin with serious attention to the phenomena of political life. For example, the practices that the Progressives and later reformers dismissed as undemocratic and thus not susceptible to defense, such as machine politics, become, for Banfield, the focus of serious attention as possibly "rational" practices in works such as *City Politics* and *Politics, Planning and the Public Interest.*[6] These works provide both a descriptive summary of the conduct of machine politics and the consequences of such practices for the character of the community. By taking such topics as machine politics for what they really are and applying "common sense" to each subject, Banfield offers an opportunity to understand the precise nature of the activities that are characteristic of, say, big city political machines or real political phenomena. For him, this is the only sensible way to understand how such organizations influence the way of life of the whole political community. To know political phenomena such as machine politics in their unalloyed form and, especially, free of utopian blinders is indispensable to an understanding of the reasons for the successes and failures of machines and their impact on the community. To Banfield, the results of such an approach will be a more thoughtful appreciation of the nature of political life itself.

Banfield leaves little doubt about the threat to an informed understanding of political life posed by the gloss applied by reformer-analysts.

His preface to *Urban Government* summarizes what he considers distinctive about his work: "Most textbooks on state and local government are preoccupied with what 'experts' think *ought* to be the case; this one is occupied with what *really is* the case."[7] Banfield sees himself returning politics, "the struggle for power and the management of conflict," to the place it ought to occupy in the study of topics such as urban government.[8] The thrust of his approach is to counteract simplistic reductionism by calling upon students of politics to begin with the basic phenomena of political life and then inquire into the relationship of existing practices to the way of life of a people—the macrodimension. This approach leads Banfield to examine and take seriously the importance of negotiation and bargaining in political affairs and to write under such headings as "The Desirable and the Possible," with an emphasis on the "possible."[9] By taking this tack, Banfield can examine the advantages that might come for the people from institutions and practices often impugned in reformist rhetoric. Because, according to Banfield, the way of life of the people and community ought to hold our attention, an approach that dismisses or depreciates the careful examination of, say, political machines due to their so-called pernicious qualities makes no sense.[10] By contrast, Banfield's position makes no sense, and indeed appears heretical, to anyone who concludes in advance that imperfectly democratic arrangements are indefensible.

In his 1954 work, *The Moral Basis of a Backward Society,*[11] Banfield studies the traits of some villagers in southern Italy in an effort to understand the critical elements that are responsible for the ethos or culture or morality of a people. Again, his point of departure is indigenous patterns of behavior and perceptions and the connection with conditions of political organization.[12] His approach contains elements reminiscent of the treatment of American society found in Tocqueville's *Democracy in America.* It is not culture or specific mores per se that intrigue Banfield, but the implications for governance and the political life of the people that follow from the culture. What emerges from his study is the conclusion that stable political structures cannot be taken for granted even in so-called developed countries. Unless a supportive culture or "way of life" is present, competence and stability in governance will be unlikely. Even in the presence of an "advanced" culture or society, chance or good luck may still be required to sustain high-toned politics (a theme to which this chapter will return).

In another early work that focuses on local political attitudes and practices, "The Dilemmas of a Metropolitan Machine," Banfield carefully identifies the calculating strategies of party officials and leaders in Chicago.[13] His use of language such as "rational" to describe the activities of political officials points again to Banfield's willingness to judge political phenomena within their own context.[14] Hence, for example, he concludes that it may make sense and certainly not be irrational for lower- and lower-middle-class persons to support machine government.[15] Here is a measure of Banfield's "realism" that challenges and is intended to mute the "idealism" of modern social science. This position is, as well, an important clue to his understanding of both human nature and politics or political activity. The possibility of supplying legitimacy to the activities of machine leaders by calling them "rational" surely flies in the face of reformist rhetoric, as does his practice of challenging the liberal hopefulness of reform thinking, and contributes to the claim that his work is "conservative" in nature.

The great tragedy that follows from the designation of Banfield's work as "conservative" is that it becomes an easy vehicle for its dismissal by persons who might benefit from the instruction he provides. In point of fact, Banfield's approach permits him and us to understand ourselves, or at least a part of our political selves, better than the rhetoric of the reformers does. The true complexities of political life come through in a way that is absent in reform rhetoric. The importance of recognizing the complex character of political life is never lost on Banfield, for he consistently emphasizes the richness of political communities. He takes great pains to reveal just how difficult it is to understand even the most ordinary tasks of political orders. The effect is to encourage deeper thought about political subjects while muting the idealism and even messianism that often accompany a simplistic view of the political world. An early effort of Banfield's that dramatizes the complexities of the city and has a sobering effect on the student of urban politics is a hypothetical case study entitled "The Case of the Blighted City."[16]

The subject of this case study is urban renewal or, more precisely, the improvement of slum neighborhoods in American cities. Using an eager reporter as the central figure in the study, Banfield presents a succession of compelling accounts of why the grandest aims of urban renewal are simultaneously attainable and unattainable. Banfield moves from one seemingly persuasive argument to another as he exposes the myriad social, economic and political considerations that constrain urban policymaking. What is especially effective about this approach is the movement through a succession of seemingly good reasons to believe that aggressive and positive public action is either needed or not needed, will be likely to succeed or not succeed. The impression that many critics draw from this approach to political study is that Banfield believes nothing can really be done by way of direct public action to solve social and economic problems. In all fairness to the critics it must be conceded that Banfield all but directly invites such a conclusion by virtually calling for the old adage, "Don't just sit there, do something" to be revised to read, "Don't just do something, sit there." Another example of such seeming pessimism can be found at the conclusion of the 1950s study of the Italian villagers in which he observes that little improvement in their community could be expected for several generations even if the most effective measures were introduced. He ends the study of this village with the remark that "nations do not remake themselves in fundamental ways by deliberate intention any more than do villages."[17] This rhetoric becomes grist for those who claim that Banfield's reasoning is that of a hard-nosed conservative who too willingly defends the status quo. Even if he can justly be blamed for not adequately protecting himself from such criticism, the merits of his substantive teaching ought finally to determine our judgment of his work.

In truth, if Banfield's approach deserves any characterization it is probably that of a "traditionalist." This appellation is not warranted so much by his emphasis on the complexity of political life or his advocacy of cautious action and his warnings about utopian idealism but by his belief that political communities ought to be judged according to the mores or qualities they cultivate in their citizens. It is unfortunate, however, that Banfield fails to adequately articulate and develop this theme in his writings and to expose the bases of desirable and undesirable mores in modernity, particularly in modern democratic orders. This deficiency, when taken together with the weight that he assigns to the complexities of public policy questions, encourages the belief that his overriding consideration is the impossibility of fully understanding and controlling political life. But to repeat, his recognition that the significant issues are connected with the mores and way of life promoted by political orders, even if not always as fully developed as might be desired, constitutes his important contribution to modern public policy analysis.

Perhaps the best representation of Banfield's political analysis, especially his attention to the mores of the people, comes in *The Unheavenly City Revisited.* Beginning with conflicting allegations about the extent and even existence of an urban crisis by the early 1970s, this book proceeds to identify the "logic of metropolitan growth" and supplies a view of public policy problems in areas such as crime and poverty based on an understanding of the major constraints on urban communities. What emerges very quickly is a stark picture of the virtual intractability of the problems of urban areas due to economic, technological and demographic considerations. Banfield effectively demonstrates that the makeup of the population in terms of age, race or ethnicity is less significant than the population's orientation to the future. Problems that arise from conflicting governmental policies, such as the commitment to reclaim inner cities while pouring billions of dollars into major highway programs that facilitate the movement of jobs and middle-class families out of the cities, receive attention. But the vivid lesson Banfield provides is the difficulty of improving the state of our urban areas in the absence of a change in human instincts, such as a desire for green space of one's own; the character of individuals; the presence in society of present-oriented, or "lower-class," types; or the commitment to democratic principles of government. Although each of these considerations is assigned considerable weight, the discussion of class types is central to Banfield's controversial analysis in *The Unheavenly City Revisited.*

According to Banfield, individuals may properly be classified according to their orientation to the future. Future orientation is treated by Banfield as a sign of normalcy, and radical present orientation is taken to be abnormal. Those who are present oriented seek immediate gratification of their desires, tend to be transients who are frequently unemployed if not unemployable, and are prone to crime.[18] Persons who are future oriented are seen as more moderate in their behavior, making calculations based on long-range considerations and finding violence distasteful.[19] Order, respect for rights and toleration are valued by the latter (upper-class) group; resentment of established authorities and an attraction to the action of the streets are characteristic of the former (lower-class) group.

Banfield combines this psychological theory with the classical argument that each society ought to be judged by the way of life it promotes and the human types to which it gives rise. "The quality of a society must be judged by its tendency to produce desirable human types; the healthy society, then, is one that not only stays alive but also moves in the direction of giving greater scope and expression to what is distinctively human."[20] In this context, Banfield argues that radical present orientation, which instinctively elevates passion over reason, represents a "pathological" condition for human beings[21] because (although he does not spell this out as explicitly as might be desired), those with this orientation cannot maintain political structures or a political community in the full sense. (Banfield finds precisely this same deficiency in the Montegrani villagers of Italy due to their *amoral familism.*) By extension, such individuals do not live fully healthy—or to use Aristotelian language, "human"—lives. To summarize, the consideration of human types becomes important not only as a way of understanding constraints on public policy but as a method of assessing the quality of society.

With this view of human nature or human types forming the essential premise for his studies, it is not surprising that he asserts that the presence of "lower-class" types constitutes a seemingly insurmountable restraint on what can be achieved through such programs as urban renewal or educational reforms. For various reasons Banfield does not expect such types to disappear soon, if at all, even in fundamentally "healthy" societies. It is this belief that prompts him not only to conclude that we should expect little to be accomplished through direct governmental action to improve the cities, but that we ought not to become dispirited or cynical for this reason. By taking these constraints seriously he believes that we will be more likely to appreciate how much has been achieved and see that it is reasonable to feel good about the American republic. Ironically, Banfield concedes his own difficulty in eliciting this much understanding because his arguments challenge the impulses of "normal" types. Persons who fall in the "normal" category are by nature inclined to champion reforms to improve or perfect society in the fashion envisaged by Woodrow Wilson and the New Dealers. To quote once more from *The Unheavenly City Revisited:* "The reformer wants to improve the situation of the poor, the black, the slum dweller and so on, not so much to make them better off materially as to make himself and the whole society better off morally."[22] Banfield candidly acknowledges that his own teaching runs into the hardened views he attributes to "normal" types.

In the end, Banfield has the unenviable task of persuading persons for whom promoting socially beneficial action is morally obligatory that the combination of human, economic, social and political constraints on public policy make it impossible to achieve the great goals typically sought by reformers and that the frustrations that come with their failures are both needless and dangerous. But unlike the call for moderation that he issues to reform-minded theoreticians, Banfield must persevere with his own task without restraint, even immoderately, because of his conviction that the rhetoric of the reformers can so easily threaten and injure a political order that is fundamentally decent, even if not perfect. Because he presumes that immoderation in the pursuit of noble objectives is the destiny of modern democratic middle- and upper-class people, Banfield seems compelled to discourage all criticism rather than merely counsel prudent criticism.

Moderation as "Prudence"?

There is, then, a markedly ironic character to Banfield's teaching with regard to the public policy process. He is determined to counsel restraint and modest expectations to a community that he understands is committed by its political principles and its Madisonian way of life to opinions that fly in the face of his teaching and that spawn reform proposals that are either useless or dangerous in his view. Indeed, he goes so far as to indicate that middle- and upper-class reformers allow their pursuit of "good" to blind them to the frequently harmful results of their actions. The desire to feel good about themselves or to do good for society becomes the all-consuming impulse.[23] Combine this with Madisonian-style interest group politics and Banfield concludes that we have a formula that virtually guarantees that society will either adopt wrong policies or avoid making the hard decisions needed to solve the really beguiling problems. Here are the "defects of [the] virtues" of the American political community.[24]

Banfield confessed to the apparent futility of efforts such as his own to mute the excesses of democratic idealism in a 1960s article entitled "In Defense of the American Party System." In what must be regarded as a cynical view of the democratic temperament, Banfield addressed the reform mentality directly: "To meddle with the structure and operation of a successful political system is therefore the greatest foolishness that men are capable of. . . . Democracy must always meddle, however. An immanent logic impels it to self-reform, and if other forces do not prevent, it must sooner or later reform itself out of existence."[25] Banfield's fear of the democratic impulse towards reform is revealing of his view of political life. Decent political orders are both rare and fragile in his estimation. It is never fully clear in his writings whether chance or good fortune, on the one hand, or great exertions of the human spirit, on the other, are principally responsible for the existence of decent political orders. That he virtually abstracts from this matter is indicative of the greatest weakness in his work—that is, a failure to probe some of the larger issues exposed by his own treatment of political life. After all, it does make a difference whether chance or fortune rules fully or at least to such a degree that reliance on the conscious direction of political life is unreasonable. For Banfield, it is sufficient to recognize that decent political communities exist on the edge of a precipice and hence cannot endure much manipulation or tinkering. The slightest jarring motion may send them over the edge. In this context, even seemingly noble reformist pleas for refining the ability of political communities to engage in reasoned discussion of the common good may threaten decent republican states. It is this harsh view of reformist thinking that adds to the criticism of his work.

Banfield's challenge to the democratic reformers cannot be emphasized too greatly. If he is right, not only the methods and proposals of the reformers but their thinking and arguments are not just problematical but dangerous. Banfield does not quibble about the stakes in this exchange with the reformers, as the following commentary on Jeffersonian thought reveals: "Jefferson may have been right in saying that democracy cannot exist without a wide diffusion of knowledge throughout the society. But it may be right also to say that it cannot exist *with* it. For as we become a better and more democratic society, our very goodness and democracy may lead us to destroy goodness and democracy in the effort to increase and perfect them."[26] What emerges once more from this observation is Banfield's endorsement of moderate expectations and a willingness to tolerate undemocratic and imperfect elements in a political order that is fundamentally decent and competent. Fundamental decency, for its part, entails order, stability and predominance of "normal" human types.

For Banfield, the quintessential model of the middle- and upper-class reformer in the contemporary period is the policy scientist or policy analyst who proposes to apply the tenets of science, mainly economic, to the policy process to improve both efficiency and effectiveness. He perceives the application of policy science to governance as the logical extension of the progressive thinking that looked to change the character of the political order—that is, "to transfer power from the corrupt, the ignorant, and the self-serving to the virtuous, the educated, and the public-spirited."[27] Beyond what Banfield sees as a defect in substantive reasoning, the methods of the policy scientist tend to substitute technique for thoughtful understanding and complicate the whole process by increasing our perception of problems while "decreasing [our] ability to cope with them."[28] The tragic result that Banfield foresees is an undermining of the possibility of commonsense political leadership or, in the best case, statesmanship. In his view, properly grounded common sense that provides a realistic view of human nature and the limits of political life is far more desirable as a guide for action than are the techniques of the policy scientist that abstract from questions bearing on these subjects and turn out to be antipolitical in character and productive of all the deleterious results foreseen in *The Unheavenly City Revisited.*

What, then, might finally be said regarding Banfield's political thought, especially his view of political life? At the least, one striking feature of his thought is the belief that reason can take us only so far in the ordering of political things and that too great an insistence on legitimizing reason as the only proper guide for political conduct is dangerous. Pleas for governance according to pure reason as well as for the institutionalization of pure democracy are unrealistic and potentially destructive according to Banfield. Clearly pervasive in his writings is the claim that a sensible theory of governance is guided by a prudent understanding of the many constraints on political action. What might be called prudence, after all, appears to be precisely what Banfield recommends. By not sufficiently articulating the distinction between abstract reason or science, on the one hand, and prudence as a form of political reasoning, on the other, however, Banfield unnecessarily weakens his argument and opens himself to the criticism that his approach amounts to a wholesale rejection of reason as a test of good governance. In short, the special quality of prudence as a form of reasoning that rests on knowledge of noble and base human actions and the variety of constraints that confine the possibilities of political order deserves more careful attention in his writing.

By devoting greater consideration to the connection between reason and prudence, especially in the context of activities in which judgments about the limits and ends of political life will determine the character of the community being given shape, Banfield would put himself in a better position to respond to critics who might charge him with the belief that chance or good fortune finally plays the decisive role in the existence of decent democratic orders. It is too easy to draw the conclusion from many of his writings that we are merely fortunate when things go well and unfortunate when they do not or that we are merely beneficiaries or victims of forces beyond our control. This thinking not only depreciates what can be achieved through human intervention in history, including the actions of the American Founders, but can easily give rise to the very cynicism or nihilism that he greatly fears and that his works are devoted in large part to muting. In fact, by virtue of the emphasis that he gives to the difficulty of improving political orders by deliberate and reasoned action, Banfield not only leaves himself open to the charge that chance governs all, including whether individuals become "normal" or "abnormal" human types, but he risks having his works too easily dismissed by potentially serious students of political life. Interestingly, Alexander Hamilton in the guise of Publius began *The Federalist Papers* with an invitation to the American people to demonstrate to all mankind that a decent democracy can be constructed and embraced by conscious design: "It has been frequently remarked that it seems to have been reserved to the people of this country, by their conduct and example, to decide the important question, whether societies of men are really capable or not of establishing good government from reflection and choice, or whether they are forever destined to depend for their political constitutions on accident and force."[29]

Presumably Banfield has no intention of depreciating the achievement of the Founders or the American people at the time of the founding, but this is a risk that he courts by his political analysis. It is also the case that exposing the distinction between the just and the unjust or the noble and the base requires more than comprehending the enormous variability of political life or treating the minutiae of politics seriously. What is commendable in his work is the teaching that tinkering with political communities and the way of life of any people is serious business and ought to be approached cautiously and with moderate expectations and that the guiding concern always ought to be to give expression to those qualities that are most distinctively human and make for decency in a community of rights. A more direct and concrete articulation of the distinctively human life as constituting more than merely free life or life in a democratic polity would add immeasurably to the contribution Edward Banfield has already made to political scholarship.

Notes

1. 198 U.S. 45 (1905).
2. 6 Cranch 87 (1810).
3. Alexander Hamilton, James Madison, and John Jay, *The Federalist Papers,* No. 49 (New York: New American Library, 1961), pp. 313–317.
4. Alexis de Tocqueville, *Democracy in America,* ed. J. P. Mayer (Garden City, N.Y.: Doubleday, 1969).
5. Edward Banfield, *The Unheavenly City Revisited* (Boston: Little, Brown, 1974).
6. Edward Banfield and James Q. Wilson, *City Politics* (New York: Vintage Books, 1963); and Edward Banfield and Martin Meyerson, *Politics, Planning and the Public Interest* (Glencoe, Ill.: Free Press, 1955).
7. Edward Banfield, ed., *Urban Government* (New York: Free Press, 1961), p. v.
8. Ibid., pp. v–vi.
9. Ibid., p. 87.
10. Banfield and Meyerson, *Politics, Planning and the Public Interest,* p. 304.
11. Edward Banfield, *The Moral Basis of a Backward Society* (New York: Free Press, 1958), p. 9.
12. Ibid.
13. Edward Banfield, "The Dilemmas of a Metropolitan Machine," in Banfield, *Urban Government,* pp. 317–324.
14. Ibid., p. 320.
15. Banfield and Meyerson, *Politics, Planning and the Public Interest,* p. 289.
16. Edward Banfield, "The Case of the Blighted City," in Banfield, *Urban Government,* pp. 553–571.
17. Banfield, *The Moral Basis,* p. 166.
18. Banfield, *The Unheavenly City Revisited,* p. 61.
19. Ibid., p. 57.

20. Ibid., p. 9.

21. Ibid., p. 63.

22. Ibid., p. 275.

23. Ibid.

24. Ibid., p. 271.

25. Edward Banfield, "In Defense of the American Party System," in Robert A. Goldwin, ed., *Political Parties, U.S.A.* (Chicago: Rand McNally, 1964), p. 145.

26. Ibid., p. 146.

27. Edward Banfield, "Policy Science as Metaphysical Madness," in Robert Goldwin, ed., *Bureaucrats, Policy Analysis, Statesmen: Who Leads?* (Washington, D.C.: American Enterprise Institute, 1980), p. 5.

28. Ibid., p. 14.

29. *The Federalist,* No. 1, p. 33.

6

C. Everett Koop:
Abortion, AIDS
and American Conservatism

Roger M. Barrus

C. Everett Koop, Surgeon General of the United States during the Reagan years, has stood at the center of two of the most heated controversies in American politics during this period, perhaps the most heated outside of the areas of economic and defense policy: the controversies over abortion and Acquired Immune Deficiency Syndrome (AIDS).

It was abortion that brought Koop into politics and government. A renowned pediatric surgeon, Koop was nominated as Surgeon General, the first person named to the position whose background was not primarily in the area of public health, principally because of his leadership in the antiabortion, or right to life, movement. Abortion emerged as a national political issue in 1973 when the Supreme Court handed down its decision in *Roe* v. *Wade*. Holding that abortion was a right protected by the Constitution, the Court overturned the abortion legislation of all fifty states. In its place the Court erected its own standards for the regulation of the practice, which prohibited any state intervention during the first trimester of pregnancy, permitted state regulation in the second trimester but only for the purpose of safeguarding the health of the mother, and allowed states to regulate abortion for the purpose of protecting the life of the unborn child only in the third trimester.

The *Roe* decision touched off a political war over abortion that was fought in Congress, state legislatures, and the federal courts, as opponents attempted to overturn the decision or to restrict the exercise of the right enunciated in it. Koop was an active participant in this war, attacking the Court-mandated regime of abortion on demand. The battle over Koop's nomination as Surgeon General by President Ronald Reagan, which lasted almost a year, was unprecedented in both its length and intensity. Among his opponents were liberal, feminist and homosexual groups. His most stalwart defenders were from the New Right.

During Koop's tenure in office as Surgeon General, the AIDS epidemic more than anything else kept him in the focus of public attention. During the struggle over his confirmation in 1981, the first reports were published of the outbreak of rare and bizarre ailments among homosexual men. It was not long before it became clear that these were opportunistic infections afflicting individuals whose immune systems had been impaired by some underlying disease. AIDS, as the condition afflicting gays came to be called, proved to be caused by a virus that was transmitted through the sharing of bodily fluids such as blood or semen. The disease spread rapidly among homosexual men.

By the mid-1980s, control of the AIDS epidemic had emerged as a political issue. It appeared to homosexuals that the plague among them was being ignored by the larger society out of a lack of concern, or even a secret delight, at their situation. They demanded increased government funding for medical care for those afflicted by the disease and for scientific research to develop new drugs to improve its treatment and a vaccine to halt its spread. At the same time, they resisted proposals for stringent public health measures, including mandatory blood testing and quarantine, to check the progress of the disease through the population. Such policies, they argued, would infringe on their civil rights and lead to widespread discrimination against them.

More broadly, AIDS became a theater of battle in the ongoing sexual revolution, an arena of confrontation for opponents and proponents of the new permissiveness. As the epidemic developed, Koop, as Surgeon General, made efforts to stir the Reagan administration into action on the problem. In 1986, President Reagan ordered Koop to write a report on the disease with recommendations for how to control it. The "Surgeon General's Report on Acquired Immune Deficiency Syndrome," published later that same year, subscribed to the arguments of homosexuals on key issues such as mandatory testing and dismayed many of Koop's erstwhile friends while gratifying his former enemies. In the controversy kicked up by the report, Koop's most severe critics were from the New Right.

Koop, first as a leading member of the medical profession and then as Surgeon General, has been an opinion leader in the controversies over abortion and AIDS in the United States. Understanding what Koop has to say about these problems, however, requires some effort in analysis and interpretation because although he has done some writing, he is principally a practical man of affairs, given to action rather than reflection. Koop is interesting because he has wrestled for a long period of time, in positions of public note and responsibility, with extremely sensitive moral and political issues. He has arrived at positions on these issues that appear to many observers to be contradictory. For his part, Koop denies any contradiction in the stands he has taken. He considers himself consistent in practice, which, he implies, discerns realities that might escape theory. In Koop's case, however, practice has its principles. Unlike many involved in public life, he reflects on the basic beliefs that inform his actions. The principles by which Koop directs himself must be discovered by examining his writings *and* his actions. Approached in this way, Koop is a useful guide—perhps the best possible guide—to the fundamental questions at stake in the abortion and AIDS problems, along with the contradictory impulses at work in the efforts to resolve those problems, for the American conservative movement and more generally for the American political community.

Tradition and Modernity
in American Conservatism

What has befallen Koop as a result of the positions he has taken on the abortion and AIDS issues is a measure of their importance for the American political community. The debates over these problems have not been simple, straightforward clashes between Right and Left; they have gone on not only between liberals and conservatives but also among the various factions of liberalism and conservatism. These issues have agitated questions of fundamental importance about which there apparently is profound disagreement. What are really at stake in the abortion and AIDS controversies are the questions of the nature of the beginnings and ends, the principles and the purposes, of the American political community.

The groups that confront one another over AIDS and abortion can be labeled "traditionalists" and "modernists." The groups differ in their approaches to the problems of government as well as in their solutions to those problems. Traditionalists understand the problems of government to be rooted in men's passions and rely on moral suasion to elevate men above their passions. Modernists, recognizing the ineluctable power of the passions, rely on political institutions—such as the governmental system of checks and balances—and economic institutions—such as the free market—to tame the passions by accommodating their demands while curbing their destructive influences. For the modernists, the traditionalists' reliance on moral uplift is naive, whereas for the traditionalists, the modernists' reliance on institutions is shallow.[1]

There are traditionalists and modernists among both those who style themselves liberals and those who call themselves conservative. On the Left, for example, there is a division between "lunch bucket" and "new class" liberals. The former are ethnic, relatively uneducated, blue collar, interested primarily in basic economic issues; the latter are WASP, highly educated, middle and upper class, interested primarily in quality-of-life issues. The divisions within the Right on this matter are more complex and interesting. American conservatism in the 1980s is composed of a number of different factions. Four of these are especially important: cultural conservatives, free-market conservatives, the New Right, and neoconservatives. The differences among these groups are serious and substantial, having to do with their respective conceptions of the origins and ends of the conservative movement.

Culture conservatism is a reaction to the abstract egalitarianism of liberalism, having as its purpose the defense of the achievements of Western civilization from the leveling influence of modernity. A representative figure in this strain of conservatism is Russell Kirk. Free-market conservatism, which advocates individual freedom and economic efficiency, opposes the incursions of the post–New Deal welfare state into the economy. Economist Milton Friedman is the principal exponent of this position. The New Right, the core of which is composed of evangelical and fundamentalist Christians, is energized by what it perceives as the secularization of American society, largely as a result of the exercise of illegitimate power by the federal judiciary. Televangelist and former presidential candidate Pat Robertson is the most widely recognized leader of this movement. Neoconservatism is basically a reaction to the failures of the Great Society, accepting its goals of containing communism and conquering poverty but rejecting as misguided its policies and programs. An important figure in this faction is Irving Kristol. As a result of these differences, there are tensions among the groups that make up the conservative movement. Cultural conservatives are disdainful of the populism that characterizes the New Right and, to a lesser degree, free-market conservatives; free-market conservatives are hostile to, and neoconservatives are somewhat bemused by, the social agenda of the New Right; the New Right scorns what for it is the elitism of neo- and cultural conservatives.

Beneath these superficial divisions, however, lies a more profound one—between traditionalist and modernist conservatives, with cultural conservatives and the New Right on the one side and free-market conservatives and neoconservatives on the other side. For traditionalist conservatives, there are certain moral requisites of civil society, decreed by God or arising from nature. The health, even the survival, of society is contingent on its ability to secure its moral foundations. To accomplish this, it must mold the human beings who compose it, shaping their opinions, practices and way of life. The political community must undertake as one of its purposes, perhaps its most important purpose, the education of its citizens in virtue. This is not inconsistent with the freedom of the citizens because true freedom—that is, self-government—requires self-control, and self-control requires moral virtue. From this point of view, questions touching on the moral formation of the citizen body are necessarily of public concern.

Modernist conservatives, in contrast, tend to deny that there are specific moral requisites of civil society. Properly ordered, society is based not so much on the moral character of the citizens as on the more sure foundation of their passions, in particular their fear of violent death or their desire for comfortable self-preservation. Society's security depends on the institutions, both political and nonpolitical, that are established to domesticate the passions. The purpose of government is to secure the individual rights of the citizens, to guarantee for them the freedom to pursue their own desires. From this point of view, questions of moral principle are best left whenever possible to the citizens' private consideration, to be resolved in their individual choice of lifestyles. To needlessly raise these questions in the public arena is recklessly inflammatory. Traditionalist and modernist conservatives agree in defending what they understand as freedom against the paternalistic statism of the Left; they disagree, however, in their understanding of the meaning of freedom and in their understanding of the political implications of freedom.

The divisions within American conservatism reflect fundamental lines of cleavage with the American political community. American society is divided over the moral value of modernity. More specifically, it is divided over the morality of the modern project: the scientific conquest of nature. The object of this effort, as Francis Bacon, one of its originators, put it, is "the relief of man's estate," the general improvement of the condition of mankind in the world. The modern project involves control of both human and non-human nature. The latter is the work of modern natural science. The former is the intention of modern political science, to which is owed the invention of the institutions that shape the political, economic and social life of modernity.

Free-market conservatives and neoconservatives accept the modern project. The modernists' conservatism is in their willingness to defend the American version of modernity against its critics from the Left, who criticize it for its weaknesses and failures, for the insufficient comprehensiveness of its objectives, for its tendency to compromise on its principles, and for the unnecessary tentativeness of its methods. Cultural and New Right conservatives, in contrast, if they do not exactly reject the modern project, have profound reservations about it. They are troubled by its nihilist implications. The conquest of nature leaves nothing above man, neither God nor nature, as a source of moral valuation by which he can order his existence: Man cannot make himself master of nature without at the same time displacing its previous proprietor as ruler over the whole; man's mastery of nature reduces it to the level of a mere instrument for the fulfillment of his needs and wants, devoid of any transcendental meaning. The traditionalists' conservatism is in their willingness to criticize modernity for its moral vacuousness.

Interestingly, Koop placed himself on both sides of the great divide in the conservative movement and the American political community. In his opposition to abortion in the years before he became Surgeon General, he appeared as a traditionalist conservative. In his policies on AIDS during his tenure as Surgeon General, he appeared as a modernist conservative. In Koop's attempt to combine in practice positions that are antithetical in theory, he represents nicely the conservative movement as a whole, which attempts to hold together within itself those same antithetical positions. His practice represents something much deeper than that, however: the struggle between traditional and modern elements within American society for the soul of the American polity. In his approaches to the abortion and AIDS problems, Koop articulates—or at least portrays—the alternatives that define the limits of politics and the boundaries of political conflict in the conservative movement and more broadly in the American political community.

Koop on Abortion

As Koop makes clear in his writings on the subject, the abortion issue raises the question of the beginnings of the American political community.[2] It compels consideration of the moral premises at the foundations of American government and politics: what it means to be a human being; the connection between human being and citizen; the relationship between citizen rights and citizen duties; the ethical responsibilities of the strong toward the weak.

Koop traces his opposition to abortion to his evangelical Christian religious beliefs. "I speak," he avows, "as a Christian." He is "an evangelical who believes that Jesus Christ was who he said he was and that he came to do what he said he came to do. Jesus Christ said he was the unique Son of God and that he came into the world to save sinners."[3] Human life is sacred because man is created in the image of God. The sanctity of human life is affirmed in the covenants between God and man, including the Law handed down to Moses on Mount Sinai. The right to life is grounded in the fact that God is the giver of life, and human beings, as His servants, have no right to destroy it. Passages in the Bible, according to Koop, demonstrate that life begins before birth. On the other side, Koop argues that the legalization of abortion on demand "will someday be looked upon by historians as the last turning point of a materialistic society in abandoning . . . a Judeo-Christian heritage."[4]

Abortion, in Koop's view, is for American society only the beginning of a long descent down the slippery slope of moral degradation. It will inevitably be followed by such practices as infanticide and euthanasia. The United States, he claims, is a schizophrenic society, one that goes to extraordinary effort and expense to save human life while at the same time preparing for or countenancing the widespread destruction of human life. The clearest manifestation of this schizophrenia is the practice of abortion on demand, which leads to the situation in hospitals all over the land that, at the same time that some physicians are laboring in operating rooms to save the lives of babies born months prematurely, other doctors in other rooms are destroying the lives of unborn babies at a similar gestational age and stage of development.[5] Koop understands that American society will in one way or another eventually resolve this moral tension. If society does not turn away from abortion, it will necessarily lose its capacity to cherish human life. This is already beginning to occur. It is reflected in the increasing acceptance, by both the medical community and the larger society, of the concept of the "life not worth living." Only life that is in some vague or undefined way "worth living" is to be preserved. This is the connection between abortion on demand and infanticide and euthanasia. The principle that only life worth living should be preserved allows for the killing, by either active or passive measure, of those whose lives are deemed not worth living, including newborns with serious birth defects and elderly persons with degenerative diseases. "It should be obvious," Koop argues, "that as soon as one questions the value of human life there really is nothing to prevent him from considering which human beings under which circumstances should be exterminated. It takes almost nothing to move from abortion, which is the killing of an unborn baby in the uterus, to the killing of the retarded, the crippled, the sick, the elderly."[6] Abortion on demand, for Koop, is part of a process by which the previously "unthinkable" becomes "thinkable," in which people "slide into each new thinkable without a jolt."[7]

Abortion contributes to the moral descent of American society, according to Koop, by occasioning a transformation of the language by which Americans speak and think about moral issues. Social acceptance of abortion requires a kind of "depersonalization" of the phenomenon. A woman carrying a baby is not with child but "pregnant." Abortion is not the killing of an unborn child but the "termination of pregnancy." The being undergoing termination is not a baby but a "fetus," an "embryo," a "zygote" or even a "product of conception." That being is described not as alive but as "viable" or "nonviable," depending on whether it has the capability of existing outside the "uterus"—not the womb—of its mother. The decision to abort, which necessarily involves the death of the being within the mother's uterus, is depicted as a "private" matter, of concern only to the mother. Abortion is portrayed as a legitimate act of "self-defense" by a woman against the "invasion" of her body by another human being, her unborn child. Pregnancy is a kind of "exploitation" of women. The language used to speak about abortion has the effect, by no means unintended, of submerging the moral questions raised by the procedure in a sea of technologisms. This intentional obfuscation has the effect of corrupting the language of moral discourse. It depersonalizes the crucial concepts of that language—concepts such as human and nonhuman, life and death, right and duty, private and public. This depersonalization makes it difficult, if not simply impossible, to deliberate about, or even to understand, serious moral issues. The depersonalization of moral discourse leads to the theoretical dehumanization of the individuals who should be the subjects of moral duties and rights. The greatest outrages of man against man have been the result of this dehumanization. Koop claims that since the *Roe* v. *Wade* decision, American society has come "to regard the unborn baby . . . in the way [it] once looked at the Indian and the Negro and in the same way that the Nazis saw the Jews. In all of these areas, if persons had treated other persons *as* persons and if they had stood for the preservation of life, there would have been no slavery, no Dred Scott decision, no Wounded Knee, and no Nazi Germany atrocities against Jews."[8]

Koop perceives more or less clearly that medical science contributes to the process of depersonalization and dehumanization. The application of medical terminology to the phenomenon of abortion insulates against the pathos of the real-life event. The subjective human reality is lost in the spurious objectivity of the terminology. The result of this loss is reflected in the experiments medical researchers have performed on aborted infants. One experiment referred to by Koop involved the decapitation of well-developed fetuses and the attachment of their severed heads to a blood oxygenator.[9]

What Koop understands as the depersonalization involved in abortion is merely one manifestation of a deeper problem of modern medicine. Modern medicine is based on the application of the methods of modern natural science to the study of the human body and the diseases that afflict it. The purpose is to improve and prolong human life by finding the means to treat or prevent disease. This is consistent with the fundamental purpose of modern natural science—to discover the means to control nature for the relief of man's estate. In order to accomplish this, modern science must conceive of nature as subject to man's control. This requires abstracting from the possible ends or purposes, what Aristotle calls the final causes, of the beings in nature. If things had their own purposes, they could never be entirely under man's control. Modern science must conceive of nature as mere matter in motion. At least implicitly it makes a distinction between man and nature, man moving in accordance with his own purposes, nature moving in the absence of such purposes. Modern science conceptually dehumanizes nature, removing the human as such—purpose or intention—from its understanding of nature. Koop understands this conceptual transformation of nature as the consequence of the denial that the world is created by God.[10]

All of this means that the progress of science, the extension of scientific knowledge, and hence the control over nature necessarily lead to the disappearance of nature as a standard for the regulation of human conduct. Human beings can find no guidance for their actions in a nature conceived as blind bodies in intentionless motion. From this it follows, however, that the application of the methods of modern science to the study of man, as in modern medicine, necessarily leads to the dehumanization of man, the conceptual reduction of the human to purposeless nature. Koop understands that the application of science to the study of man leads to the conclusion that "there is no good reason why mankind should be perceived as special."[11] The result, according to Koop, is reflected in the new science of sociobiology, which holds that "people do what they do because of the makeup of the genes, and the genes (in some mysterious way) know what is best for keeping the gene pool of the species flourishing." "Ethics and behavior patterns," according to sociobiology, should be "put into the realm of the purely mechanical, where ethics reflect only genes fighting for survival." Koop insists that the teachings of sociobiology follow logically from the idea that "man is only a product of chance in an impersonal universe."[12]

Koop's argument concerning the moral degeneration of American society brought about by abortion on demand points to a fundamental problem in the Lockean theory of government by which the American political community takes its bearings. Lockean political theory begins with the assertion that all human beings are created equal. Because they are equal, the are naturally endowed with certain rights: All have an equal claim to life and what conduces to life, liberty and property. Equality further means that there are no natural duties that human beings owe to one another. Certainly there are no absolute duties, the kind owed by an inferior to a superior being. From this it can be concluded that men are not by nature inclined toward life in society; they are by nature asocial. Human beings enter civil society only because their situation in nature is so dire. The natural condition is a state of war, or is very close to a state of war, because in the order of nature men possess rights that they may assert against one another, unrestrained by any duties toward one another. Human beings enter into civil society by covenanting together to respect each other's rights. This covenanting is the basis for the duties of citizens in civil society. Duties are essentially conventional, founded not in nature but in agreements among men. The laws of the political community are the clearest, and most forceful, expression of these agreements. A more profound expression is in the linguistic conventions of society, the generally accepted meanings of the words that are used in the deliberations about society's common concerns—right and wrong, good and bad, justice and injustice. Because society and the duties that accompany it are contrary to human nature, they are experienced as oppressive. Human beings in civil society tend to rebel against their duties and even against society itself. It is necessary to defend the civilizing conventions that make civil society possible. In Lockean theory, this is the cause for which government is organized and given power to enforce the laws. The problem is that there is nothing in Lockean theory to protect the more fundamental conventions, in particular the linguistic conventions, that on the level of the moral sentiments define the duties of citizens and hold society together. These conventions are subject to erosion as human beings in society follow their natural inclinations, seeking to exercise their rights while forgetting about their duties. This problem is the root of what Koop perceives as the moral slippery slide down which American society is speeding as a result of the practice of abortion on demand.

In his approach to the issue of abortion, Koop appears as a traditionalist conservative. He perceives certain moral weaknesses in the foundations of American society, at least insofar as these foundations are in modernity, modern natural science, and modern political theory.

Koop is of the opinion that these foundations must be reinforced from outside modernity, from the traditional heritage of the American political community. For Koop, the means to reinforcement is Biblical religion, what he calls the "Judeo-Christian tradition," with its teaching that "every life is precious and worthwhile in itself—not only to us human beings but also to God" and that "every person is worth fighting for, regardless of whether he is young or old, sick or well, child or adult, born or unborn, or brown, red, yellow, black, or white."[13]

Koop on AIDS

The controversy, with Koop as Surgeon General at its center, over the AIDS epidemic has agitated the question of the purposes of government in the American political community. The underlying issue in the controversy over how to handle the epidemic is the question of how far government can, or should, go in imposing a way of life on the members of society and whether any part of the purpose of American government is to shape the ethos or the mores of the American people. The policies that Koop has recommended were premised on the understanding that government cannot or should not attempt to impose a particular way of life on society. It was his acceptance of this essentially limited conception of the purposes and powers of government, more than any of his specific recommendations, that has endeared him to gay rights and other groups that were among his opponents in the confrontation over his nomination as Surgeon General, while outraging many of his allies from that battle, especially his friends from the New Right.

AIDS is a political issue in the United States because of the way the disease has spread in this country, appearing first among, and continuing to principally afflict, gay men. AIDS is caused by a virus that attacks certain white blood cells, T-lymphocytes, that are crucial in the functioning of the immune system. Present in blood, semen and other body fluids, it is transmitted only by direct contact with the bloodstream. The virus spreads readily through anal intercourse, the rectum providing easy access to the bloodstream. Since the outbreak of the epidemic in the United States, a majority of its victims have been homosexual or bisexual men.[14] Gay sex is not, of course, the only means of transmission for the AIDS virus. An increasingly common cause of infection is the sharing of hypodermic needles by intravenous drug users. From this it appears that government, by legally prohibiting the gay sexual practices that have been the principal means of transmission for the disease, while not entirely halting its spread through the population, could at least slow its progress and save many lives in

the process. There is, however, an organized homosexual rights movement that will resist anything it might interpret as discrimination
against homosexuals. Whatever political influence the gay rights movement may enjoy is due in large part to the fact that it appeals to an
opinion held by many, perhaps a majority, in American society that
matters of sex are entirely private. Sex is outside the sphere of public
control, an issue to be settled strictly on the basis of personal preference.
Any effort by government to attempt controlling the spread of AIDS
by directly or indirectly suppressing the practices of gay sex would
meet with opposition not just from homosexuals but more importantly
from the far larger group in society subscribing to the opinion that sex
is a private matter. This opinion, in turn, is derived from the understanding, fundamental in American politics, that the end or purpose
of government is to secure the rights or the freedom of its citizens.
The AIDS epidemic effectively focuses the issue of the respective realms
of the public and the private in the American political community.

Koop, in his recommendations on the functions of government in
the control of the AIDS epidemic, subscribes to the common conception
of the relationship between the public and the private. Government,
according to Koop, is to confine itself to monitoring the progress of
the epidemic, organizing research efforts to develop vaccines and drug
treatments, and educating the public about the disease. Public education
is to commence in the schools, beginning at the "lowest grade possible,"
and to include "information on heterosexual and homosexual relationships," with emphasis on the "prevention of AIDS and other sexually
transmitted diseases."[15] The public is to be given information on the
ways AIDS is spread and on the ways it is not spread. This is necessary
in order to allay irrational fears and prevent discrimination against
victims of the disease or against gays and other groups in which the
disease is common. Public education is to feature the message that
"the most certain way to avoid getting the AIDS virus and to control
the AIDS epidemic in the United States is for individuals to avoid
promiscuous sexual practices, to maintain faithful monogamous sexual
relationships."[16] At the same time, public education is to include specific
information on the means for avoiding infection, for example by the
use of condoms, for those engaged in promiscuous or high-risk sexual
activities. In general, the public education campaign is to avoid moralizing about the disease. In particular, it is to be emphasized that
AIDS, in spite of its incidence among gays, is not a homosexual disease.

Koop is forthright not only about what government should do but
also about what it should not do to try controlling the AIDS epidemic.
This includes mandatory blood testing, which he opposes because it
would drive away from the medical system many potential carriers of

the disease. He favors instead voluntary testing, with guarantees of confidentiality for those undergoing the test. Koop argues for what can be characterized as a "public health," as opposed to a "moralistic," approach to the AIDS problem. In urging the necessity of a public health approach, he has contributed, if only indirectly, to the development of controversial publicly sponsored programs that attempt to control the AIDS epidemic by distributing condoms to the sexually active and clean hypodermic needles to intravenous drug users. Koop's recommendations have met with approval by homosexuals. The Surgeon General's "report turned out better than we could possibly have hoped for," commented Richard Dunne, executive director of Gay Men's Health Crisis.[17]

Koop is clear about what brings him to his recommendations on AIDS. In part it is the inordinate danger from the disease. Sexually transmitted diseases such as AIDS have spread rapidly in recent years. Unlike more common venereal diseases, such as syphilis and gonorrhea, AIDS, because it is caused by a virus, cannot be treated with antibiotics. Estimates are between 50 and 100 percent of those infected with the virus eventually go on to develop AIDS. A vaccine effective against the virus is probably years away. Something must be done immediately to contain the spread of the disease and save lives. Changing the moral standards governing sexual activity, if it can be accomplished, will be a long process. For the immediate future, the only defense against the spread of AIDS is the modification of sexual behavior, encouraging individuals to be more careful in their choices of sexual partners, use condoms, and avoid high-risk sexual practices.

At least as important for Koop, however, in making his recommendations on AIDS, is his conception of his power or authority as a government official. Defending his recommendations to a conservative Christian audience at Jerry Falwell's Liberty University, in his first public address after the issuance of his report, Koop argues that "I cannot indulge in the luxury of what I feel as an individual. Rather, I have to speak as a health officer."[18] It is Koop's opinion that he cannot bring "ideology or morals" into his job, "especially with the sort of threat we have with AIDS." "When you walk into a lab to do a sterile technique," he explains, "you do a sterile technique. When you walk into a health job, you make pronouncements about health based on facts."[19] Koop understands his government position to require him to sterilize his pronouncements of "ideology and morals." As he sees himself, he is "the surgeon general, not the chaplain of the public health service."[20] Koop's understanding of what is allowed to him as the chief public health official of the federal government is based on a distinction between "facts" and "values." He may seek to educate citizens as to the "facts" of the disease—what it is, how it is transmitted, how its transmission can be prevented. But he may not attempt to impose his, or anybody else's, "values" on the citizens with respect to the question of how they ought to live their lives.

Koop, in his recommendations for attacking the AIDS epidemic, combines faith in science with nonpartisanship in government. This is by no means a chance combination; rather, it reflects the underlying structure of the modern project, in the Lockean synthesis that forms the basis of American political thought and practice. Koop, it appears, is at least aware of a necessary relationship between scientific progress and governmental nonpartisanship.

Modernity holds that human happiness requires the mastery or conquest of nature because mankind is enslaved by nature, subjected by nature to the yoke of cruel necessity. The natural endowment of the human race is, as John Locke termed it, a "very narrow and scanty" thing. Nature is for mankind not an indulgent mother but a wicked stepmother. The horrors of AIDS indicate just how heartless nature is toward the human race. What man receives from nature is altogether insufficient to meet, if not his needs, then certainly his wants. The principal instrument for the emancipation of humanity from the bondage of natural necessity is modern natural science. Modern science aims at knowledge of how nature operates in order to find ways to control its operations for the alleviation of the pressing needs of mankind. The principal tool of the new science in this enterprise, the basis of its method, is controlled experimentation, which aims at catching nature and its operations in the toils of human art. Scientific method is universal in its applicability. The employment of the method presupposes a world without distinctions of kind, quality or rank—that is, a world intelligible in the light of a universal method. The new science begins by abstracting from the heterogeneous forms that compose the natural world of human experience. This science conceives of its objects as constructs of mere matter in motion and thereby homogenizes beings who are in reality heterogeneous. Treating nature in this fashion brings it within the reach of man's power and makes it at least in principle manipulable by man's reason while removing the moral restraints, related to the heterogeneity of form, on its manipulation by man. On its deepest level, modern natural science is a kind of warfare against nature. One front in this warfare is the effort to control and ultimately conquer the AIDS virus through the development by scientists of drugs for its treatment and a vaccine to halt its spread.

Nonpartisanship in government, at least in the Lockean synthesis, is an essential concomitant of the conquest of nature in modern natural science; it is the means by which human beings are able to ally together in civil society in order to more effectively make war on nature. Government is a human invention created by the consent of those who are to be subject to it in order to escape what Locke calls the "inconveniences" of the natural condition. The artificiality of government is implied in the claim, fundamental to Lockean political theory, that all human beings are created equal. Because all men are equal, there is no one who possesses any right, by natural or divine endowment, to rule over others; government, on this assumption, can have no other basis than consent. Because government is artificial, it is inherently nonpartisan. It has no moral or political purposes of its own that it might attempt to impose on its subjects. Having no opinions of its own concerning the moral purposes of society, it takes no side in the disputes over the matter that might erupt among its subjects. It cannot be used as an instrument to impose a way of life on society.

This is the basis for Koop's resistance to demands that government in the effort to contain the AIDS epidemic move to suppress sexual practices that contribute to the spread of AIDS. Legitimate government, on this line of argument, necessarily represents the opinions or interests of society as a whole. The principal purpose of most human beings most of the time—what then will be principally represented in legitimate representative government—is comfortable self-preservation. This, in passing, is why Koop as Surgeon General, while being unwilling to lead a moral crusade to reform the sexual mores of American society, has been zealous in conducting a campaign to stamp out smoking in the United States. The Lockean tradition puts government in the service of the needs or wants of the many without conceding to the many the right to rule over the few—that is, without conceding to the many the right to impose themselves and their way of life on the few.

Nonpartisanship in government ensures the freedom, crucial to the development of science, of scientists to pursue their investigations. At the same time, nonpartisanship in government prevents the few, in particular the few scientists, from ruling over the many, from imposing themselves on the many. It assuages whatever fears the many might harbor toward the scientists, who are, after all, potentially dangerous because of the power at their command. Thus, nonpartisanship in government reconciles science and society and lays the necessary foundation for the progress of the modern project of human emancipation through the conquest of nature by modern natural science. This conclusion is reflected in Koop's insistence that the effort to contain the AIDS epidemic must rely on the voluntary consent of groups that are at special risk for the disease, rather than applying coercive measures against them.

Koop, in his approach to the AIDS crisis, appears as a modernist conservative. He relies on the power of science to take care of the problem presented by the disease. As a result, he acquiesces in the essentially limited conception of the powers or purposes of government that is prerequisite for the progress of science.

Conclusion

It is clear why Koop has been criticized as inconsistent in his position on abortion and AIDS, appearing as a traditionalist conservative on the former issue and a modernist conservative on the latter. Deeply offended by the criticism, he claims that he has not changed his basic position.[21] Koop may be wrong in this claim; he might, without realizing what he was doing, have moved from his original stand. If Koop is correct, however, his practice reflects an underlying consistency between traditionalist and modernist conservatism, more generally between traditionalism and modernism, in the American political community.

What is consistent for Koop in his stands is his altruism, his selfless devotion to the welfare of those who suffer—unborn children destroyed in abortion, homosexuals and others struck down by AIDS. The measure of his devotion is his unwillingness to abandon what he understands as their causes, in spite of the criticism and obloquy that have been heaped at him at one time or another from all sides. It is Koop's altruism that moves him, in wrestling with these problems, between traditionalism and modernism. It appears from what can be gathered from Koop's practice that traditionalism and modernism are both somehow defective from an altruistic point of view and that each somehow requires the other to complete itself in its altruism. This is just the kind of understanding that might present itself more readily to a man of affairs, confronted by the sobering demands of practice, than to one whose concerns are essentially theoretical. The altruism of traditionalism exists in the way that it teaches human beings the duties that they owe to others, duties that traditionalism insists have priority over their own needs. This altruism teaches them to succor others without heed for themselves.

The defect of traditionalism from the point of view of its altruism is its impotence in the face of the evils—famine, plague, pestilence and the rest—that afflict mankind; traditionalism offers nothing to human beings by which they can fulfill their duties toward others to succor them in their afflictions. Traditionalism needs something like modern science, which discovers the means by which man can control nature, to complete its altruism. Thus it is that traditionalism requires modernism. The altruism of modernism is in the power that it puts at the disposal of the human race. It makes this available to all through the progress of science.

The defect of modernism from the point of view of its altruism is its inability to guarantee that the few who discover the powers of nature, the scientists, will not use those powers to rule over and oppress the many, the intended beneficiaries of those powers. The only hope modernism offers is its claim that there is a convergence of interest between the few and the many, that the few will achieve their most important goods as they faithfully serve the needs of the many. This amounts, however, to the assertion of a kind of hidden providence in the cosmos, an underlying order beneficial to man. This is contrary to the explicit teaching of modernism concerning the place, or rather the lack of a place, for man in the world, what for modernism points to the necessity of the conquest of nature through the instrumentality of the new natural science. Modernism needs something, if only on the level of its rhetoric, like the traditional teaching of a providence for man in order to complete its altruism. Thus it is that modernism requires traditionalism. Koop's actions in addressing the problems of abortion and AIDS reflect the fact that traditionalism and modernism, in spite of their contradictions in theory, are inextricably intertwined with one another in practice.

Koop, in his approaches to abortion and AIDS, is no more and no less consistent than is the American conservative movement or, for that matter, the American political community. The issues with which he has wrestled bring to light a basic tension in conservatism and in the larger society between their modernism and their traditionalism, their appreciation of the power of modernity and their recognition of its moral problems. More fundamentally, however, what Koop has done in his struggles over these issues illuminates the reality that holds together in practice the theoretically disparate elements of American conservatism and the American political community.

Notes

1. On the difference between traditional and modern approaches to the problems of politics, see Leo Strauss, *What Is Political Philosophy?* (Glencoe, Ill.: Free Press, 1959), pp. 9–55.

2. Koop's writings on abortion are found in two books: *The Right to Live, the Right to Die* (Wheaton, Ill.: Tyndale House, 1976), and *Whatever Happened to the Human Race?* with Francis A. Schaeffer (Old Tappan, N.J.: Fleming H. Revell, 1979).

3. Koop, *The Right to Live,* p. 19.

4. Ibid., p. 98. Also see Koop, *Whatever Happened to the Human Race?* pp. 20–24.

5. Koop, *The Right to Live,* p. 17.

6. Koop, *The Right to Live,* p. 99; and Koop, *Whatever Happened to the Human Race?* pp. 31–37.

7. Koop, *Whatever Happened to the Human Race?* p. 17.

8. Koop, *The Right to Live,* pp. 85–86.

9. Ibid., p. 90.

10. See Koop, *Whatever Happened to the Human Race?* p. 27.

11. Ibid., p. 29.

12. Ibid., pp. 27–29.

13. Ibid., p. 195.

14. C. Everett Koop, "Surgeon General's Report on Acquired Immune Deficiency Syndrome" (Washington, D.C.: GPO, 1986), pp. 15, 19.

15. Ibid., p. 31.

16. Ibid., p. 26.

17. *New York Times,* April 6, 1987, p. B3.

18. *New York Times,* Jan. 20, 1987, p. C11.

19. *New York Times,* April 6, 1987, p. B8.

20. *Washington Post Magazine,* November 15, 1987, p. 46.

21. Ibid., pp. 20, 26.

PART TWO

The Neoconservative Movement

In recent years a number of thinkers popularly labeled "neoconservative" have emerged as effective and very influential policy spokesmen. Unlike many traditional conservatives who are content to live, learn and write in the world of ideas, neoconservatives have sought to play an active role in the policy environment. The three neoconservatives studied here—Irving Kristol, Norman Podhoretz and Jeane Kirkpatrick—take part in both the "war of ideas" and public policy debates.

The neoconservatives hold a tenuous position in the American conservative movement. Given their prominent positions in the national news media and their abilities to propagate ideas through such publications as *Commentary, The Public Interest, The National Interest* and even *The New Republic,* these opinion leaders are enormously influential. Nonetheless, many traditionalist conservatives question the conservative credentials of Irving Kristol, Norman Podhoretz, Jeane Kirkpatrick and others. Kristol is a former Trotskyite, Podhoretz a former Leftist, and Kirkpatrick an heir to the Hubert Humphrey, liberal Democrat tradition. Podhoretz and Kirkpatrick are still supportive, to different degrees, of big government and the welfare state.

Jeffrey J. Poelvoorde examines the political development of America's leading neoconservative, Irving Kristol. Like many neoconservatives, Kristol's political thought went through a period of profound change. Kristol's conversion to the political Right coincided with the rise of a threatening, Marxist superpower state, the Soviet Union. For Kristol, the Soviet model of government called into question his earlier utopian political views.

Mark J. Rozell analyzes the political ideas of Norman Podhoretz and Jeane Kirkpatrick. As with Kristol, Podhoretz's political development was influenced by a reexamination of foreign policy principles.

101

Podhoretz's political thought can be attributed as well to his reaction against the political and cultural excesses of the Left movement in the late 1960s and 1970s.

Whereas Podhoretz made a clean break with his radical past, Kirkpatrick holds on to many of the domestic policy views she espoused years ago as a Humphrey Democrat. She broke with the Democratic Party mostly over foreign policy and national security postures. Nonetheless, Kirkpatrick maintains that since the Reagan era began she has developed a stronger affection for market economics.

7

Irving Kristol's Neoconservatism

Jeffrey J. Poelvoorde

"There are no benefits without costs in human affairs (though there are frequently costs without benefits)."[1]

"Faith is less concerned with the truths of Reason than with the fate of man— the mortal, finite creature who cannot volatilize himself into Reason."[2]

An unflattering account of neoconservatism describes Irving Kristol as its "standard bearer."[3] It is probably an accurate description, not only with respect to the role that Kristol has actually played in the rise of an intellectually active and politically effective conservative movement but also with respect to how he is perceived by others. Although Kristol did not coin the term *neoconservative,* he has embraced it as the best description of his thinking and has consciously sought to fashion a definable position and a movement around it. As an essayist, editor and participant in research foundations and "think tanks," he has become extremely influential in the academic, literary and political worlds. In fact, he is arguably the single most important individual in the growing prominence of American conservatism. Our task is to understand why this "journalist-administrator" has become so influential and to see if his thought may fulfill his desire to become a shaping force in politics.

Kristol has never written a book, if by "book" we mean an extended, systematic and complete explanation of his thought. Instead, his writings (which span the entire array of important human concerns or, at least, those concerns that touch the world of politics) are scattered across four decades of editorials, articles, speeches and essays, which he has occasionally collected in book form. His latest effort, *Reflections of a Neoconservative,* stands as the most complete presentation of himself as a neoconservative and of neoconservatism as a coherent public philosophy. The book's title reveals an important aspect of its contents, especially the word "reflections." This suggests "questions" rather than "conclusions," "problems" rather than "solutions." As we shall see, it is no accident that Kristol's books are essentially collections of prior essays. Nor does this necessarily imply that his intellectual powers are limited to light exposition.[4] There is a harmony between the style of Kristol's writing and the core of his thinking as a neoconservative. Neoconservatism is not only a way of thinking about politics; it is a way of thinking about thinking and, as such, reaches to the deepest questions that the human mind is capable of raising. Of course, neoconservatism in general—and Kristol's thought in particular—presents grave difficulties. But this is true of all sustained approaches to the problems of human identity and action in the world, an insight upon which neoconservatism itself rests.

What does Kristol mean when he calls himself a "neoconservative"? Clearly the term calls attention to the differences—and the similarities—between himself and those who have always called themselves "conservative." He has not always *been* a conservative; he came to conservatism or discovered it. *Reflections* is an account of that discovery and is therefore something of an autobiography. His experience and development are typical of many who have redefined themselves along the ideological spectrum. Perhaps this is one reason he has become so influential: His thinking articulates the transformations occurring in many of his generation. Yet, neoconservative does not simply mean "new conservative." For if Kristol feels more comfortable with the substantive portion of the term than with some other term locating him ideologically, he is nevertheless not willing to identify himself unhesitatingly with the existing strands of American conservatism. For the same reason that he ceased to be a "liberal" he refuses to become a "conservative": the rejection of ideology.

Kristol begins his account of his intellectual development with a description of himself as a student at the City College of New York in the late 1930s. The focus of his emerging identity was not his classes but his participation in an informal lunch group of radical "Trotskyist" students who ate at "Alcove No. 1" in the student cafeteria. Kristol displays a nostalgic fondness as he describes the endless debates and the dialectical striving for ideological purity. It was obviously a time of intense mental energy and self-discovery, passionate waltzing with ideas of grand historical sweep, and, perhaps most importantly, uplifting moral fervor. It was, in short, adolescence. More accurately, it was an example of the particular form of consciousness born of the adolescent's disdain for the dirty reality of the world combined with his optimistic reforming fervor unencumbered with concern about the real effects of his ideas: romanticism.

Romanticism is a simplification of the complexity of the world, both a flight from reality and an attempt to conquer it. The romantic views the world from the lens of his imagination, whether that lens takes the shape of a beautiful image or a compelling ideal. When the inevitable confrontation with the intractable complexity of the world comes, the romantic either suffers disillusionment, denies the unpleasant reality, or matures into a sober and qualified acceptance of the limited possibilities of the real world. Although Kristol does not teach that radicalism is simply a disease of adolescence (which would be an easy and smug way to dismiss his opponents), he nevertheless does suggest that its fundamental impulse is romantic.[5] In the other chapter of the opening section of *Reflections* (a defense of his activities as a "cold warrior" during the 1950s), Kristol implies that it was just this kind of sobering that freed him from Trotskyism and converted him to opposition to the Soviet Union: the confrontation with a real—brutal, ugly, aggressive—Marxist society.

"Ideology" is the attempt to relate (and justify) all social and political phenomena to a single idea or set of ideas. Although ideology and romanticism are not identical, they are closely akin to each other. An ideology can very easily become an unforgiving standard for practice, demanding absolute consistency in the name of purity. Kristol observes that this tendency is probably rooted in political life itself. It is, however, a tendency to which modern social and political life is especially prone. Why this is so we shall subsequently explore, but let us at least note here that Kristol believes that he has located the fundamental disease from which all modern societies must be protected. When untempered, the ideological underpinning of modern society surfaces as the desire to reshape all human activities and institutions by abolishing any imperfections in practical life. In other words, it surfaces as "radicalism"—the passion to "root out" all divergences in practical life from a principled ideal. Radicalism does so no matter what the consequences because it hopes that destroying the distinction between the ideal and the real will eliminate any bad consequences.

Kristol's journey from radicalism to neoconservatism by way of contemporary liberalism was initiated when he saw that radicalism can, indeed, unleash very bad consequences upon humanity and was completed when he saw contemporary liberalism losing its sounder instincts and dissolving into radicalism. Modern radicalism desires to create the community of perfect equality and liberty. All its members will actively unite in truly democratic institutions of rational self-rule superintending an economy of communalized abundance, all will swim in a culture of unlimited freedom and creativity, all will be graced with a happiness heretofore unknown among humans as their psyches experience the liberation from all repressions of their natural instincts. In a diluted form, Kristol would argue, the same vision of society animates today's liberalism. Conservatism's task is to recover the possibility of sobriety by holding up an alternative view of society.

The problem with conservatism, however, is twofold. One, in the extent to which conservatism tries not to be ideological, it is unappealing to the majority of modern people. The "moral sense" of modern people vibrates to the progressive content of radicalism. A nonideological conservatism, therefore, simply looks like a form of faintheartedness about justice. Two, to the extent that conservatives hold up an alternative ideology of society, that ideology tends to be inapplicable to modern life or just as rigid as that of its opponents. If a conservatism is to be truly successful, Kristol argues, it must find a way to appeal to the moral vision at the ground of modern society at the same time that it expresses that vision in a nonromantic form.

Neoconservatism, then, is a reaction to the ideologization of politics, the fusion or refounding of politics purely upon ideology. It is an attempt to chart a path toward the good society without simple dependence upon any single image of justice or the human good. No ideological picture, Kristol would argue, is capable of articulating the reality of the world's complexity and therefore of guiding human beings and society toward their good. Of course, there might still be better and worse ideologies. Kristol, as we noted, feels closer to the principles of American conservatism than liberalism, but even so, conservatives are capable of demonstrating an ideological rigidity destructive of the true good of the nation as much as liberals or radicals. From the standpoint of a conceptual ideal, all reality is blemished. And, of course, ideology aside, reality *is* blemished. But as we stand and confront reality's blemishes, we can ask ourselves two very different questions: What can we do to make the world perfect? What can we do to improve the good that exists, or more likely, what can we do to prevent the present imperfect reality from getting worse? The former question is ideological and romantic. The latter is the fountain of neoconservatism.

In the rest of this chapter, we shall examine how Kristol has fashioned a neoconservative disposition in each of his major areas of concentration: politics, economics, culture and religion. We shall conclude with an examination of the deepest grounds of his thinking and an assessment of its practical possibilities and its theoretical coherence.

The Defects of Ideological Politics

Two revolutions signaled the arrival of modern politics: the American and the French. They had much in common, but for Kristol, their differences may be more important than their similarities. Both revolutions were "democratic"; both were devoted to the same core of modern principles, best expressed in the concept of "natural rights," which teaches that human beings are by nature free and equal. Therefore, the cumulative standards by which both revolutions measure the health of politics are best spoken in the questions: How free are the people in their daily lives? How equal are they in their conditions? To what extent is the will of the people the actual basis of operation of the government? Whereas the American Revolution embodied these standards in an act of sober constitutionalism, the French Revolution culminated in a wave of radical political terror followed by imperial despotism. For Kristol, the decisive difference between the two revolutions consisted of how radically they interpreted these principles and how realistic the leaders and thinkers of either revolution were about the frailties of human nature.

The leaders of the American Revolution considered civil freedom more important than equality or democracy; the former is a more attainable end for government and requires less of an overall transformation of society. Moreover, they conceived of equality mainly in terms of political equality or the absence of aristocratic classes. This moderated the passion for equality that found its expression in France in the relentless descent of the guillotine's blade. And most important, the leaders of the American Revolution—who by and large were also the framers of the American Constitution eleven years later—thought that sound politics required institutional attention to values other than popular will or majority rule. They were capable of taking a hard look at the people's limitations in terms of the conduct of public policy. Because good government requires qualities such as stability, farsightedness, deliberation, fairness and a capacity to deal prudently with complex issues, and because public opinion (or the will of the people) is often transient, fickle, shortsighted, passionate, shallow and factional, the framers preferred a popular government based on complex republican institutions rather than on democracy. The former, although rooted ultimately in the people's will, is sufficiently distant from it so that the final products of popular government do not possess the limitations of public opinion polls.

Although much of this century's democratization of American institutions has been for the good, according to Kristol, our contemporary politics has increasingly come to abandon the complex prudence of the framers. Fed by the dogmatic democratism of the last generations of American historians and the immoderate populism of today's liberals, American institutions have become progressively attuned to the vagaries of public opinion. Combined with the greater centralization of functions in the federal government and more complex activity of government, this democratization has rendered public policy more simplistic and ideological, more inconsistent and often simply foolish and self-destructive. In domestic policy, greater governmental activity combined with greater incompetency has led to public disenchantment and cynicism about the health of our institutions. Especially in foreign affairs, the nation's interests have often been sacrificed to moral posturing and fits of public enthusiasm.

Neoconservatism seeks to temper contemporary democratism and its ill effects by resurrecting the political wisdom of the framers. By recovering their prudential and restrained embrace of popular institutions, Kristol hopes to restore public attachment and confidence in our governing institutions at the same time that the institutions are free to govern in the genuine national interest. This is a project both of national self-education and education of the world in the great advantages of free, republican government—properly understood. It is also the link between domestic and foreign policy. The internal threat to the health of American politics is the same threat to American interests abroad: a radicalism or radicalized liberalism whose aim is the abandonment of the advantages of moderate republicanism in the name of freedom, equality and democracy.

The Virtues and Limitations of a Free Economy

Kristol's economic teaching begins with raising again the question of what the fundamental purposes of economics are. Of course, economics is about creating the material conditions of life, and aims, or should aim, at generating productivity and prosperity. But for Kristol, these purposes are subordinate to larger considerations: political economy and morality. By "political economy" he means the question of what kind of economy is appropriate for what kind of political order. Specifically, if we desire a republican political system characterized by broad civil liberty and limited authority, what kind of economic arrangements do we need to bolster and support it? By "morality" Kristol does not mean what many contemporary economists, Marxist or otherwise, mean: the "just distribution" of the goods and services of society (although he does reflect upon this question). Rather, he means the kind of moral *character* or *qualities* that a particular economic system encourages in its participants.

His economist of preference is Adam Smith, the "father of capitalism," because Smith's qualified embrace of the free market is guided by each of the three preceding considerations. Kristol finds Smith's economics much richer and more complex than that of either his capitalist or socialistic successors. Post-Smithian theoretical capitalism has suffered from its indifference to political conditions or moral consequences and its reduction of economic thinking to the calculation of the mathematical relationships among imaginary "rational" (self-interested) consumers. Hence, post-Smithian theory generates shallowness in the minds and characters of the participants and advocates of the free market about the requisite conditions for the market and the market's effects on larger society. Conversely, socialism, which contemplates a utopian world in which self-interestedness has dissolved into communalized superabundance, undermines the conditions of political liberty and moral self-reliance that a republican citizenry demands. When confronted with the polemical denunciations of their socialist critics, the contemporary ideologists of the free market stammer about the greater productivity and prosperity under capitalism—which, according to Kristol, are undeniable and utterly to be expected, given the free market's firm grasp of the nature of "incentive"—and have nothing interesting to say about political liberty and moral fiber.

The latter points, however, to some problematic tendencies in capitalism in practice. As capitalism creates general conditions of affluence in the world, it begins to eat away at the reserve of moral character in its participants. Kristol calls this particular moral character "bourgeois virtue," a combination of the habits of a responsible businessman with the values of family attachment and religious sentiment. But it was exactly this kind of individual who worked so hard and made capitalism such a successful and productive system. Affluence tends to make us wallow in self-regarding consumerism, which, Kristol believes, will not sustain a people either as responsible citizens or as effective producers (or investors). Moreover, developed capitalism wants ever greater opportunities for the creation of wealth, so it develops a way of pooling investment and productive forces: the modern corporation. But the structure and operation of a large corporation, like any bureaucratic organization, encourage neither entrepreneurial imagination nor bourgeois virtue. Even worse, the leaders of the corporate world do not perceive how uncomfortably the large corporation rests with American democratic sentiments. Hence, they are politically naive about the forces in the political world that seek to regulate and redistribute the corporation out of existence. Could it be that capitalism evolves into something that cannot sustain itself?

Kristol's neoconservatism resorts to the economic perspective of Adam Smith just as it resorts to the political perspective of the framers. It seeks to fashion a moderated capitalism that is more humane (he argues that one can embrace several major features of a welfare state without the essential loss of the free market), more politically aware (modern corporations should seek to modify themselves so as to dispel the potential antagonism in American politics against them), and more sophisticated in its own principled defense against its socialist critics. But it should be a capitalism that can also admit, and therefore address, its own genuinely problematic effects upon the human character, which might require transcending a purely economic perspective on the economy.

The Unraveling of Bourgeois Culture

As we have seen, Kristol argues that modern capitalism may undermine its own capacity to thrive by dissolving the culture of bourgeois virtue that sustains its operation and secures popular attachment to its institutions. Capitalism substitutes for the sturdy, if dull, culture of the middle class a universal "urban" culture of novelty and self-gratification. The problem is that everyday people lose their bearings as to what is important in life. Standards of self-restraint and the feeling of connectedness with others become significantly diluted, so that individuals are gratified and empty at the same time.

Capitalism also produces another interesting cultural effect: the "class" of artists and intellectuals, which is increasingly hostile to capitalism (and moderate republicanism, too) and open to the radical criticisms lodged against capitalism by socialism. Kristol calls this class the "New Class."[6] As affluent children of the productive middle class, the members of the New Class have benefited from the wealth generated by capitalism, but because they have no clearly defined productive function, they feel insecure about their place in capitalism and do not understand its advantages. Because most artists and intellectuals take their bearings from the intellectual culture of the academic world, they come to live in the realm of abstracted ideas, which, in the context of modern thought and life, means the more radical versions of modern ideology. Moreover, in the name of liberty, the representatives of the New Class come to despise "bourgeois virtue" for its "repressive" restrictions on free expression. In the name of progress, these intellectuals support the abolition of restraints on pornography and obscenity. Expression of any thought or passion, no matter what its origin in the psyche, becomes a good for its own sake. Hence, many intellectuals in American society stand in an adversarial relationship to the economic and cultural life around them and become committed to the radical revision of bourgeois culture.

Kristol argues that the preservation of a healthy culture requires some forms of restraint, especially the kinds of restraints that prefer the family over sexual license. When the adversarial efforts of the New Class are added to the wider cultural effects of capitalism, he worries that our culture is sliding toward decadence. The symptoms of decadence are not only visible in a civilization that is indifferent to its own preservation but also in the lives of individuals who cannot restrain their passions, who cannot express serious and sustained interest in each other, and who cannot find in their own lives a minimum nobility that deserves to be passed on to their children. But upon what should that restraint, that interest, that nobility rest?

The Necessity of Religious Belief

Kristol has written much about the Jews. This is not simply because he is a Jew and is therefore indulging himself in a clumsy and obvious ethnocentrism. Rather, he believes that the experience of the Jews confronting modernity is a concentrated example of what the rest of humanity has experienced (or will experience) as modernity unfolds itself in the world. One might wonder, for example, what a chapter entitled "Is Jewish Humor Dead?" is doing in a book intended to be a comprehensive and serious introduction to neoconservatism. Yet, this little obituary for what the world and the Jews themselves view as one of the most characteristically Jewish traits points to the sacrifices that humanity will make as it succumbs to the lures of modernity. Jewish humor was the result of the attempt to affirm the precariousness of life against the background of an occasionally insupportable faith in God. It was a form of nobility, rational cynicism and faith all at the same time. Looking, however, at contemporary Jewish life in America, Kristol notes that this distinctive humor is rapidly fading—as is the faith that provided its horizon.

In the last section of *Reflections,* "Religion and the Jews," we see what Kristol believes modernity offers as the most serious claimants to replace religion as the grounds of human happiness in this life: bourgeois affluence, psychoanalysis, modern science (as modern physics) and socialism. Aside from the first, into which the Jews as a people can be said to have thrown themselves wholeheartedly, the irony of these alternatives is that they were decisively formulated by Jews: Sigmund Freud, Albert Einstein and Karl Marx. In varying degrees, each of these individuals understood himself to be fashioning a rational and secular replacement for the old faith that would prove to be the refoundation of the human condition. Each of them claimed to represent Reason at its peak and therefore to represent the ultimate expression of man's power over his world and himself. Also, these alternatives are widely viewed as modernity's decisive refutation of religious faith, before which even the leading representatives of religion have come to bow and reshape the core of their ancient faiths. For Kristol, all four alternatives probably do represent the modern world's most powerful formulations. Yet, each is liable to grave theoretical and practical reservations.

Bourgeois affluence promises a world of personal liberty and consumer gratification to replace the religious conception of humanity governing and restraining its passions in the light of eternal truth. Psychoanalysis promises a world of non-neurotic individuals to replace the world of superstitious repression of natural instincts. Moreover, because psychoanalysis reveals religious belief itself to be a form of psychic disorder, it frees mankind from the fear and guilt attached to the concept of sin. Modern science promises a world whose secrets have been pried open by methodical reason and in which we find our satisfaction contemplating nature's design and manipulating it according to our will instead of experiencing religious mystery and pious reverence. Socialism promises a world of perfect community, justice and abundance attainable on earth to replace the religious hope for an otherworldly paradise purged of human wickedness and suffering.

What do we find in practice instead of the promises? In bourgeois society, we find humans reduced to (humorless) bored and boring pigs.[7] Socialism, as we have seen, digs a pit of tyranny, sterility, poverty and bitter disillusionment. And as for psychoanalysis and modern science, Kristol presents Freud and Einstein themselves as tragic figures whose unrelenting pursuits of their visions of human reason led to despair and loneliness. Moreover, the theoretical foundations of each of these potential replacements for religion turn out not to be as rigorous as their modern adherents believe; they are shot through with assumptions and unproven (and unprovable) assertions about reality that—even in the case of Einstein—derive as thoroughly from "intuition" as religion. They are, in other words, not truly "rational" replacements for religious faith as much as they are other species of faith. The only difference between them and the old faith is their inability to generate the kind of society and individual life in which humans can attain happiness and nobility.

Religion, therefore, according to Kristol, must remain a permanent feature of human life. The pious attention to the eternal is the only attitude that can shape moral character sufficiently so as to hold society together by generating citizens with sufficient love and concern for each other. Religion is the only force capable of teaching people to be more than their appetites and out of which dignity and the capacity for sustained attention to serious matters flow. Religion is the only source of the gentle consolations of the heart that enable our species to bear the endless—and unavoidable—agonies of this life and to face the stark reality of the eternal silence of the grave. This is true not only for the masses but even for the enlightened minds of humanity as well. For there is one other benefit derived from religious faith, both as a cultural element and as a component of human consciousness: Faith reminds us of the limits of our reason and our power in the world.

This, then, is the great error of modernity: its unmoderated belief in the unlimited power of human reason to understand and govern the world. All the political, economic and cultural movements and forces of the modern world—and their effects, for great good and greater evil—stem from this impulse. Uncontained, this impulse leads to the belief that this earth, through rational restructuring by human beings, can be a heaven with only benefits and no costs, which leads in practice to a hell with only costs and no benefits. A society in which religious faith is an active element will not succumb to the romantic temptation to cure all of its ills or master the universe. An individual in whose mind religious faith lives will not lose a sense of the ultimate insufficiency of his reason to penetrate the mysteries either of the cosmos or of the heart.

There is, however, perhaps one other reason the Jews figure so prominently in Kristol's thinking. In his wider meditations about the insufficiency of modern rationality to guide the human world in politics and economics, to shape the moral dimensions of culture and character, and to provide the consolations and grounds of integrity that the religious faiths supplied, Kristol might appear to argue for a return to premodern society. Several strands of conservatism conclude in such a way by expressing a preference for the society of community and virtue in which ancient thought and practice culminated and by rejecting the individualism and secularity implicit in the modern concept of natural rights.

Yet, premodern society was by and large an intolerant society. In particular, the Western world for two millennia was a civilization that had no room for the Jews. It tried to burn, starve and intimidate the Jews out of existence. Of course, the Jews were not alone in this dilemma, as any other number of sects and religions can testify. They are, however, perhaps the clearest examples of the victims of the premodern world's impatient otherworldliness, which, if it elevated the soul and uplifted the moral tone of society, also unleashed immeasurable brutality. Kristol's neoconservatism, therefore, is a self-conscious attempt to preserve the benefits of a religious contribution to human society at the same time that it is *not* a call to return to premodern foundations. As it does with democracy, capitalism and liberty, neoconservatism tries to affirm the essential goodness of religion at the same time that it restrains its power in the world.

Neoconservatism as Theory and Practice

Kristol's neoconservatism is an uneasy dance of precariously balanced practical arrangements: a cautiously democratic republic, a moderately free market, a mildly censored culture of freedom and a fairly religious society. We may assess his efforts along two lines: the likely success of neoconservatism as a political movement capable of reshaping American politics and as an approach to the enduring problems of human life and identity, in short, as practice and as theory.

What is to be done? What would a "neoconservative" America look like? Kristol would probably conclude that American society in the late twentieth century is, or with minor modifications could be, the best of all possible worlds. America is a republican polity that is reasonably attuned to the common good and often forceful and thoughtful enough to do some good and prevent some evil around the globe at the same time that it occasionally manages to secure its self-interest; an essentially free economy that has been moderated (improved) by institutions of public charity and regulation and bolstered by the apparent putrefaction of its chief economic alternative in the world; a free culture that appears to allow almost every part of the human psyche its expression at the same time that it echoes with reverberations of religious faith that at least keep alive the question of the meaning of virtue.

The practical task is to preserve the basic character of present society, restrain the ideological excesses of liberalism, and reinforce some of the traditional elements of social life that have languished under the influence both of capitalism and liberal culture. There is, therefore, no grand "program" at the heart of Kristol's vision of American life. Rather, neoconservative policies are piecemeal and specific: governmentally supported or encouraged medical and child care, for example, instead of a federally sponsored and run national health system or day care (examples of a "conservative welfare state");[8] a less active national judiciary that would leave states and localities the latitude to regulate cultural expression or support religious activity; a more assertive foreign policy divorced from moral fervor. Overall, it is true that most of these would share the theme of the reduced activity of the federal government. It is, after all, through and in the federal government that most ideologically liberal or radical sentiment in American society finds its expression. What practical developments would have to take place for American government and society to assume a neoconservative direction?

First, neoconservatism would have to become a political party. Because the Democratic Party represents a contemporary liberalism the instincts of which have drifted toward ideological radicalism, Kristol (somewhat ambivalently, to be sure) embraces the Republican Party as the one most likely to embody neoconservatism. Several difficulties immediately present themselves: (1) The "backbone" of the modern Republican Party, he suggests, suffers from an irritating limpness; it is often more devoted to a blasé managerialism than to the political leadership of the nation.[9] (2) The major ideological components of the neoconservative synthesis (free-market conservatism and religious or social conservatism) may not, in fact, consent to being synthesized. Although neoconservatism's aversion to ideology may permit Irving Kristol to embrace both elements, the truly "committed" in either camp are deeply suspicious of the other. (3) As with any other party, the Republican Party requires a pool of able and enlightened leadership. The most likely sources for this in American society would be intellectuals (see below) and corporate leaders. Corporate leaders, however, tend to be singularly narrow and uncomprehending, if not ambivalent, about the nature of their own free-market activity and the requirements of politics.[10] (4) A party requires mass participation, which means that it must appeal to the sentiments and interests of a majority of American citizens. Neoconservatism's ambience is probably a little too arid and complex to become the basis of a boisterous rally. Kristol might suggest that neoconservatism's embrace of general economic liberty and prosperity, patriotism, decent abhorrence of pornography and religious sentiment would be sufficient to draw out a "populist" conservatism. It might; the question is, however, whether these elements can outweigh the moral appeal and palpable advantages to self-interest that an active federal government dispensing regulation and subsidies can.

Second, as many of the ill effects of liberal or radical ideology have entered American politics and society through the New Class of alienated intellectuals, there would have to be a significant reorientation of the educated elite in America. Although this is not impossible, it is also not likely. If Kristol's analysis of the cultural tendencies of capitalism is accurate, the sociological conditioning of intellectuals does not render them particularly open to diminished antipathy to capitalism or to tempered moralism. Especially in the legal community—that portion of the academic or "professional" intellectual world (besides journalism) that most directly affects the culture of government and governmental effects upon the wider culture—there is little evidence that the "progressive" disposition can be moderated. There may be more organized and visible conservative and neoconservative intellectuals today than there were twenty years ago, but the fundamental dynamics of America's intellectual class appear to be permanent.

Third, and most difficult, Kristol would also have to succeed in making the sobriety present in earlier stages of modern thinking obvious and appealing both on the level of intellectual analysis and popular consciousness. This is difficult not only because Kristol is willing to say what most other conservatives are *not* willing to say—that America (even with the genuine strands of decadence) is a better country in the twentieth century than it was in the nineteenth or eighteenth century— but also because the core principles of modern thought make the later radicalizations of those principles appear "purer" and more morally satisfying than the earlier stages. Even if it can be shown that the thought of Adam Smith or James Madison is more complex, more *prudent* than that of Karl Marx, it is less inspiriting. The very character of democratic politics suggests—as Kristol is aware—that principles that fail to inspire the people will not move them. So, even if by a searching examination of the *Wealth of Nations* Kristol can demonstrate that early capitalism is preferable to later capitalism and certainly to socialism, it is doubtful that sobriety can become the impetus for a popular political movement.

And what of neoconservatism as a "theory" of human nature? As we saw at the beginning, Kristol's writing does not take the form of a sustained and elaborated philosophical system. Neoconservatism comes to light more as a series of topics raised by practical problems in politics. As he develops the questions raised by these problems, Kristol's deeper intellectual work has more to do with showing the problematic effects of certain theories than with building his own theory of human nature, with defending healthy practice against the influence of bad theories. His enterprise is really "quasi-theoretical" or "quasi-philosophical" rather than philosophical. His thinking, in other words, makes use of philosophical analysis of texts and arguments, but only in a very partial sense.

Is this finally a failing? How one answers this question depends upon one's understanding of one of the greatest mysteries raised by political philosophy, if not human life itself: the relationship between theory and practice. The problem, simply put, is this: Human life is "practical" in that we live in a world that forces us to act and therefore to choose a course of action. But "practice" must become clear as to the grounds or reasons for choosing a particular course of action. The act of clarifying the basis of choice is "theory," which proceeds by a rational examination of what we are and need. Without theory, the ultimate basis of knowing what is truly good and evil for us will never become apparent to us. But "theory" itself can become so divorced from actual choice, so "abstract," that it loses the ability to guide choice and may even destroy the possibility of practical action in the world.

The capacity to act well in the world is called "prudence." It is Kristol's aim to foster prudence by using theoretical reason to examine the various ideologies that contend for dominance in the political and social world. Yet, as we have seen, Kristol believes that "Reason" untamed and uncontained is itself the cause of the modern world's loss of prudence. Neoconservatism in this sense presents itself as a reasonable skepticism about reason whose aim is to permit reasonable action in the world.[11]

Kristol may finally be aware of all the problems to which his "neoconservative" approach to human life is liable. Consistent with the grounds of that approach, his reply might well be: What one can do may not be enough to supply the world with what it needs; nevertheless, it is enough to do what one can do.

Notes

1. Irving Kristol, *Reflections of a Neoconservative: Looking Backward, Looking Ahead* (New York: Basic Books, 1983), p. 167.

2. Ibid., p. 310.

3. Peter Steinfels, *The Neoconservatives: The Men Who Are Changing America's Politics* (New York: Simon and Schuster, 1979), pp. 81–107.

4. Ibid., pp. 72–79. This is Peter Steinfels's suggestion as to the character of Kristol's, and other neoconservatives', writing: It is a form of literary "fast food"—tasty in the consumption but empty of nutrition and content. Steinfels, however, himself lapses into sterile and shallow polemicism that leads him to underestimate the depth and importance of the objects of his criticism.

5. Kristol, *Reflections,* pp. 4, 13.

6. Irving Kristol, *Two Cheers for Capitalism* (New York: Basic Books, 1978, pp. 27–28). The original analysis along these lines can be found in Joseph Schumpeter, *Capitalism, Socialism and Democracy* (New York: Harper & Row, 1942).

7. Also see Kristol, *Two Cheers for Capitalism,* pp. 250–254, for an account of the combined influence of bourgeois affluence and psychotherapy.

8. Kristol, *Reflections,* p. 76.

9. Ibid., esp. p. 111. Also see Kristol, *Two Cheers for Capitalism,* pp. 130–135.

10. Kristol, *Reflections,* pp. 214–215.

11. No doubt Kristol would distinguish between the philosophical reason of the ancient philosophers and that of the moderns. His own thinking resembles, and even relies upon to some extent, the thought of Plato and Aristotle. Compare, for example, Kristol's discussion of Einstein with Aristotle's criticism of Hippodamus in Book II of the *Politics,* especially at 1267b26. Yet, the

background of Aristotle's *Politics,* one might say, is the *Metaphysics.* Aristotle's political teaching does not exist in a vacuum; it stands upon the notion of the intelligibility of nature. It would not be inaccurate, perhaps, to say that for Aristotle, theoretical reason or wisdom supports and forms the horizons for practical reason or prudence. Kristol, on the other hand, really does appear to point to religious faith as the only faculty capable of addressing the issue of the nature of existence itself without destroying the grounds of practical wisdom. This is the critical question regarding his entire enterprise: Is Kristol's thought "theoretical" enough to reveal the insufficiency of the positions that he wishes to criticize and to establish the preferability of his own?

8

Norman Podhoretz's
Polemical Commentaries

Mark J. Rozell

Norman Podhoretz is a leading figure of the so-called neoconservative movement. But he dislikes the label "neoconservative" and instead refers to himself as a "liberal centrist." He portrays himself as a traditional Democrat in the John F. Kennedy mold: committed to strong national defense, anti-Communist containment and the modern welfare state. Nevertheless, Podhoretz is known for his support of foreign policy causes popular with contemporary conservatives and for his highly polemical arguments against the ideological Left. Podhoretz, in fact, is properly regarded as a literary critic and political polemicist, not a major political thinker. As a polemicist Podhoretz influences the development of ideas through his editorial position at *Commentary* magazine, his extensive literary and political writings, and his frequent participation on televised public affairs and news programs such as the "MacNeil/Lehrer News Hour." Podhoretz rarely shies away from any opportunity for a spirited political debate with an opponent. He appears to genuinely enjoy the public exposure he receives from participating in such exchanges.

A review of the writings of Podhoretz and his critics reveals a quality of public discourse that is rarely elevating. In large part this level of discourse is attributable to the nature of the debates in which Podhoretz engages. He writes for and speaks to an audience much broader than the scholarly community. He tries to influence both opinion leaders and the general public. It is not uncommon for Podhoretz to resort to such characterizations as "appeasers," "Stalinists" and "totalitarians" to describe his opponents. These characterizations understandably offend those on the receiving end of Podhoretz's invectives.

Many of Podhoretz's critics exhibit even less rhetorical restraint than he does. Writing for *The Nation,* Christopher Hitchens refers to "poor Norman's" political views and arguments as "rotten," "lousy," and "tenth-rate," as well as "dingy, sloppy, and unconvincing."[1] In another article, Hitchens refers to Podhoretz as a "fool" and asks, "Who the hell does Podhoretz think he is?"[2] A *Saturday Review* article labels Podhoretz the "highbrow hitman for the neoconservative movement."[3] Anthony Lewis asserts that regarding U.S. involvement in Vietnam, Podhoretz seems "almost sorry that the bombs are not actually falling."[4] Historian Arthur M. Schlesinger, Jr., refers to Podhoretz's arguments on the Vietnam War as "really dumb."[5] Another critic of Podhoretz claims that *Commentary* reads as though "it were written by one person, a solemn and dyspeptic sourpuss."[6]

It is unfortunate that much of the debate between Podhoretz and his critics is cheapened by inflammatory rhetoric. Despite his polemical argumentative style, Podhoretz raises serious issues and questions that must be addressed seriously. My purpose is to analyze and assess Podhoretz's political views and to examine his role as an influential critic of the ideological Left.

Podhoretz began his literary career in the 1950s as a political liberal who, out of "boredom," moved to radicalism in the 1960s. As the radical Left became excessive in its attacks on American culture and society in the 1960s, Podhoretz broke away from that movement. Today, Podhoretz regrets the role he once played in disseminating radical ideas and finds it difficult to accept that he once "believed all that stuff" about America as a "sick society." Podhoretz now grudgingly accepts the label "neoconservative" as descriptive of his political philosophy. He professes to hold a "realistic" outlook toward the Soviet government. He defends the welfare state against libertarian attacks, yet he never characterizes egalitarianism as a virtue.

Podhoretz distinguishes his neoconservatism from the New Right movement associated with figures such as Richard Viguerie and the Reverend Jerry Falwell. Podhoretz argues that the New Right, which allegedly seeks to limit the civil rights and liberties of Left-oriented groups, only generates sympathy and support for the counterculture. By contrast, Podhoretz adds, neoconservatives seek to elaborate an intellectually viable alternative to the "radical-chic" he believes pervades modern literature and academic teachings.

As this chapter shows, Podhoretz is primarily concerned with the influence of the radical Left on American culture and politics. To understand Podhoretz's contemporary views, however, requires a review of the development of Podhoretz's thought.

Podhoretz's Political Development

The story of Podhoretz's move from political liberalism, to radicalism, to his current philosophy is well known to his devoted readers. Podhoretz candidly discusses the development of his thought in *Breaking Ranks: A Political Memoir.*[7] The book begins as a letter to Podhoretz's son John who wants to know if his father really did once believe "all that stuff" about America as a sick society. Podhoretz confesses:

> I visibly and enthusiastically participated in the swing to radicalism in the early 1960s. . . . Yes, once upon a time I really did believe in all that stuff. In fact, I played a not inconsiderable part in spreading it around, beginning with a number of articles I wrote in the late fifties and then, much more importantly, through *Commentary* after I became its editor in 1960.[8]

Podhoretz attributes his radicalization to restlessness and "boredom" with the predictable ideas of traditional liberalism. His boredom led to a search for new, exciting ideas to disseminate in *Commentary.* In 1960 Podhoretz described *Commentary* as a forum for writers to criticize "existing institutions of every kind, to expose their shortcomings, their weaknesses, and their inadequacies as measured by the degree to which they are contributing or failing to contribute to our own future potentialities."[9]

Podhoretz became uncomfortable with traditional liberalism's hardline anticommunism and began blaming U.S. foreign policy for the development of the cold war. Furthermore, taking his cues from radical thinkers such as Paul Goodman, Norman O. Brown, Lillian Hellman and Norman Mailer, Podhoretz blamed American "cultural malaise" on traditional political and social institutions. He confesses that he encouraged writers to be "perverse and impious."[10] Yet Podhoretz does not accept full responsibility for his self-professed intellectual failings. He claims that the force of radicalism "pushed" him into defending the proposition that "surrender to the Soviet Union would be preferable to a nuclear war if it ever came to such a choice."[11]

The Vietnam experience was critical to the development of Podhoretz's thought. In the early 1960s Podhoretz identified his own views of the Vietnam conflict as a virtual "copy-cat" of Hans J. Morgenthau's reasons for opposing the war. Podhoretz portrays Morgenthau as the "intellectual leader" of the position that the Vietnam War was the "wrong war in the wrong place at the wrong time."[12]

Podhoretz became increasingly uneasy with the character of the opposition to the Vietnam War. Podhoretz recalls that he lost his temper in a "drunken public scene" upon hearing Jason Epstein compare U.S. policy in Vietnam to the Nazi atrocities:

> This comparison was later to become a commonplace of radical talk, but I had never heard it before, and it so infuriated me that I literally roared in response. . . .
>
> Not only did I reject the view that the United States was an evil society in its way as Nazi Germany had been; I even objected to the idea that it was evil in any degree. That there were many things wrong with the country I had been saying for a long time now. But *evil*? Beyond redemption? In need of and deserving to be overthrown by force and violence? I could not believe that the condition of blacks, let alone of the young, justified any such apocalyptic verdict. . . . I did not and could not see the American role in Vietnam as evidence that the United States and its leaders were evil.[13]

Because of his "breaking ranks" with the radical movement, Podhoretz explains that he was "cut off from the most fashionable and in some ways most influential circles in New York."[14] This falling out with the New York literary crowd also occurred because, Podhoretz explains, he dared "tell it like it is." In his autobiographical work, *Making It,* Podhoretz allegedly shamed the New York literary crowd by exposing their "dirty little secret." According to Podhoretz, sexual lust used to be *the* dirty little secret. "For many of us, of course, this is no longer the case. . . . Ambition seems to be replacing erotic lust as the prime dirty little secret of the well-educated American soul."[15]

Podhoretz says that at the "precocious age of thirty-five" he stumbled upon an "astonishing revelation": he preferred success over failure, wealth over poverty, recognition, fame and power over anonymity.[16] Podhoretz wants us to believe that the difference between himself and other literary critics is that he is open about his ambitions while the others are not. And by exposing the "dirty little secret" Podhoretz asserts that he "weaken[ed] its power to shame."[17] This revelation allegedly crippled the literary class. For years, Podhoretz maintains, this class thrived on the belief that its pursuits were intrinsically valuable and wholly unselfish. The literary class could claim superiority to the business class whose interests it perceived as selfish, base and materialistic.[18]

The literary community, shocked by Podhoretz's revelation, allegedly tried to block the publication of *Making It*. Several noted authors advocated the suppression of the manuscript. After publication, Podhoretz asserts, the literary community unleashed "the terror" on him. Famous writers ostracized Podhoretz from fashionable literary circles and retaliated with vicious reviews of *Making It*. Podhoretz claims that Norman Mailer agreed with *Making It* yet did not defend the book because Mailer "realiz[ed] that in defending it he would in all probability unleash the 'terror' against himself as well."[19]

Making It also provides considerable ammunition to critics who believe that Podhoretz adopts positions because of his ambition, not because of his convictions. Podhoretz admits he finds fame "unqualifiedly delicious" and loves money, power and prestige. Curiously, Podhoretz adopted hard-line anti-Communist views in the mid- to late 1950s, radical views in the 1960s to early 1970s, and neoconservative views during the mid- to late 1970s. Some critics contend that Podhoretz exhibits his ambition by adopting intellectually fashionable positions. This accusation is, of course, difficult to substantiate. It is based upon mere speculation about Podhoretz's motives which only Podhoretz understands. Also, it is too simple—and irresponsible—to dismiss someone's views by questioning his motives. It is important instead to examine the substance of a person's thought to provide a foundation for intellectual criticism.

As Podhoretz explains, his views began to change when a "plague" descended upon the United States in the 1960s. This "plague" of excessive radicalism took root in the intellectual community and spread until it became "the conventional wisdom of the seventies. . . . Its ideas and attitudes are now everywhere." Podhoretz explains that he "came to hate" and "fear" this movement.[20]

Undoubtedly, Podhoretz's current philosophy is profoundly influenced by his earlier participation in "the movement." Because of his "fear" and "hatred" of that movement Podhoretz continues his battle with the "adversary culture." He maintains that overconfidence and complacency among conservatives could lead to a resurgence of the "appeasement culture" hostile to the core values of Western civilization. Podhoretz believes that the views of the "common man" are more accepting of the core values of our civilization than are the views of the intellectual. He therefore proposes that a major goal of *Commentary* is to make the views of the "common man" intellectually defensible and thereby increasingly influential on public opinion and policy. Podhoretz's views are compatible with William F. Buckley, Jr.'s assertion that the country could be better governed by the first two thousand families named in Boston's telephone directory than by the faculty of Harvard University.

The Present Danger and the Adversary Culture

Podhoretz directs much of his writing against what he calls the adversary culture. He asserts that this group comprises intellectuals and their followers who use their command of language to transform conventional values. This adversary culture makes good seem evil, noble seem base. Podhoretz examines, for example, intellectual attitudes toward capitalism and the business community. In a *Harvard Business Review* article he argues that an ideologically leftist, antibusiness bias pervades most American academic institutions.[21] Podhoretz attributes this intellectual bias to two factors: intellectuals are by nature hostile toward capitalism; and the business community is intellectually complacent in confronting academic challenges to capitalism.

To promote his argument Podhoretz characterizes the modern intellectual as contemptuous of the material aspects of life, resentful of those who value materialism, and willing to use rhetorical skills to convince people that the business community is greedy, selfish and corrupt. According to Podhoretz, "hostility toward capitalism has almost always been one of the defining characteristics of intellectuals."[22] Apparently, Podhoretz does not include "intellectuals" as a part of the literary class that harbors a "dirty little secret."

Significantly, the only empirical evidence Podhoretz provides contradicts his own arguments. Podhoretz cites a study by sociologist Seymour Martin Lipset that shows that close to 90 percent of university professors today "consider themselves friendly to capitalism."[23] Podhoretz asserts that Lipset's findings are unpersuasive: "My own impression is that intellectuals are generally still hostile in some degree to capitalism. Certainly, this is true of the intellectuals of whom—and from whom—we usually hear."[24]

Podhoretz charges businessmen to become involved in the "war of ideas" and to stop standing idly by while intellectuals undermine the foundations of capitalism. Podhoretz warns that every institution subjected to the "moral assault" of the ideological Left in the past twenty to thirty years "collapsed into silence or apology instead of mounting a self-respecting defense of its role and character."[25] Podhoretz asserts that businessmen must turn to "the new defenders of capitalism," such as Irving Kristol and Peter L. Berger, or else witness the demise of free enterprise: "The very survival of private enterprise in the United States may depend on whether this newly sympathetic view of capitalism ultimately prevails in the world of ideas over the traditional hostility."[26]

Podhoretz therefore believes that the "survival of private enterprise" depends upon the development of an intellectually viable defense against the hostility of the ideological Left. In the same article Podhoretz proclaims that the arguments of the ideological Left are so weak that hardly anyone pays attention to their views. One page prior to asserting that the "moral assault" of the ideological Left overturned many traditional institutions, and threatens to do the same to capitalism, Podhoretz argues that the "ideas and policy prescriptions" of leftist intellectuals "are so stale that even the converted to whom they preach must have trouble staying awake."[27] Thus, at one point Podhoretz argues that the ideas of the ideological Left are powerful enough and pervasive enough to threaten the survival of the business community. He then implies that the sedative effect of these ideas is more likely to make disciples of the Left roll over and fall asleep than to incite a "moral assault" on free enterprise.

Podhoretz is also concerned about the adversary culture's influence on the direction of U.S. foreign policy. The adversary culture lost a great deal of influence during the Reagan years. Podhoretz believes that the resurgence of this group could mean national "suicide" or "surrender" of the United States to Soviet domination. The focus of his foreign policy writings is the Soviet threat. Podhoretz outlines his views on the U.S.-Soviet conflict in a series of well-known *Commentary* articles: "The Present Danger," (later revised and expanded into book form), "The Future Danger" and "Appeasement by Any Other Name."[28] A certain degree of alarmism pervades each of these articles. Arthur M. Schlesinger, Jr. humorously compares Podhoretz to a cartoon character who carries a placard proclaiming: PREPARE TO MEET THY DOOM.[29]

In his 1980 article, "The Present Danger," Podhoretz explains that during the era of détente the Soviet government embarked upon the largest peacetime military buildup in recent history. The United States failed to keep pace with Soviet military advances. He largely blames détente for the increase in Soviet military power. Unless the United States wakes up and shows a willingness to spend "the many billions more in defense systems," Podhoretz warns, the Soviets may achieve "an unobstructed road to domination." But Podhoretz bleakly proclaims: "It may, as I say, already be too late."[30]

This possible Soviet domination will not be achieved by the arrival of Soviet troops. Rather, Podhoretz adds, it will occur during a period of a few years through the negotiation of Strategic Arms Limitation Talks agreements, transfer of technology to the Soviets, new grain deals, and democratically elected Communist parties in Western Europe. Podhoretz again adds: "Let us, however, suppose—let us pray—that it is not already too late."[31]

American complacency toward the Soviet military buildup, Podhoretz believes, is fueled by the fear of nuclear weapons. Rejecting the notion that nuclear weapons are radically different from other conventional weapons, Podhoretz points to the "apocalyptic visions" of the post–World War I era of what "another war would be like" and quotes individuals who predicted that aerial bombing would end "civilization as we know it."[32] Podhoretz compares today's "nuclear pacifism" to the pacifistic tide that swept much of Europe and the United States in the post–World War I era. The major effects of "nuclear pacifism," he concludes, are the common beliefs that war is the ultimate evil and that Western civilization is not worth fighting for if during the next war all civilization will evaporate in a mushroom cloud.

Podhoretz's principal warning is that we must not once again be duped by the seemingly persuasive appeals of the adversary culture. For Podhoretz, Ronald Reagan's 1980 election to the presidency constituted the beginning of a "new consensus" on defense and national security issues. The new consensus comprises a renewed appreciation for the moral legitimacy of force and a belief in the moral superiority of Western democracies over totalitarian regimes. Podhoretz is not confident that the new consensus will be a long-lasting one. He believes that the major centers of opinion leadership—the media and the universities—remain "mired in yesterday's conventional wisdom."[33] According to Podhoretz, the media's standard impulses are "to deny or even cover up evidence of Soviet malevolence" and to "leap at and magnify even the faintest indication of American wrongdoing."[34] Also, columnists, editorialists and academicians look to Communist victory as "the inevitable wave of the future."[35]

Podhoretz characterizes the modern Soviet leadership as no different than "Hitler with nuclear weapons."[36] Imagine, Podhoretz asks, Adolf Hitler with nuclear weapons facing an opposition afraid to fight because of the potential effects of nuclear war. Hitler's opponents would have two choices: surrender or suicide. Podhoretz warns that this is the choice we eventually face unless the arguments of the "appeasement culture" or adversary culture are muted:

> For the moment the counsels of appeasement are muted, but this school of thought will always be potentially influential. . . . A scare similar to the Cuban missile crisis, only this time with the roles reversed and the United States forced to back away from an "eyeball-to-eyeball" confrontation, could energize the case for appeasement overnight, smoothing our

side into Finlandization with the assurance that if we surrendered all that would happen is that we "would live less well, but live."[37]

For Podhoretz the great crime of détente is that it robbed U.S.-Soviet conflict of its moral dimension. He contends that the Nixon-Ford policies started the United States down the slippery slope of acquiescence to the Soviet Union's grand designs. Podhoretz now refers to himself as a "dissident Democrat" who longs for the days of John F. Kennedy when our president was willing to "pay any price, bear any burden, meet any hardship, support any friend, oppose any foe, to assure the survival and success of liberty."

The noted Kennedy proclamation is a favorite Podhoretz citation. Podhoretz believes that this proclamation set a standard for all presidents, including Kennedy. In *Why We Were in Vietnam* Podhoretz accordingly criticizes Kennedy for fighting the Vietnam War "on the cheap" militarily. Podhoretz never seriously considers that Kennedy's performance in the Bay of Pigs operation revealed the President's unwillingness to live up to his own standard.

Podhoretz celebrated Ronald Reagan's 1980 election as the opportunity for the United States to once again affirm the principles of anti-Communist containment. Many disgruntled Democrats, "saw in Reagan the hope that the Republican Party would now assume the responsibility for containing Soviet expansionism that had originally been shouldered by the United States under Democratic leadership but that the Democrats since Vietnam had been increasingly eager to evade."[38]

The "new consensus," in Podhoretz's view, made the Reagan presidency possible.[39] Reagan's early anti-Soviet rhetoric accurately reflected that consensus. Podhoretz asserts that Reagan's denunciations of Soviet leaders as "liars" and "cheats" reflected a common and correct perception of the Soviet regime's moral depravity. Podhoretz characterizes critics of Reagan's rhetoric as the victims of "a campaign of disinformation."[40] Critics in the media and the universities allegedly stimulated American and Western European suspicions of the Reagan Administration's motives. A negative public reaction to administration rhetoric, combined with the President's sensitivity to public opinion, undermined the Administration's "minimal steps" to redirect U.S. foreign policy.

Podhoretz also blames Reagan for failing to exploit Soviet weaknesses at appropriate opportunities. For example, the Reagan Administration chose to focus its efforts during the "honeymoon period" on domestic economic policy. Reagan also revoked the Soviet grain embargo imposed by Jimmy Carter. Podhoretz approvingly cites George F. Will's devastating assertion that the Reagan administration "loves commerce more than it loathes communism."[41] Failure to accept domestic eco-

nomic hardship in order to fight the Soviet threat made incredible the
Administration's request that Western European democracies make eco-
nomic sacrifices by halting construction of a gas pipeline to the Soviet
Union. "Either Reagan wanted to declare 'economic warfare' on the
Soviet Union or he did not. But if he did he could not ask the Europeans
to shoulder the burden while decreeing a special exemption for the
American farmer."[42] Podhoretz also faults Reagan for not exploiting the
Polish crisis of 1981–1982. Instead of furthering the process of disintegration within the Soviet empire, Reagan "cooperated with the Soviets
and their Polish surrogates in quieting the situation down instead of
stepping aside and letting an internal rebellion against Communist rule
take its course and work itself out."[43]

Podhoretz makes clear his preference for "Reagan the ideologue"
over "Reagan the politician." In Podhoretz's view, "Reagan the politician" too easily retreated in the face of mounting pressure from public
opinion. Allegedly sensitive to political pressures and what historians
will someday teach about his presidency, Reagan continually retreated
from anti-Communist ideology and sought unwise arms control agreements with the Soviets. In Podhoretz's assessment, Reagan took the
"appeasers" too seriously.

Podhoretz believes that a vigorous anti-Communist strategy, aimed
at exploiting the Soviet regime's weaknesses, "holds out the hope of a
breakup of the Soviet empire."[44] He assumes that the Soviet empire is
not eternal because "the Roman empire was not eternal" and "the
British empire was not eternal."[45] The alternative to seeking to undermine the Soviet empire is "horrifying . . . a universal Gulag and life
that is otherwise nasty, brutish, and short."[46]

Political scientist Richard Melanson observes that Podhoretz professes "a moral outlook that demands absolute solutions."[47] This assertion is reasonable. Podhoretz appears to equate political pragmatism
with appeasement and fails to appreciate that presidents cannot direct
foreign policy unconstrained by domestic political pressures. Moreover,
he asserts that we must be willing to take "great risks" to help
undermine the Soviet regime, yet he fails clearly to identify what these
risks should be.

To properly understand Podhoretz's "moral outlook" requires an
examination of his controversial book, *Why We Were in Vietnam.* In
Podhoretz's view, rewriting the "lessons of Vietnam" is the first step
toward curing the United States of defeatism and moral guilt. He
believes that before the United States once again accepts the moral
legitimacy of force, it must prove that its earlier use of force against
totalitarian expansionism was morally justifiable. Relearning the lessons
of Vietnam, therefore, is a means of reestablishing the American will

to resist totalitarianism. *Why We Were in Vietnam* is intended to "reopen the debate over Vietnam."[48]

Podhoretz believes that the debate over Vietnam became a closed subject once the liberal orthodoxy of the media and higher education prevailed. Liberal orthodoxy replaced the "legacy of Munich" with the "lessons of Vietnam." For Podhoretz, the legacy of Munich is the perception that democratic societies must be willing to resist totalitarian expansionism. The lessons of Vietnam include the notions that force is immoral, ideologically based foreign policies are dangerous, and anti-Communist crusades are futile. "Instead of learning humility about the extent of their power, Americans were to learn renunciation. . . . The lesson of Vietnam was that the United States, not the Soviet Union and certainly not Communism, represented the greatest threat to the security and well-being of the peoples of the world."[49]

Podhoretz asserts the common thesis that the United States became involved in Vietnam out of an "excess of idealism." During the early stage of U.S. involvement there existed in this country a strong belief in the moral superiority of democracy over communism and in democracy's ability to guard against the spread of communism. Podhoretz portrays the legacy of Munich as essential to President Kennedy's worldview. Thus, Kennedy perceived the lessons of Munich as applicable to Vietnam as they were to Korea.[50]

In Podhoretz's view, nobility of intent is sufficient to vindicate U.S. involvement in Vietnam. He also acknowledges the impossibility of any U.S. military-strategic victory. "In short, it seems reasonable to conclude that the only way the United States could have avoided defeat in Vietnam was by staying out of the war altogether."[51]

Podhoretz's arguments are somewhat confused. He praises President Kennedy for "acting prudently" by going into the war "slow and small," but "it was the wrong prudence at the wrong time in the wrong place."[52] Despite his argument that the Vietnam War could not be won by the United States, Podhoretz asserts that staying out of Indochina "would have meant conceding South Vietnam to the Communists."[53] At times Podhoretz blames policymakers, the media and the antiwar movement for the Vietnam failure and implies that the U.S. war effort could have succeeded. For example, he argues that President Lyndon Johnson's failure was trying to fight the war "on the political cheap"; that is, fearing political repercussions, Johnson failed to make the appropriate moral arguments in favor of the war effort. "*To be fought successfully,* the war had to have a convincing moral justification, and the failure to provide one doomed the entire enterprise."[54] Podhoretz also asserts the common complaint that the media and the antiwar movement "lost" the war for the United States. He notes that President Johnson "was right" in declaring that the United States helped defeat itself in Vietnam through self-criticism.[55]

Podhoretz saves his harshest criticisms for the radical opponents of the Vietnam War. Many of these critics, he asserts, carried Vietcong flags and endorsed enemy propaganda, "all without being subjected to any legal penalty or even much public censure. On the contrary, in the intellectual community the people who did these things were often treated as heroes. . . ."[56] For many of these critics, the Vietnam War became an excuse to bring out into the open anti-American hysteria that existed even prior to the war. Podhoretz concludes that "the antiwar movement bears a certain measure of responsibility for the horrors that have overtaken the people of Vietnam."[57]

Why We Were in Vietnam portrays the antiwar movement as strong enough to influence public opinion, Congress, the press and intellectuals. Podhoretz also maintains that three presidents (Kennedy, Johnson, Nixon) made crucial decisions regarding the war uninfluenced by public opinion and pressure. A "failure of leadership" by each of these three presidents allegedly doomed the war effort:

> Kennedy failed in prudential wisdom; Johnson failed in political judg-ment; Nixon failed in strategic realism. These were all the more failures of leadership in that the actions were taken without any pressure from below. The decision to enter the war was made by Kennedy and his advisers; the decision to escalate the war was made by Johnson and his advisers; and the decision to withdraw gradually was made by Nixon and his advisers. None of these major decisions owed much, if anything at all, to popular pressure.[58]

Podhoretz characterizes U.S. involvement in Vietnam as both "moral" and "imprudent." This aspect of his thesis is problematic. Podhoretz wants to vindicate the moral legitimacy of force by showing that our actions in Vietnam were moral. Yet he fails to recognize that morality in foreign policy requires attention to the prudence of our actions. A number of political "realists" criticized U.S. involvement in Vietnam on the basis that our efforts were imprudent. Serious critics of the war such as Reinhold Niebuhr and Hans J. Morgenthau were unconvinced that the national interest was served by our involvement in Vietnam. These critics never denied the moral legitimacy of force. They believed that the nation should not be subordinated to foreign policy ideals such as global anti-Communist containment. Podhoretz does not take the arguments of these realists seriously. In fact, he accuses "moderate" critics (his qualifying quotation marks) such as Morgenthau of com-mitting "left-wing McCarthyism" with their arguments against the war.

Podhoretz thereby fails to carefully distinguish those critics of the war who addressed both the strategic and moral problems with American involvement from the radical war opponents who marched in rallies "carrying Vietcong flags."

Why We Were in Vietnam is additional evidence of Podhoretz's preoccupation with the influence of the ideological Left. In his view the adversary culture has had a disproportionate and negative influence on U.S. foreign policy since the 1960s. His study of the Vietnam War attempts to discredit the ideological Left and rewrite the "lessons of Vietnam." Until that war's history is revised, he concludes, intellectuals, opinion leaders and policymakers will fail to heed the necessity of confronting totalitarian expansionism.

Podhoretz's Commentaries

Norman Podhoretz is first and foremost a political polemicist devoted to influencing currents of thought and opinion. He is eminently successful at this task. Podhoretz directs much of his effort against the influence of the ideological Left. He laments the alleged influence of the ideological Left in both the "establishment press" and the universities. Ironically, Podhoretz's own position in the "establishment press" is prominent. He is now a syndicated columnist appearing in many influential news dailies.

As a polemical writer Podhoretz often engages in spirited debates with opponents. He occasionally resorts to the use of characterizations such as "appeasers" and "adversaries" to describe his opponents. Some of Podhoretz's critics, such as Gore Vidal and Christopher Hitchens, respond by calling Podhoretz unflattering names. Podhoretz is not blameless for the often uninspiring level of debate in which he and his opponents engage. In *Breaking Ranks* Podhoretz asserts that "the elements of tone and literary grace . . . are not supposed to count in political debate or for that matter in intellectual analysis generally. What is supposed to count there is the logical soundness of the argument, its coherence, and the extent to which it fits the available evidence."[59] Yet literary tone and grace are relevant to the clarity, logical soundness and empirical soundness of one's arguments. Writers who ignore the need for evidence and pay little attention to the logical coherence of their analyses are likely to make their arguments by resorting to the use of characterizations and name calling.

Podhoretz is now among a number of prominent Democrats and former Democrats who openly support Republican candidates for public office. Many "disaffected" and former Democrats want the Democratic Party to reaffirm its once strong support for anti-Communist containment. For Podhoretz, turning the Party back to its traditional stance requires relearning the "lessons of Vietnam." It also requires a new Party leadership willing to resist pandering to popular fears of super-power hostility by promoting ill-advised arms control agreements. Podhoretz believes that Ronald Reagan's election and reelection marked a temporary yet insufficient decline in the adversary culture's political influence. He perceives considerable evidence of a resurgence of the "adversaries." For this reason Podhoretz continues to vigorously challenge the arguments of his philosophical opponents.

Notes

1. Christopher Hitchens, "No End of a Lesson," *The Nation,* April 3, 1982, pp. 403–404.

2. Christopher Hitchens, "On Anti-Semitism," *The Nation,* October 9, 1982, p. 3236.

3. Robert R. Harris, "Podhoretz on Vietnam: The Enemy Was US," *Saturday Review* (April 14, 1982): 61.

4. Anthony Lewis, quoted in Arnold Beichman, "Their Present Danger," *National Review,* September 3, 1982, p. 1088.

5. Arthur Schlesinger, Jr., "Make War Not It," *Harper's* (March 1982): 72.

6. Quoted in Beichman, "Their Present Danger," p. 1088.

7. Norman Podhoretz, *Breaking Ranks: A Political Memoir* (New York: Harper & Row, 1979).

8. Ibid., p. 3.

9. Quoted in Jane Larkin Crane, "One Man's Commentary," *Saturday Review,* October 27, 1979, p. 40.

10. Podhoretz, *Breaking Ranks,* p. 37.

11. Ibid., p. 175.

12. Ibid., p. 186.

13. Ibid., pp. 216, 219.

14. Ibid., p. 320.

15. Norman Podhoretz, *Making It* (New York: Harper & Row, 1980), pp. xvi–xvii.

16. Ibid., p. xi.

17. Ibid., p. xvii.

18. Podhoretz, *Breaking Ranks,* p. 227.

19. Ibid., pp. 264, 267.

20. Ibid., p. 361.

21. Norman Podhoretz, "The New Defenders of Capitalism," *Harvard Business Review* (March-April 1981): 96–106.

22. Ibid., p. 97.

23. Ibid.

24. Ibid.

25. Ibid., p. 106.

26. Ibid.

27. Ibid., p. 105.

28. Norman Podhoretz, "The Future Danger," *Commentary* 71 (April 1981): 29–47; "The Present Danger," *Commentary* 69 (March 1980): 27–40; and "Appeasement by Any Other Name," *Commentary* 76 (July 1983): 25–38.

29. Schlesinger, "Make War Not It," p. 71.

30. Podhoretz, "The Present Danger," p. 37; also see pp. 32–33.

31. Ibid., p. 38.

32. Podhoretz, "Appeasement by Any Other Name," p. 27.

33. Podhoretz, "The Future Danger," p. 34.

34. Podhoretz, "Appeasement by Any Other Name," p. 36.

35. Ibid., p. 34.

36. Podhoretz, "The Future Danger," p. 35.

37. Ibid.

38. Norman Podhoretz, "The Reagan Road to Detente," *Foreign Affairs* 63 (1985): 449.

39. Podhoretz, "Appeasement by Any Other Name," p. 25.

40. Podhoretz, "The Reagan Road to Detente," p. 450.

41. Ibid., p. 459; and Podhoretz, "Appeasement by Any Other Name," p. 26.

42. Podhoretz, "Appeasement by Any Other Name," p. 27.

43. Podhoretz, "The Reagan Road to Detente," pp. 456–457.

44. Podhoretz, "The Future Danger," p. 47.

45. Ibid., p. 45.

46. Ibid., p. 44.

47. Richard Melanson, "Paul H. Nitze to Norman Podhoretz: The Tradition of Anti-Communist Containment," in Kenneth W. Thompson, ed., *Traditions and Values: American Diplomacy, 1945 to the Present* (Lanham, Md.: University Press of America, 1984), p. 174.

48. Norman Podhoretz, *Why We Were in Vietnam* (New York: Simon and Schuster, 1983), p. 15.

49. Ibid., p. 14.

50. Ibid., pp. 42, 48.

51. Ibid., p. 62.

52. Ibid., p. 63.

53. Ibid.

54. Ibid., pp. 107–108.

55. Ibid., p. 129.

56. Ibid., pp. 85–86.

57. Ibid., p. 205.

58. Ibid., p. 171.

59. Podhoretz, *Breaking Ranks,* p. 175.

9

Jeane Kirkpatrick's Public Philosophy and Rhetoric

Mark J. Rozell

Former United States permanent representative to the United Nations, Jeane Kirkpatrick, is popularly regarded as an articulate supporter of unremitting anti-Communist foreign policies. George F. Will describes Kirkpatrick as a "woman whose intellectual gifts and attainments at least match those of Dean Acheson and Henry Kissinger."[1] Will proclaims that "she unites thought and action, theory and practice, better than anyone in government in this generation."[2] Will's enthusiasm for Kirkpatrick's thought is countered by leftist critics who view her foreign policy outlook with alarm. Writing for *The Nation*, Penny Lernoux calls Kirkpatrick a "self-appointed apologist for Latin American dictators."[3] The *New Republic*'s Jefferson Morley argues that Kirkpatrick perceives the murderers of lay missionary Jean Donovan as "heroes" for acting to restore order to El Salvador.[4]

To find diverging interpretations between a political thinker's sympathizers and detractors is not surprising. Yet the divergences in interpretations of Kirkpatrick's views are striking in tone. Kirkpatrick's followers and detractors tend to become emotional and highly polemical when discussing her perceptions of U.S. foreign policy.

The nature of these debates can be attributed to two factors. First, Kirkpatrick has developed a generally well thought-out, yet controversial public philosophy. Second, Kirkpatrick employs a rhetorical approach that draws clear lines of division between her supporters and detractors.

My purpose is to lend some perspective to the debates over Jeane Kirkpatrick's policy views and political rhetoric. In what follows I identify and discuss the major tenets of Kirkpatrick's public philosophy. I then critically assess Kirkpatrick's views after considering the views of her supporters and detractors. Finally, I examine the effectiveness of Kirkpatrick's rhetorical approach.[5]

The argument presented here is that Jeane Kirkpatrick is what George F. Will calls a "big government conservative." Kirkpatrick is optimistic about the state's ability to contribute to both the national security and the public welfare. She believes that public officials are morally responsible for adopting foreign policies based upon the principles of political "realism" and for promoting social and economic justice at home. Although Kirkpatrick advocates government action to promote a just society, she recognizes the inherent limitations on government's ability to ensure a perfectly just social and economic order.

To begin, an examination of the major tenets of Kirkpatrick's public philosophy reveals several persisting themes: rationalism versus realism, the relation of liberty to equality, the importance of tradition, ideas and their consequences, and present dangers emanating from Communist ideology. The distinction between rationalism and realism is the major foundation of Kirkpatrick's thought.

Rationalism Versus Realism

Kirkpatrick perceives two general tendencies in political thought. First, there is "rationalism," or the belief that abstract, imaginary laws and principles can become operational in the "real world." For Kirkpatrick, the "rationalist perversion in modern politics" is attributable to the efforts of idealistic reformers to implement policies based on oversimplified views of human behavior.[6] Second, there is "realism," or the belief that policymakers should always begin with an assessment of "what is" rather than "what ought to be."[7]

According to Kirkpatrick, rationalist thinkers harbor many illusions, including the belief that anything conceivable to the human mind "can be brought into being."[8] Rationalists fail to see the distinction between the realms of thought and experience. They also confuse the domains of politics and rhetoric. Rationalists are so "blindly optimistic" that they fail to perceive the need for empirical verification of their assumptions. Rationalists do not begin their analyses by examining how to move away from a known and concrete problem toward an improved state of affairs. Rather, they discourse about ultimate solutions and how these solutions can perfect society.

Kirkpatrick equates rationalism with utopianism. She writes that "rationalism not only encourages utopianism, but utopianism is a form of rationalism."[9] Rationalist utopians, she argues, fail to perceive people "as they are" and portray human nature as extremely malleable. Kirkpatrick explains that Plato's *Republic* provides extreme examples of rationalist-utopian prescriptions for overcoming human imperfections.[10]

Kirkpatrick also equates rationalism with political tyranny. In her view, rationalists are "arrogant" because they presume to understand the needs of other human beings. Rationalists assume that arrangements agreeable to themselves are beneficial to others as well. Such arrogance, she contends, results in tyranny when rationalists gain control of governing institutions and enforce their own views on the polity. Rationalists may have noble motives, but their attempts to improve the human lot and perfect society inevitably do more harm than good. Kirkpatrick is particularly concerned about rationalists gaining political power in the modern era because of society's great advances in the arts, sciences and technology. These advances may provide political elites armed with "a sense of righteousness" more efficient means to manipulate symbols and extend their power.[11]

Kirkpatrick distinguishes herself from the so-called rationalists of this world. She portrays herself as a political realist.[12] Kirkpatrick explains that political realists begin examining a problem with a clear understanding of how the problem exists rather than how it can be "solved." Realists are concerned with "what is" rather than with "what ought to be." Political realists are piecemeal, practical reformers who seek to improve upon the status quo rather than try to create a new, ideal political or social order. Realists understand that public policy-making involves difficult and often unpleasant choices among competing moral claims. Realists also understand that such choices are problematic because satisfying all moral claims is impossible. Sometimes, the most that we can accomplish is the least objectionable of a number of unpleasant policy options. Kirkpatrick concludes that rationalist utopians are never satisfied with such a state of affairs and that they therefore allow the best to become the enemy of the good.[13]

The Relation of Liberty to Equality

According to Kirkpatrick, rationalist utopians, in seeking to combine the worlds of thought and action, advocate "absolute equality" as a social good. But attempts to achieve absolute equality are doomed to fail because "so many of the inequalities among humans are rooted in nature and accident that it is quixotic to imagine they can be eliminated by government policy."[14] In her view, "Equality is easy to conceive, literally impossible to achieve."[15]

Unlike many conservative thinkers,[16] Kirkpatrick does not perceive a conflict between equality and liberty. Kirkpatrick proclaims that these two objectives "are compatible, mutually reinforcing values which can and, in fact, must exist and grow together."[17] She disagrees with conservatives who believe that the evolution of modern liberalism constitutes the triumph of equality over liberty. In both classical and modern welfare-state liberalism we find a commitment to the values of liberty and equality:

> Welfare-state liberalism and social democracy incorporated the classical liberal's emphasis on individual liberty and individual rights. They did not supplant it, but added to it a further egalitarian thrust. Freedom from severe economic and social deprivation was sought for all; providing the basic elements of the good life—hot lunches, old-age pensions, education, medical and dental care—became a major goal of public policy.[18]

For Kirkpatrick, the major virtue of the modern welfare state is that it allows government to use its regulatory powers to expand the realms of both equality and liberty. In the modern welfare state, the desire to enhance equality is "identical" to commitments to individual freedom and liberty.[19] While liberty and equality appear incompatible in the abstract, Kirkpatrick asserts that these values "prove salutary in practice."[20] Interestingly, Kirkpatrick refers to herself as a "welfare state conservative."[21] In her words:

> A welfare-state liberal is much more ready than a conservative to maximize the power of the central government, and to minimize the role of individuals and voluntary associations, while a welfare-state conservative seeks central government as the last resort, not as the first resort, and is wary of the high cost and uncertain side effects that often attend centralized programs.[22]

Kirkpatrick proclaims that society should resist the temptation to pursue either equality or liberty as its sole aim. She warns that a too zealous pursuit of one objective undermines other desirable goals. For example, a vigorous pursuit of equality may destroy political and social freedoms. A completely free society, unregulated by government, can never enhance equal opportunity. Restating Barry Goldwater's famous political maxim, Kirkpatrick exclaims that "extremism in the pursuit of justice (or any other political value) is a vice; and moderation in the defense of liberty (or any other political value) is a virtue."[23]

Kirkpatrick relates her discussion of liberty and equality to the pitfalls of political rationalism. Rationalists easily succumb to the temptation to pursue one political value to its extreme. In seeking to perfect society, rationalists are inclined to pursue absolute goals. The danger here, she explains, is that in trying to achieve absolute goals rationalists devalue "imperfect but real goods."[24] Political realists, in contrast, understand that the political and social environments are not conducive to the achievement of absolute goals. Because absolute material equality is impossible to achieve, Kirkpatrick believes, policymakers should seek instead to enhance equal opportunities.

The Importance of Tradition

Understanding the traditions of a society, Kirkpatrick notes, is a prerequisite for dealing with its social and political problems. Cultural values, mores, and political institutions and practices are all rooted in a society's traditions. Policymakers need to be aware of these roots before proposing political or social reforms.

However, like philosopher Edmund Burke, Kirkpatrick insists that tradition cannot be the ultimate or only guide to political analyses. We should not accept any "bestial conception" as legitimate simply because it is grounded in the traditions of a particular society.[25] Kirkpatrick warns political analysts to resist cultural relativism: the belief that all traditions and practices are equally acceptable and that we have no right to make moral or ethical distinctions between different traditions and practices. As Kirkpatrick humorously asserts, it is incorrect to argue that "cannibalism is only a matter of taste."[26]

Another hallmark of rationalism, Kirkpatrick maintains, is its failure to consider the profound influence of political and social traditions on a society's institutions. Rationalists look toward a future ideal order and neglect the potentially dangerous effects of upsetting practices that took generations to develop. While Kirkpatrick respects the importance of tradition, she recognizes that there are practices in every culture (such as racial and sexual discrimination) that are unworthy of support and in need of change. "Tradition, to be sure, does not filter out bestial conceptions any more than it eliminates brutal practices. . . . But traditional ideas have at least the merit of being integrally related to actual societies and social practices."[27]

Ideas and Their Consequences

A major theme in Kirkpatrick's thought is the notion that "ideas have consequences, bad ideas have bad consequences."[28] One of the most disturbing aspects of rationalism, she argues, is the tendency to cut ideas loose from the realm of experience. Abstract ideas are rooted not in everyday experience but in the minds of philosophers. Is it necessarily improper to have ideas that are not based upon experience? Kirkpatrick answers, "Not always." Philosophers are "free to be foolish" as long as they do not have the opportunity to see their abstract ideas implemented.[29] If abstract principles are not verified by real conditions, they are harmless.

Kirkpatrick's point is that political analysts should not be persuaded by appealing abstract conceptions of the world. Instead, political analysts must take a serious look at existing realities. Rationalist ideas can delude policymakers into believing that problems can be solved by well-planned policy interventions. More often than not, rationalists adopt their plans with a reckless disregard for facts. The consequences of their ideas, therefore, are frequently "disastrous." Kirkpatrick concludes that all practical political thought is grounded in the realm of experience: "Theories cut loose from experiences are usually blindly optimistic. They begin not from how things are but how they ought to be, and regularly underestimate the complexities and difficulties concerning how you get there from here. They tend also to be abstract and unembarrassed by the need for empirical indicators of their major assumptions."[30]

Kirkpatrick asserts that many rationalists are overly concerned with purity of intention as opposed to the consequences of their actions. In arguing that the rationalist approach is both irresponsible and dangerous to the welfare of the polity, she suggests that good results are likely to be produced by a realistic appraisal of what can be achieved under existing conditions. She concludes that the aim of our policy interventions is not to make us feel good about ourselves simply because our motives are noble. Rather, we should be concerned with having real effects on real situations. In fact, our only "realistic" policy options may not conform to our ethical ideals. Ethical ideals are not always useful guides to political action in a world inhospitable to the greatest possible good.[31]

Present Dangers Emanating from Communist Ideology

Policy Review writer Adam Wolfson sympathetically describes Kirkpatrick as "an unrepentant cold warrior."[32] Seymour Maxwell Finger observes that Kirkpatrick perceives most foreign policy issues and problems in the context of U.S.-Soviet competition. Like many of former senator Henry M. Jackson's followers Kirkpatrick believes that détente was a mistake.[33]

Kirkpatrick observes that the Soviet Union's leadership is motivated by a "strategy of domination." The Soviet "grand strategy," she asserts, "derives from a tradition of Oriental despotism, from czarist synthesis of economic, social, and bureaucratic state power."[34] In an interview with *Encounter* Kirkpatrick elaborates: "We are unfortunately not fully at peace with the Soviet Union. We are engaged in a serious and potentially deadly competition that is not a shooting war. That is all. 'Cold War' strikes me as a highly adequate description."[35]

Kirkpatrick condemns Western liberals for their lack of any "inordinate fear of communism." She argues that it is ironic that Western liberals, "who are often such smart people," are also "slow learners about communism."[36] Many Western liberals, she maintains, once so concerned about liberating South Vietnam and Cambodia from General Thieu and Lon Nol, expressed little anguish over Pol Pot's ascension to power.[37] Kirkpatrick speculates that perhaps defenders of the rationalist doctrine feel a special affinity with tyrannical regimes professing to establish perfectly egalitarian societies. Yet the Soviet model of change and reform, she adds, is proof of the difficulties associated with trying to alter traditional institutions and norms of behavior: "[Soviet] rulers have had more than half a century to employ formal education, habit, imitation, group pressure, mass media, terror, and other environmental controls to bring about internationalization of new norms and new behavior patterns."[38]

The social and economic condition of the modern Soviet regime, according to Kirkpatrick, attests to the impoverishment of Communist ideology. Motivated by external conquest rather than internal reform, the Soviet regime presents the most imminent danger to Western civilization. Seymour Maxwell Finger observes that Kirkpatrick is committed to the view "that the American concepts of democracy and freedom are superior to Marxism or any other collectivist society."[39]

Rationalist utopians allegedly fail to recognize the clear difference between the moral character of liberal democracy and that of a collectivist system. Kirkpatrick portrays rationalist utopians as both naive and dangerous: naive in the sense that they are easily duped into believing the sincerity of adversaries' motives; dangerous in the sense that their idealistic visions often influence the direction of U.S. foreign policy. Kirkpatrick therefore seeks to expose the sham of idealism so that policymakers can realistically confront present dangers to American security.

Kirkpatrick's Policy Views

Jeane Kirkpatrick is most widely recognized as a controversial critic of U.S. foreign policy. She is also a recognized scholar of American national government and politics. The previously identified tenets of Kirkpatrick's thought are reflected in her writings on foreign and domestic policy. I turn now to a brief review of some of these writings.

Kirkpatrick's most well-known publication is her November 1979 *Commentary* article, "Dictatorships and Double Standards." That article is a critical assessment of U.S. foreign policy toward Iran and Nicaragua during the Carter years. According to Kirkpatrick, President Jimmy Carter's noble aspirations for these two countries "were moderation and democracy; and the results were Khomeini and the Ortegas."[40] She lists several reasons for the Carter Administration's failure to achieve its objectives.

First, Carter adopted an overly expansive definition of human rights. Rather than try to secure limited, tangible personal and legal rights for citizens in these countries, Carter focused on political and economic "rights" and all the good things in life "promised by socialism," including education, food, health care and shelter.[41]

Second, Carter failed to adequately consider the nature of the Communist threat to these countries. For example, Carter Administration officials refused "to take seriously, or even take into account, the commitment of Fidel Castro or Nicaragua's Sandinista leadership to Marxist-Leninist goals and expansionist policies."[42] The Carter Administration supported progressive forces, "regardless of the ties of these revolutionaries to the Soviet Union."[43]

Third, the Carter approach failed to take into account how particular social and political traditions in these countries inhibited sudden and successful reform. The reason for this neglect is that Carter's foreign policy approach "derived from an ideology rather than from tradition, habit, or improvisation."[44] Carter should have tried to achieve gradual, peaceful change, "rather than democracy over night."[45]

Finally, the Carter approach derived from rationalist philosophy, expecting that noble objectives and a blueprint for reform would produce desired policy outcomes. Carter's policies toward Iran and Nicaragua therefore failed due to Carter's "lack of realism" and his unwillingness to acknowledge the differing natures of totalitarian and authoritarian regimes.[46] Kirkpatrick concludes, "Obviously, President Carter and his advisers should have moved beyond the invocation of universal values and general principles to the knotty business of applying them in this notoriously imperfect, intractable world."[47]

In a lesser known article, "The Hobbes Problem," Kirkpatrick reveals that her brand of political realism is influenced by Thomas Hobbes's philosophy. This article assesses the difficulties associated with establishing order in El Salvador. Kirkpatrick declares that El Salvador's problem is similar to a problem that Hobbes identified: how to establish order in a society in which fraud, force and violence prevail and in which no conception of legitimacy exists. Like Hobbes, Kirkpatrick asserts that "order" is the first of all political and social goals. Order, in fact, is "the precondition for all other public goods."[48] Without authority and legitimacy, Kirkpatrick explains, "whoever successfully claims the power of government is given obedience."[49] Under such a situation—as it exists in El Salvador—a government may have to rely upon force, fraud and violence to secure and maintain order.

Kirkpatrick's argument is controversial among critics who believe that order and stability can be achieved in El Salvador (or other countries lacking legitimacy and authority) through peaceful democratic means. Kirkpatrick believes that indigenous political and social conditions in nation-states such as El Salvador inhibit our ability to effect peaceful, democratic change. We therefore must seek incremental progress even if that progress does not conform to our own democratic ideals.

On the domestic front Kirkpatrick is cautiously optimistic about the government's ability to effect beneficial change. In "Regulation, Liberty, and Equality" she praises modern liberalism's contributions to social and economic equality. The administrative apparatus of the welfare state "demonstrates that it is possible to use government's regulatory power to expand liberty as well as to serve egalitarian goals."[50] Ironically, in 1979 Kirkpatrick wrote that she resisted becoming a Republican because many members of that party never accepted the necessity of the modern welfare state. Republicans lacked a clear philosophy of the public good and failed to show how decentralization, free markets and mediating structures enhanced the common good rather than served privileged citizens' interests. Kirkpatrick exclaims, "Since the New Deal, it has almost always been the Democrats who moved first to provide economic aid, social status, and political rights to the deprived members of the society. Almost always, it has been the Republicans who complained."[51]

Kirkpatrick became a Republican in 1985 anyway, citing her differences with the Democratic Party's defense and national security postures. In a recent interview on her "welfare state conservative" philosophy, Kirkpatrick also explains that her domestic policy views have evolved to the point where she feels most comfortable in the Republican Party. She maintains that she has developed "a much greater appreciation of market economics" and that the Reagan experience "demonstrates that even incremental enhancement of reliance on the market stimulates the economy and helps achieve goals like lower unemployment far more effectively than any kind of state action."[52]

The rise of a "new Democratic elite" also influenced Kirkpatrick's decision to become a Republican. The Democratic Party's "new breed" leadership, she asserts, is largely composed of anti–party politics ideologues. Since Senator George McGovern's 1972 presidential nomination the Democratic Party has witnessed the rise to power of "large numbers of new men and women whose motives, goals, ideals, and patterns of organizational behavior are different from those of the people who have dominated American politics in the past."[53] Kirkpatrick refers to this group as the "new class." These individuals constitute a cultural rather than an economic class. They are largely intellectuals and masters of media, language and wit who manipulate the symbols of politics and culture to pursue their political objectives. Many members of the new class, she believes, embrace counterculture values founded in the antiwar movement and civil rights demonstrations.

The new class, according to Kirkpatrick, poses a potential danger to democratic liberties in that its members embody aspects of the rationalist-utopian ideal. For example, they adopt a "moralistic" preference for motives over results. They also measure policy alternatives against abstract ideals. The new class, in fact, is a highly paternalistic elite that expresses "caring that coerces."[54] She warns that the ascension to power of symbol specialists and "intellectuals" historically leads to excessive government control of the polity.[55] Kirkpatrick fears that the rise of counterculture values may result in a society devoid of meaningful values, and "only the completely dispirited would fail to defend their way of life against an enemy."[56]

Kirkpatrick holds "new class" activists largely responsible for reforms of the presidential selection process during the past twenty years.[57] The proliferation of primaries, she notes, is attributable to the efforts of reformers to make the presidential selection process increasingly open, democratic and representative of rank-and-file members. The reformists' actions embody the "rationalist approach to politics." Believing political institutions and human nature to be more malleable than they are, these reformers seek "to perfect the political process" while failing to understand that "the consequences of any reform are not entirely clear."[58] Consequently, they unintentionally created a presidential selection process that focuses too much on personality, charm and other media-based skills and too little on the kinds of skills needed to govern effectively. The new "issue activists" who now dominate presidential selection, Kirkpatrick argues, are more concerned with the ideology than with the electability of their candidates. As a counterreform, Kirkpatrick proposes abolishing presidential primaries:

> I propose that the Congress by national legislation provide that the nominating convention of each party consist of its elected public officials and party leaders—its congressmen, senators, governors, state party chairs and possibly members of the national committees.[59]

Any input from the primaries would create a situation in which the elected public and party officials would be very vulnerable to charges of illegitimacy if they did not reach a decision that was consistent with the outcome of whatever participatory process were devised.[60]

Finally, Kirkpatrick is concerned about issues of racial and sexual discrimination. She believes that government's coercive power should be used when necessary to overcome discrimination:

I agree with the civil rights laws of the 1960s. I think they have been positive and I think they were necessary. This was an example where massive use of the coercive power of government was necessary to solve an unsolved problem. We had given ourselves a long time to end our racial discrimination by other means, and we hadn't succeeded. . . .
I always say that I am in favor of affirmative action if it means a helping hand to people who have been historic victims of discrimination, especially discrimination based in law. It is appropriate for government to eliminate discrimination. But it is never appropriate to sacrifice merit to affirmative action or to substitute quotas for merit-based evaluation.[61]

In *Political Woman* Kirkpatrick praises "historic trends" moving society toward a "progressive inclusion of women" in political decisionmaking.[62] She argues that government can help "accelerate the trend toward increased participation of women in public power processes."[63] For example, government can deny funding to universities and colleges practicing sexual discrimination, and government can also resort to legal intervention in private-sector employment practices. She even suggests that abstract conceptions of the "possible" play an important role in the development of "goals and strategies" to achieve political equality for women.[64] She concludes that society need not be blinded by the past with regard to notions of sexual equality: "Past and present provide data on probabilities; the future involves possibility as well. The future need not reproduce the past, particularly in contemporary times when the principle of equality dominates political culture."[65]

This passage reveals that Kirkpatrick's thought is not devoid of rationalist tendencies. Yet this passage also appears consistent with Kirkpatrick's argument that in the modern era tradition cannot always be the ultimate guide to our actions.

Kirkpatrick's Thought: A Critique

Kirkpatrick's political conservatism is unusual by contemporary American standards. She disputes contemporary conservatism's rejection of big government and defends the modern welfare state's contri-

butions to liberty and equality. Kirkpatrick believes that government—
when properly directed—can have a positive influence on our lives. A
vigorous, enlightened government can protect the national security and
provide for basic human needs at home. It can enhance public affection
for the community, patriotism, and belief in the superiority of liberal
democracy over collectivist systems by adopting policies that uphold
the equal worth and dignity of all members of society. Kirkpatrick
therefore criticizes Republicans who fail to articulate an "inclusive
vision of the public good":

> There has been a continuing Republican embarrassment about expressing
> an inclusive concern for the whole. Some Republicans feel that they are
> not quite being conservative unless they are Spencerian, Darwinian sur-
> vival-of-the-fittest individualists. They seem to think that social goods
> are incompatible with respect for individual freedom or adherence to the
> principle that individual initiative is the most effective motor for accom-
> plishing social goals.[66]

Many conservatives may object to Kirkpatrick's defense of the welfare state and to her belief that the values of liberty and equality can
be mutually reinforcing. Yet Kirkpatrick understands that there are
limitations on government's ability to achieve these values. She recognizes that although government can enhance the public welfare,
government cannot, and should never, try to attain "absolute equality."
She contends that distinctions in ability, attainment and ambition will
always result in important and salutary differences between human
beings. Kirkpatrick wants government to enhance equal opportunities
without trying to create equal outcomes.

Kirkpatrick's defense of liberty is evidenced by her criticisms of
rationalist thought. She fears the loss of liberty posed by a paternalistic
government that exercises "caring that coerces." Excessive government
control of the polity, she assesses, destroys the fundamental principles
of a liberal democratic regime.

Kirkpatrick's thought appears to pose a classic line-drawing dilemma.
She defends government's use of "coercive power" to solve problems
such as racial and sexual discrimination. She likewise fears excessive
government control over society. Nonetheless, although Kirkpatrick is
neither a strict libertarian nor a welfare-state liberal, her arguments are
not necessarily contradictory. Apparently she believes that government
actively needs to use its moral and legal authorities to overcome
discrimination. She is also uncomfortable with the extent to which new
class proponents wish to use government to pursue their social and
economic agendas. Reasonable people disagree over where to draw the

line between necessary and excessive government intervention. Kirkpatrick wants government to affirm conservatism's principles of national security, liberty and opportunity.

Contemporary conservatives respond enthusiastically to Kirkpatrick's foreign policy views. They are most impressed with her unremitting, hard-line anti-Communist beliefs and with her skepticism of international organizations and treaties. Kirkpatrick portrays herself as a political realist. Yet Kirkpatrick's worldview is not wholly compatible with the principles of political realism as developed by its major framers and practitioners. For example, while it is incorrect to assume that a political realist is necessarily an "unrepentant cold warrior," Kirkpatrick equates realism with hard-line anticommunism. In fact, in the 1950s and 1960s many prominent political realists, including Reinhold Niebuhr and Hans J. Morgenthau, assessed worldwide anti-Communist containment as a too costly foreign policy ideal that conflicted with the national interest. While very committed, as Kirkpatrick is, to the principles of liberal democracy, they opposed U.S. involvement in Southeast Asia on the basis of fundamental realist principles.

Kirkpatrick's well-known criticisms of Carter Administration foreign policies appear to lack balance. She offers a controversial distinction between authoritarian and totalitarian regimes—a distinction worked out by earlier writers including Hannah Arendt—and declares that authoritarian regimes, such as Somoza's Nicaragua, are less violent, less oppressive, and more likely to evolve into democracies than are totalitarian regimes. Many of Kirkpatrick's critics read this analytic distinction as nothing more than an unabashed defense of U.S. support for right-wing autocracies, despite the levels of government-supported violence committed within such regimes.

The major difficulty instead is that the distinction between authoritarian and totalitarian regimes is not as clear and unambiguous as portrayed by Kirkpatrick. For example, there is substantial evidence that authoritarian governments are capable of levels of oppression that Kirkpatrick equates solely with totalitarian systems. It is not clear that levels of government-instigated oppression are always significantly worse in some "totalitarian" Eastern European countries than in some "authoritarian" regimes such as Somoza's Nicaragua. Kirkpatrick also believes that liberalization and democratization are possible in authoritarian-ruled societies, whereas no totalitarian regime has ever evolved into a democracy. Yet some Marxist-ruled societies (for example, Hungary and Yugoslavia) have become more pluralistic throughout the years. The prospects for democratization in some traditional authoritarian-ruled countries (such as Zaire) are not very promising.

Kirkpatrick also maintains that the Carter Administration "actively collaborated" with totalitarians in the overthrow of friendly autocracies. In her view, Carter had an ideological preference for revolutionary regimes in Iran and Nicaragua rather than for "traditional" regimes. This view is challenged by Richard Melanson who writes that in the case of Nicaragua, the Carter Administration engaged in a lengthy and "unsuccessful search for a 'democratic' alternative."[67] Kirkpatrick's belief that the Carter Administration enthusiastically welcomed the Sandinistas' rise to power is unsubstantiated. A Carter Administration State Department official told Melanson, "Nobody was pleased. It was clearly a defeat for United States policy. . . . There were some younger FSOs in the Latin American Bureau who did look on the Sandinistas as maybe not so bad, but none was in a policy position."[68]

In the case of Iran, Carter clearly did not want the Shah removed in favor of a revolutionary regime. Kirkpatrick's argument disregards the Carter Administration's extensive initial support of the Shah which was given in an attempt to solidify the Shah's rule. Early in Carter's term human rights activists frequently criticized the President for a different kind of double standard than that envisioned by Kirkpatrick: In their view, human rights violations in Teheran were ignored while transgressions in Siberia were condemned. Despite Kirkpatrick's belief that Carter had a special "affinity" for leftist revolutionaries, the record clearly indicates that Carter frequently reserved his harshest condemnations for rights violations taking place behind the Iron Curtain.[69]

Kirkpatrick's Rhetoric and the United Nations

It is appropriate to conclude by assessing how Kirkpatrick's thought and rhetoric influenced her diplomatic effectiveness at the United Nations. As U.N. observer Seymour Maxwell Finger observes: "Clearly, Kirkpatrick's political philosophy . . . had a decisive impact on her attitude and actions at the United Nations."[70]

Kirkpatrick often criticizes the role of the United Nations in resolving international conflicts. Her assessment of U.S. influence at the United Nations is that we "have none at all."[71] She also points out that the United Nations never evolved into what its creators believed they were building after World War II: "Very quickly after 1945, it became very clear that the vision of a fundamentally united world of basically peaceloving nations could not be sustained."[72]

Rather than resolve conflicts, Kirkpatrick believes that the United Nations creates additional opportunities for international tensions. The United Nations allegedly contributes to conflicts by pressuring all states to participate in debates on various issues that may or may not affect vital national interests. Being forced to vote and take sides on a number of issues dramatically raises the quantity of disagreements among participating nation-states. Bloc formation in particular, she adds, heightens the realm of conflict and disagreement.[73] Kirkpatrick contends that the inability to resolve conflicts such as the Iran-Iraq war, Arab-Israeli disputes, the Soviet invasion of Afghanistan and Central American tensions clearly exhibits the U.N.'s impotence.

Kirkpatrick's yardstick for measuring the U.N.'s success is somewhat inflated. The United Nations has not lived up to its framers' expectations, but its lesser achievements should be recognized. An antidote to Kirkpatrick's view of the United Nations is Finger's perhaps exalted view of that organization's contributions to conflict resolution:

> One could add a host of other examples, such as the peaceful settlement of the dispute between Indonesia and the Netherlands on West Iran, the Iranian agreement to allow a U.N. referendum which resulted in the independence of Bahrain, and the presence of a U.N. peacekeeping force to stop the conflict between Saudi Arabia and Egypt in Yemen. In fact, of more than 150 disputes submitted to the Security-Council and the General Assembly, only a dozen long-range problems have thus far defied solution. The others have been resolved from the United Nations or between the parties themselves.[74]

Kirkpatrick's negative perception of the United Nations unquestionably influenced her operating style as U.S. permanent representative. Delegates criticized her confrontational style (often compared to that of former ambassador to the United Nations Daniel P. Moynihan), lack of accessibility, and "lecturing" of other representatives.[75] Richard N. Gardner assesses that during Reagan's first term the U.S. delegation to the United Nations developed a reputation for "ideological zeal."[76] Finger agrees and adds that based on a series of interviews with other U.N. representatives Kirkpatrick was perceived as overly ideological in her approach and too confrontational. In his view, Kirkpatrick's diplomatic approach often made "cooperation difficult even for friendly delegations."[77]

As a political thinker, Jeane Kirkpatrick exhibits a strong commitment to the fundamental principles of liberal democracy and convincingly exposes the social, economic and political failings of collectivist systems. Her domestic policy writings display a healthy skepticism of expansive government, yet she rejects the views of libertarians who do not accept government's legitimate role in caring for the public good. Her foreign policy views exhibit a consistent, although less moderate posture. She has been aptly described by a sympathetic writer as an "unrepentant cold warrior." Kirkpatrick's critics contend that her hard-line foreign policy views and corresponding rhetoric undermined her effectiveness as a diplomat. The art of diplomacy indeed values the time-honored principles of moderation, toleration and compromise. Kirkpatrick is generally not credited by her critics with fostering an atmosphere at the United Nations conducive to advancing these three crucial principles.

Notes

1. George F. Will, "Kirkpatrick Should Stay at the Table," *Washington Post,* November 25, 1984, p. C7.

2. George F. Will, "A Place for Kirkpatrick," *Washington Post,* November 22, 1984, p. A27.

3. Penny Lernoux, "The Kirkpatrick Doctrine for Latin America," *The Nation,* May 28, 1981, p. 361.

4. Jefferson Morely, "Jean vs. Jeane," *The New Republic,* January 28, 1985, p. 39.

5. See Seymour Maxwell Finger, "The Reagan-Kirkpatrick Policies at the United Nations," *Foreign Affairs* 72 (Winter 1983-1984): 435–446; and Richard Gardner, "A Memorandum: U.N. Diplomacy," *New York Times,* March 8, 1985, p. A35.

6. Jeane Kirkpatrick, *Dictatorships and Double Standards: Rationalism and Realism in Politics* (New York: Simon and Schuster, 1982), p. 11.

7. Jeane Kirkpatrick, "Regulation, Liberty, and Equality," *Regulation* (November-December 1977): 14.

8. Kirkpatrick, *Dictatorships and Double Standards,* p. 11.

9. Ibid.

10. Ibid., p. 12.

11. Ibid.

12. Ibid.

13. Ibid., p. 233.

14. Ibid., p. 14.

15. Ibid., p. 15.

16. See, for example, Milton and Rose Friedman, *Free to Choose* (New York: Avon Books, 1980).

17. Kirkpatrick, "Regulation, Liberty, and Equality," p. 11.

18. Ibid., p. 12.

19. Ibid., p. 14.

20. Ibid.

21. *Time,* March 25, 1985, p. 39.

22. An interview with Jeane Kirkpatrick, *Policy Review* 44 (Spring 1988): 2–3.

23. Kirkpatrick, "Regulation, Liberty, and Equality," p. 14.

24. Ibid.

25. Kirkpatrick, *Dictatorships and Double Standards,* p. 9.

26. Ibid., p. 241.

27. Ibid., p. 9.

28. Ibid., p. 8.

29. Ibid., p. 10.

30. Ibid.

31. Jeane Kirkpatrick, "Why Not Abolish Ignorance?" *National Review,* July 9, 1982, p. 830.

32. Adam Wolfson, "The World According to Kirkpatrick: Is Ronald Reagan Listening?" *Policy Review* 31 (Winter 1985): 70.

33. Finger, "The Reagan-Kirkpatrick Policies," p. 437.

34. Wolfson, "The World According to Kirkpatrick," p. 70.

35. Ibid.

36. Kirkpatrick, *Dictatorships and Double Standards,* p. 18.

37. Ibid.

38. Ibid., p. 122.

39. Finger, "The Reagan-Kirkpatrick Policies," p. 436.

40. Kirkpatrick, "Why Not Abolish Ignorance?" p. 829.

41. Jeane Kirkpatrick, "U.S. Security and Latin America," *Commentary* 71 (January 1981): 33.

42. Ibid., p. 35.

43. Jeane Kirkpatrick, "Dictatorships and Double Standards," *Commentary* 68 (November 1979): 43.

44. Kirkpatrick, "U.S. Security and Latin America," p. 29.

45. Kirkpatrick, "Dictatorships and Double Standards," p. 44.

46. Ibid., p. 34.

47. Jeane Kirkpatrick, "Selective Invocation of Universal Values," in Ernest W. Lefever, ed., *Morality and Foreign Policy: A Symposium on President Carter's Stance* (Washington, D.C.: Ethics and Public Policy Center, 1978), pp. 24–25.

48. Jeane Kirkpatrick, "The Hobbes Problem: Order, Authority, and Legitimacy in Central America," *Across the Board* 18 (September 1981): 29.

49. Ibid.

50. Kirkpatrick, "Regulation, Liberty, and Equality," p. 13.

51. Jeane Kirkpatrick, "Why We Don't Become Republicans," *Commonsense* 2 (Fall 1979): 30.

52. An interview with Jeane Kirkpatrick, p. 5.

53. Jeane Kirkpatrick, *The New Presidential Elite: Men and Women in National Politics* (New York: Russell Sage Foundation, 1976), p. 3.

54. Kirkpatrick, *Dictatorships and Double Standards,* p. 202.

55. Ibid., p. 203.

56. Jeane Kirkpatrick, "The Revolt of the Masses," *Commentary* 55 (February 1973): 61.

57. Jeane Kirkpatrick, *Dismantling the Parties* (Washington, D.C.: American Enterprise Institute, 1978).

58. Ibid., p. 31.

59. Jeane Kirkpatrick et al., *The Presidential Nominating Process: Can It Be Improved?* (Washington, D.C.: American Enterprise Institute, 1980), pp. 16–17.

60. Ibid., pp. 18–19.

61. An interview with Jeane Kirkpatrick, p. 3.

62. Jeane Kirkpatrick, *Political Woman* (New York: Basic Books, 1974), p. 247.

63. Ibid., p. 251.

64. Ibid., p. 242.

65. Ibid.

66. An interview with Jeane Kirkpatrick, p. 2.

67. Richard Melanson, "World Order Theorists and the Carter Administration," in Kenneth W. Thompson, ed., *Traditions and Values: American Diplomacy, 1945 to the Present* (Lanham, Md.: University Press of America, 1984), p. 137.

68. Ibid., pp. 136–137.

69. Carter, in fact, won praise from a number of conservative writers for his emphasis on Soviet rights abuses. George F. Will exclaimed that by "focusing attention on [the Soviets'] contemptuous disregard for international undertakings," Carter distanced himself from the "preemptive appeasement" of the Kissinger years (*Washington Post,* March 3, 1977, p. A23). Marvin Stone assessed that Carter's rights campaign could teach the Soviets "that humane leadership is the way to strength and respect in the civilized world" (*U.S. News & World Report,* July 31, 1977, p. 71). The *Wall Street Journal*'s editors maintained that Carter's rights campaign "has given U.S. foreign policy a principled tone and has put the Soviet Union, a prime offender, on the defensive" (March 21, 1977, p. 18).

70. Finger, "The Reagan-Kirkpatrick Policies," p. 438.

71. Jeane Kirkpatrick, "The United Nations as a Political System: A Practicing Political Scientist's Insights into U.N. Politics," *World Affairs* 146 (Spring 1984): 359.

72. Ibid., p. 361.

73. Finger, "The Reagan-Kirkpatrick Policies," p. 439.

74. Ibid.

75. Ibid., pp. 446–447.

76. Richard N. Gardner, "A Memorandum: U.N. Diplomacy," *New York Times,* March 8, 1985, p. A35.

77. Finger, "The Reagan-Kirkpatrick Policies," p. 448.

PART THREE

Capitalism and Economics

There is an inherent tension within American conservatism between defenders of laissez-faire economics and advocates of "big-government conservatism." The chapter on George F. Will revealed, in part, some of the bases of this tension. For example, whereas many defenders of laissez-faire economic policies believe that government should play a relatively small role in most areas of individuals' lives, many thinkers on the Right, especially some prominent neoconservatives, contend that an activist government can be a tool to achieve conservative policy ends.

The following analyses of Milton Friedman and Michael Novak as political and economic thinkers dig more deeply into the nature of a fundamental debate in American conservative thought. A. Craig Waggaman and Sidney A. Pearson, Jr., show that these two thinkers differ significantly on matters both political and economic. Friedman, a classical Liberal in the tradition of nineteenth-century thought, joins with conservatives to criticize the collectivist character of much twentieth-century progressive liberalism. Yet unlike Novak, Friedman does not link democratic capitalism to civic virtue. Novak believes that democratic capitalism is characterized by a "spirit" that reflects the moral qualities of human beings. Novak's defense of democratic capitalism stands as a powerful critique of utopian, socialist visions.

10

Milton Friedman and the Recovery of Liberalism

A. Craig Waggaman

I am in no way a conservative. . . . I am a liberal in the strict sense of the word . . . since, above all, I put all of my faith in human liberty.[1]

As an observer of the relationship between economics and politics, Milton Friedman is best known as a defender of the close affinity between competitive capitalism and a free polity. His writings on political economy show a remarkable consistency and fidelity to a few simple truths, which he states again and again in his popular works. For many years Friedman was primarily a gadfly on the sluggish horse of Keynesian economic orthodoxy, issuing repeated warnings about the bad effects of even well-intentioned government intervention. Now that Friedman's views have been embraced (although not necessarily implemented) by some of the defenders and advisers of the Reagan and Bush Administrations, this might be a good time to reconsider Friedman's contribution to a conservative political economy.

There is an obvious irony in the inclusion of a chapter on Milton Friedman in a book on contemporary conservatism. Friedman is a classic nineteenth-century Liberal in almost every sense of the term. It is only the collectivist character of twentieth-century liberalism that allows him to join forces with some conservatives in defense of what Friedman considers the original principles of the regime.[2] Thus, while Friedman has been a leader in the criticism of the economic agenda of contemporary progressive liberalism, he stops short of people such as George Gilder or even Michael Novak in linking capitalism to private or public virtue. His generally libertarian sentiments also make Friedman more openly suspicious of large corporations and their connection to large government than some of his fellow defenders of democratic capitalism are.

Reading Milton Friedman in the late 1980s is still a challenging experience for both liberals and conservatives. His clear and closely reasoned arguments bring us quickly back to a consideration of the most basic question of political philosophy—the proper character and ends of government.

Freedom, Economics and Politics

Concentrated power is not rendered harmless by the good intentions of those who create it.[3]

An analysis of Friedman's thought brings back all of the old dilemmas of liberalism that have made it vulnerable to attacks from both the Left and the Right. Friedman's liberalism begins with the assumption that freedom is a necessary condition for the realization of the good life. He does not pretend that free individuals are always going to make good choices, but he does question whether any choice not freely arrived at can be considered a good one. The function of government is to allow the pursuit of individual preferences regarding the good life. This vision of the purpose of government leads Friedman to the conclusion that good government is nearly identical to limited government.

When politics attempts to move beyond its admittedly limited boundaries, even in the name of other goods such as equality or economic justice, Friedman condemns it for two reasons. First, the attempt by a centralized authority to put into practice any particular vision of the good life necessarily involves limiting the freedom of those who disagree with or do not share that vision. This would be true even if the vision were shared by a majority of citizens. If there were not legitimate competing conceptions of what is good for human beings, the case for freedom might be weakened. But Friedman clearly sides with James Madison in arguing that freedom and faction go hand in hand and that controlling the effects of faction is preferable to attempting to eliminate its cause. Second, government intervention is often ineffective and in many cases has effects opposite to those intended. This view has been elaborated in Friedman's frequently stated positions on public policy issues such as housing, education and welfare. It also allows him to be fairly congenial with his opponents, admitting that they are well intentioned while condemning the results of their actions and proposals.

The central thesis of Milton Friedman's political economy is that competitive capitalism and the free market are essential to the maintenance and expression of individual freedom. A market economy permits millions of decisions to be made daily based on nothing more than individuals' expression of their own preferences. A competitive market allocates resources "efficiently" based on those accumulated decisions by consumers. Such a system allows for the wide diversity in tastes that one would expect to be a product of a pluralistic regime, and it allows for the satisfaction of a multitude of desires, however trivial or vulgar. If the primary end of a regime is individual liberty, or if freedom of choice is seen as a prerequisite to other goods, such a variety of choices is either good in itself or good because freedom of choice regarding unimportant things is a supporting condition of freedom of choice regarding important ones.

Are the individuals making these decisions responsible people? Some are and some are not. A regime that posits freedom as the primary political good must assume either that most adults are responsible or that freedom is the only logical condition for the development of responsibility. Friedman believes that most people spend their own money more efficiently than if someone else spent it on their behalf. Arguing that most people are responsible consumers is not the same as saying that they are virtuous ones. Friedman admits that most people's motivations are self-interested. But, he argues, this is the way it always has been. Freedom is the condition for the expression of what is highest in men and women, but it allows as a consequence the expression of what is lowest or is in between. For this reason, despite the enormous accomplishments of a free polity, it will always come up short when compared to some vision of the perfect order.

A political benefit associated with the combination of freedom, a free market and self-interested activity is a prosperous economy. As long as most of us are at least partially self-interested in a material sense, this combination helps make governing easier. Of course, the political legitimacy attached to economic success may be fragile and may be affected both by the possibility of economic failure and by the distribution of economic benefits. One is also never completely sure in a free and prosperous regime whether freedom or prosperity is the most cherished good. Friedman clearly favors the former and assumes that the latter will almost take care of itself.

A prosperous and competitive economy also creates numerous small centers of economic power and influence that help to prevent concentration of political power. The liberal tradition that Friedman belongs to asserts that the individual's right to private property is essential to the protection of other natural rights. He rejects the notion shared by much of the Left and some of the Right that democratic capitalism limits our choices and conditions our behavior. Quite the contrary, its preoccupation with material success actually liberates those who wish to pursue nonmaterial visions of the good life.

Friedman's praise for capitalism is not as unqualified as some would think. While he believes that a prosperous economy is a nice benefit of a free polity and economy, it is individual freedom that should be the primary goal of politics. Friedman realizes that taken individually, there are many financial and industrial corporations as well as labor unions that decry government intervention and praise free competition only as long as their own interests are involved. "The two greatest enemies of free enterprise in the United States . . . have been, on the one hand, my fellow intellectuals, and on the other hand, the business corporations of this country."[4] The conditions of freedom must therefore be defended against economic as well as political concentrations of power.

Friedman and His Critics

Underlying most arguments against the free market is a lack of belief in freedom itself.[5]

Much of Friedman's polemical writing is aimed at a group he refers to in one article as "Tory Radicals." A standard-bearer of this group is Friedman's longtime nemesis and friend, John Kenneth Galbraith. Friedman's criticism of Galbraith's assumptions provides the reader with one of the most interesting statements of Friedman's own philosophical foundations.[6]

According to Friedman, the problem that so many intellectuals have with freedom and a free market is that they simply do not like the results. They consider themselves a natural aristocracy whose values and tastes are superior to those of the multitude. There is nothing new here, of course. The aristocratic claim is a long-standing one, and even many traditional liberals believe that freedom will bring forth a natural, as opposed to a hereditary, aristocracy. Many contemporary pundits who call themselves liberal, however, are uncomfortable with the antidemocratic character of the belief that some people are more fit to rule. Using Galbraith as an example, Friedman suggests that these modern aristocrats look for ways to explain why the common folk do not share all the aristocracy's allegedly superior values. One easy solution is the popular argument that the market does not reflect what people really want. Instead, it shows what consumers are manipulated into wanting by the propaganda of large corporations. As one of my students recently explained to me, could anyone in his right mind ever actually want to buy a "hot-topper"? (If you have never heard of this device that will *spray* butter over your popcorn, count yourself fortunate.) Good people cannot possibly be responsible for the myriad bad decisions that are made. Freedom cannot be the cause of good people making those bad decisions. Hence, the market cannot be a free one. Once this reasoning is completed, the way is left wide open for guiltless intervention by the new aristocracy. All this is done, of course, in the name of freedom. Freedom has now become an end, however, rather than a condition. This "authentic freedom" now carries with it a variety of preconditions, none of which is seemingly satisfied by traditional arrangements.

The argument of the Tory radicals is deepened and widened by contemporary radical critics of capitalist societies. For them, Friedman is merely an apologist for a system that ignores the poor in favor of the rich, creates an unhealthy competitive environment instead of an authentic human community, and promotes the evils of racism, sexism and poverty. The freedoms that exist under democratic capitalist regimes only mask our alienation and our lack of genuine freedom. Karl Marx argued in *Capital* that systems such as ours are characterized by a despotic workplace and an anarchical marketplace. He assumed that a community has a right to bring production under "social control" in the name of the common good. This social control of production is the beginning of a just regime, and freedom is impossible without justice. Freedom is also impossible under capitalism because work is still tied to necessity, although orthodox Marxists accept that the development of tremendous productive capacity under advanced capitalism is a prerequisite to socialism.

Most contemporary radicals do not give as much credit to capitalism as Marx did. This is partly for political reasons—it would be unseemly to defend the extension of democratic capitalism as a solution to Third World problems—and partly because of a deeply held moral antagonism to modern industrial societies that takes the Marxist concept of alienation and extends it to assume that all the problems of modern men and women are systemic.

Friedman's critique of New Deal liberalism and of socialism complements his defense of freedom. There are a variety of opinions regarding the good life. To choose one and call it justice and name it as a prerequisite to all other goods is to begin the dismantling of a free regime. This does not mean that limiting freedom in the name of justice is not philosophically defensible. But it does suggest that you may choose to forego the implementation of a particular vision of the just regime for a couple of reasons. The first is that your opinion is not shared by others. You may therefore have to subject a number of people to a vision of the good life with which they do not agree. This may force you to take actions that are repugnant to you, and you may therefore choose to forego ends that are not consistent with your definition of acceptable means. The second reason is that you do not know how to get from point A to point B. These problems are actually related. Many well-intentioned reformers genuinely believe that as soon as their truth is presented to the people, the veil will fall from their eyes and everything will fall into place. Contemporary liberals often fall into this category, believing that good intentions are sufficient and blaming others when good intentions lead to less than wonderful results.[7]

Friedman is the first to admit that liberal reformers and even socialists may be very well-motivated people. Good motivation does not make them any less the enemies of freedom, however. If government intervention could create a significantly "better" polity, some sacrifices in freedom might be theoretically justifiable. What makes Friedman so adamant in his criticism of such intervention is his reading of the historical record regarding such attempts. Friedman was a forerunner of contemporary critics of the welfare state such as George Gilder and Charles Murray, arguing at least since the publication of *Capitalism and Freedom* in 1962 that paternalistic government intervention in the name of justice and equality often has effects opposite to those intended. He also supports the use of economics as a science to demonstrate the costs and benefits associated with such government action. His conclusion is that government intervention of the type typified by New Deal liberalism, far from being necessary to "save" capitalism, has had deleterious effects on freedom and on those groups it was meant to benefit.[8] More intervention cannot possibly be the solution to problems caused by intervention. This argument has been relatively effective in recent years against New Deal liberals who have lost the policy initiative, if not their moral self-righteousness, in the area of federal welfare programs. Friedman's arguments are less useful in responding to the radical Left, however, which insists that problems will continue as long as the basic institutional expressions of a capitalist economy remain intact.

Even more ominous a result of larger government for Friedman is the formation of new centers of power and influence that lie outside of normal political channels of accountability. The creation of additional "programs" and the bureaucracy needed to administer them, coupled with the increase in middle-class welfare such as subsidized student loan programs, has led to a widespread acceptance by many Americans of the responsibility of government to provide for us in a variety of ways. As soon as all problems, whether economic, social, racial or whatever, are assumed to have political solutions, the very notion of limited government disappears. This tendency of government to grow creates new constituencies that benefit from that growth and are unwilling to give up those benefits. Those who are hurt by the growth of government have been more quiet because the costs of a larger government are more difficult to point to—lost opportunities and fewer jobs in the private sector, for example. This situation creates what Friedman refers to as the "tyranny of the status quo."

There is also a strong libertarian component in Friedman's thinking that suggests that the growth of government in the name of the poor actually leads to an increase in the power of the rich and the power and influence of large banks and corporations at the expense of middle-class and lower-middle-class taxpayers. He argues, for instance, that government agencies set up to protect the worker or the consumer are often captured by the very organizations they are designed to regulate. Although Friedman is cautious in delving too far into a populist political economy, he understands the mutual attractions of large capital, bureaucracies and intellectuals to a "regulated" polity that approaches state capitalism or socialism. Whether the impetus for such a regime comes from the positivistic desire for the rule of "experts" or whether it comes from the moral claim of the just to rule in the interest of others, Friedman realizes the profound effect that such a political economy has on the character of the regime.

The radical critique of capitalism is not as fully addressed by Friedman. He does point out that socialist countries have found no good substitute for the price mechanism to allocate resources and that attempts to overcome the "anarchy of the market" have only produced widespread poverty, a new privileged class, and a glaring lack of civil and political freedoms. This is especially evident in the Third World, where the orthodox Marxist precondition for socialism—advanced capitalism—simply does not exist. Friedman's flirtation with the military dictatorship in Chile that attempted to implement many of Friedman's laissez-faire and monetarist suggestions led him to reformulate the argument he made in *Capitalism and Freedom.* Where he once argued that economic liberty was a prerequisite to political liberty, he suggests now that the opposite may be the case and that a free-market experiment cannot be maintained successfully for long in the absence of political liberty.

Friedman is sensitive to the moral criticism of advanced capitalist society that forms a significant part of the Left's argument. It is also one that he rejects unequivocally. A humane society, according to Friedman, is one that allows people to be good. This is not the same as forcing people to be good. It is also not the same as manipulating through law and force the external appearance of the regime to conform to one particular standard of justice. Individuals pursue goodness and excellence in a variety of ways according to the promptings of their own souls. Only freedom will allow those few who choose a life of nobility, virtue, charity or excellence to pursue their own visions of the good life. In a free society many will choose more vulgar ends or some combination of the material and the spiritual. For many would-be reformers or moralists, this is unsatisfying. For Friedman it points the way directly to a principled support of limited government. Friedman has genuine sympathy for these high-minded souls, but he continually reminds us of the importance of prudence—the relationship between ends and means—and its central role in political life.

Friedman does not neglect the problem of justice or the plight of the poor. What he does suggest is that we consider separately the questions of equity and efficiency. Capitalist production is the source of our wealth and our jobs. Social justice should not be pursued in a way that assumes that those who produce are the enemies of a just order. The suggestion that questions of production and distribution can be separated is a direct challenge to Marxist orthodoxy and is still not accepted by a large number of those on the moderate Left. Friedman's public policy proposals are premised on the assumption that the pursuit of justice, equity and social welfare should begin with a commitment to affecting individual liberty and market allocation as little as possible.

Three brief examples can be given to illustrate Friedman's approach. The first addresses the issue of welfare. Like many contemporary critics, Friedman argues that current welfare programs create dependency and disincentives to work and paternalistically suggest that welfare recipients are not capable of making rational decisions regarding how to spend welfare income. Much of the welfare dollar goes to the maintenance of a middle-class bureaucracy established to administer the system; this bureaucracy constitutes a powerful lobby against basic changes in the system that might be in the public interest.

Friedman's solution to the welfare muddle—negative income tax— is simple and controversial. It is premised on the assumption that the job of welfare is to get money into the hands of people who need it. Assuming that they are mentally competent, Friedman argues that they should be given the money and allowed to spend it as they please. Most of the welfare bureaucracy could be dismantled and the money returned to the taxpayers or given to the poor as part of the program. The negative income tax would be administered in the same fashion as regular income tax is; only the cash flow would be reversed. The negative tax payment would constitute a percentage of a base amount that could be adjusted based on the cost of living or on the charitable inclinations of the citizens.

Those who make more than this base amount would pay taxes and those who made less would not. If the negative income tax rate was 50 percent and the base income was $15,000, everyone would be guaranteed an income of $7,500. The disincentive to work would be partially removed because one would get (in this example) fifty cents of every dollar earned until one reached the minimal taxable income. Part-time jobs would help the negative income tax recipient to get experience and earn money without jeopardizing his or her participation in the program. There would be little or no paperwork involved in getting the money, and income would be reported and dispensed in a fashion very similar to the way taxes are removed from our paychecks currently.

Very few people I have talked to like the negative income tax idea. Liberals are afraid for the social workers who will lose their jobs and smell a plot by conservatives to get rid of welfare altogether. Conservatives fear human nature will drive half of us onto the dole. Friedman argues, however, that such a plan would be consistent with the demands both of justice and of freedom.

The second example of Friedman's public policy suggestions is changes in the social security system. At the very least, Friedman suggests that there is no reason the government should have a monopoly on providing old age annuities to its citizens. The government could provide the individual with a variety of private-sector investment funds, make participation in some plan mandatory, and remove payments for that program from the individual's paycheck in the normal fashion. If the negative income tax was in place to protect older people from extreme poverty, Friedman would support abolition of social security altogether.

The third example is Friedman's now famous educational voucher system. Friedman argues that parents should have a choice of where they want their children educated. Public and private schools would compete for the same dollars, which would be allocated to the parents in the form of a voucher worth a certain amount of money. Friedman believes that this would make education more accountable to parents and provide for a greater freedom of choice. While there are a variety of questions and concerns that might be raised about such a plan, it again represents the assumptions that individuals male the best choices regarding themselves and their own children and that the market is the best way to allocate resources based on those individual choices.

Friedman's liberalism is often called conservatism by those who voice the kinds of criticisms of laissez-faire capitalism discussed previously. It is also true that many who identify themselves as conservatives of one sort or another embrace many of Friedman's positions on specific issues. The common ground that is shared by Friedman and many conservatives is the belief that the country is turning away from its founding principles. The debate is thus over the character of the American regime. Within this debate, the temporary political alliance of Friedman with conservatism begins to weaken.

If contemporary liberals reject Friedman's old-fashioned liberalism because of its lack of emphasis on justice, many conservatives worry about Friedman's liberalism because of its lack of concern with virtue, either civic or moral. Should the regime be concerned with the character of its citizens? Is it possible that a free regime can be "corrupted" from within? Can even a liberal regime survive without passing along certain beliefs from one generation to the next, and can this occur under the kind of society that Friedman would favor? These questions are as old as political philosophy itself and cannot be answered here. But they are at the heart of a theoretical uneasiness about liberal democracy that is an important component of contemporary conservatism.

The quote from Friedman that begins this chapter might lead one to believe that he has an optimistic view of human nature. Elsewhere in his writings, however, this optimism is qualified. The majority of people act out of material self-interest the majority of the time, and "the problem of social organization is how to set up an arrangement under which greed will do the least harm."[9] Friedman suggests that democratic capitalism is such a system. This connection between self-interest and political stability identifies Friedman closely with the ideas of many of the Founders and draws him away from the most optimistic strains of Enlightenment thought. The issue of human nature is confused a little more by Friedman's discussion of what he calls the "myth of the robber barons." He suggests here that the extreme laissez-faire character of the last century was connected to an outpouring of charitable activity even without the encouragement of income tax deductions, as there was no income tax.[10]

Friedman's inconsistencies with regard to the character of a free people leave him open to criticisms from both the Left and the Right. Would the world be better off if fewer people were materialistic? Do most people really know what to do to achieve happiness? Does advanced democratic capitalism broaden the choices available to individuals regarding the good life, or does it narrow them?

In his recent book *The Closing of the American Mind,* Allan Bloom argues that if this regime is founded on the principle of natural rights, it may be essential that the regime encourage through education and public discourse the passing on of an understanding of that idea to as many of its citizens as possible.[11] A vague defense of freedom may not be enough because self-interest can lead people just as well to tyranny as to liberty. Irving Kristol makes a related point in his wonderful essay entitled "When Virtue Loses All Her Loveliness" by asking this question: "But can men live in a free society if they have no reason to believe it is also a just society?"[12] Is self-interest an adequate bond to maintain a political community, however narrowly defined? Kristol doubts that it is.

The criticism of the lack of community in a democratic capitalist regime is not confined to the neoconservatives. Traditional Catholic social thought decries the excessive individualism of regimes such as ours, a criticism recently reaffirmed by John Paul II. Socialists, democratic or otherwise, consider the competitive nature of a capitalist economy to be a distortion of the social character of human beings and therefore a cause of a variety of social ills. The search for justice and for some mythical organic community in which human beings will rediscover themselves still has the power to draw people away from liberal regimes, despite the dismal historical record of attempts to found such perfected cities.

The longing for community that defines or helps to define the meaning of one's life is a very real one. To suggest that we need no help in our quest for the good life is open to serious question. It is difficult sometimes to decide where the legitimate expression of culture and community ends and where despotism begins, but the implications of that difficulty are not easy to draw out. The connection among freedom, individualism, community and happiness appears more complex than Friedman makes it out to be.

Where political economy fits into these issues is a difficult question. Marxists, contemporary liberals and many conservatives do not seem hostile to a "managed" economy. The Left sees such management in terms of government intervention to achieve desired social and economic goals. The position of the conservatives is less clear. Many who claim neoconservative status accept the need for such intervention but are critical of the efficiency with which it has been done in the past and wish to limit its extent. Conservatives who have reservations about democracy or those who are otherwise suspicious or even contemptuous of the "vulgar many" might be willing to grant large capital certain privileges as one section of a ruling elite whose purpose is to guide the community toward some vision of the common good or at least away from certain alternative visions.

Conclusion—Pluralism and Community

On the whole, the formal restrictions on governmental activity should be most severe at the federal level, less so at the state level and least of all at the local level.[13]

Milton Friedman is usually thought of as a champion of (or apologist for) the freedom of the individual, a capitalist economy and limited government. Although all of these compliments (or accusations) are true, each one can be qualified in important ways. I think that these qualifications hint at a rapprochement between Friedman and some conservatives.

The centerpiece of Friedman's politics is his defense of individual freedom, which he sees as a more important goal of his public policy suggestions than economic prosperity. An important component of individual freedom is choice. If, as Friedman assumes, individuals find happiness in a variety of ways, it is good that a great variety of ways be available for the individual to choose from. The problem arises when one assumes that some of those ways depend on the existence of a community that does more than build roads and provide police protection. Any social group that pursues a vision of a common good is likely to put restrictions on freedom of choice that are objectionable to some people. If Friedman in any way accepts the possibility that there is a social component to freedom, his understanding of individual liberty may have to be qualified. What if you want to sell dirty books in a community in which a majority of the citizens do not want a dirty bookstore? Does freedom mean the right of the majority to choose to live in a community without dirty bookstores, or does it mean the right of individuals to purchase whatever they wish in their own community and the right of others to sell it to them? If a community wants to preserve a certain flavor of architectural style, should it have the right to limit the kind of home that you build on your own property?

Can a liberal regime address the tension between freedom and community? Three possibilities present themselves. The first is to try building a national community without sacrificing individual freedom. The second is to allow greater expression of community at the local level—giving smaller political communities the right to make a variety of decisions about what kinds of places they wish to be. The third is to depend only on "private communities" or associations to satisfy the social needs of human beings.[14]

There is no doubt that Friedman rejects the first alternative, which is the one that has generally been adopted by the contemporary liberals of whom Friedman is so critical. A national community oriented toward a common vision of the good life is simply not consistent with his understanding of liberty. That he also sees liberal prescriptions inconsistent with their own goals makes him even less likely to be sympathetic to them. The failure of New Deal liberalism to create and sustain anything like a national consensus puts liberals in the awkward position of having to argue that their critics are bad or stupid people. Neither implication is likely to win friends. Even if gifted Democrats are able to rekindle the passions of the majority in favor of their vision, the problem of means is still there. If the Democrats revert to taxing and spending after being so critical of Republican deficits, even many who applaud their motives may revolt against their methods.

When we move to the last two means of addressing the question of community, Friedman's views are less clear. The quotation that opened this section suggests that despite his reputation as a libertarian, Friedman might be willing to allow the public expression of community on a local level. A simple explanation for this would be that power is less concentrated at those levels and therefore less dangerous to liberties. Although this is true, why not go all the way and argue that all levels of government should be as limited as possible? This is certainly consistent with much of what Friedman says, especially his views on government intervention in the economy and on issues such as schools, in which his proposed voucher system would tend to take away from the local community the power to use public schools as a symbol and as a promoter of that community. But Friedman's view of freedom seems to accept the extension of the concept of pluralism to include giving individuals significant choices regarding the kind of community in which they want to live. These choices must remain at the subnational level, however, so that individuals can freely choose to live elsewhere if a certain community is not to their liking.

The right of local communities to pursue or promote a certain way of life is currently a conservative rather than a liberal cause. This is why I suggest a rapprochement between Friedman and these "new federalism" conservatives. Not all conservatives fall into this category, of course. Some wish to mold the national community as much as the liberals do. Others would support local community as a political ploy to prevent liberal homogenization rather than as a principled defense of this kind of pluralism.

Friedman's defenses of individual liberty and of limited government need to be considered, I think, within these larger questions about the meaning of pluralism and the nature of community. That Friedman is not consistent in responding to these questions only places him squarely within a liberal tradition that has always been ambiguous about these things. Friedman's eloquent defense of that tradition does not resolve these ambiguities, but it does challenge those who pretend that they do not exist.

The last qualification that can be made to Friedman's reputation concerns his defense of capitalism. Friedman has a healthy suspicion regarding the intentions of large corporations. He knows that they will pursue monopoly advantages where they can. In fact, Friedman fears that the growth of the federal government, part of which is defended in order to protect us all from big corporations, leads not to control but to collusion. This fear of Friedman's that a "managed" economy is a danger even where socialist politics are not triumphant lends his analysis a complexity that is often ignored and asks us to recall the days when the debate over political economy was not simply an ideological clash between capitalism and socialism.

Milton Friedman's attempts to recover the perspective of the older liberalism is a useful counter to the historical amnesia of contemporary liberals. It is also a challenge to self-identified conservatives to decide whether their opposition to contemporary liberalism is a defense of freedom or simply a desire to replace one vision of the good regime with another one.

Notes

1. This quotation is taken from an interview with Friedman that appeared in the Chilean magazine *Cosas,* no. 149 (June 17, 1982): 15. The quotation was translated by the author.

2. For a brief review of Friedman's view of these principles, see Milton Friedman, *Tyranny of the Status Quo* (New York: Harcourt Brace Jovanovich, 1984), pp. 16–17. For a general overview of the role of government, see Milton Friedman, "The Economic Responsibility of Government," in *Milton Friedman and Paul Samuelson Discuss the Economic Responsibility of Government* (College Station, Tex.: Center for Education and Research in Free Enterprise, 1980), pp. 1–13.

3. Milton Friedman, *Capitalism and Freedom* (Chicago: University of Chicago Press, 1962), p. 201.

4. From a February 9, 1977, address at Pepperdine University entitled "The Future of Capitalism" and reprinted in Milton Friedman, *Tax Limitation, Inflation & the Role of Government* (Dallas: Fisher Institute, 1978), p. 11.

5. Friedman, *Capitalism and Freedom,* p. 15.

6. Friedman, *Tax Limitation,* pp. 52–81.

7. This is a particular problem in foreign affairs, where good intentions seem enough to convince many on the moderate Left in the United States to accept restrictions on civil and political liberties in other countries that they would never condone in their own.

8. Besides books and chapters already cited, see Milton and Rose Friedman, *Free to Choose* (New York: Avon Books, 1979).

9. Milton Friedman, *Bright Promises, Dismal Performance: An Economist's Protest* (New York: Harcourt Brace Jovanovich, 1983), p. 50 (from an interview published in *Playboy,* February 1973).

10. Friedman, *Free to Choose,* pp. 129–131.

11. Allan Bloom, *The Closing of the American Mind* (New York: Simon and Schuster, 1987), Introduction.

12. Irving Kristol, *Two Cheers for Capitalism* (New York: Mentor Books, 1979), p. 246.

13. Friedman, *Bright Promises, Dismal Performance,* p. 57.

14. My thanks to my colleague Peter Schultz for first suggesting this way of looking at the distinctions between national and subnational communities and how this distinction helps us to think about the meaning of pluralism.

11

Michael Novak:
On Democratic Capitalism and
the Things That Are Caesar's

Sidney A. Pearson, Jr.

For American Catholics the social teaching of the American bishops since Vatican II in the 1960s have been the subject and object of unprecedented controversy. The bishops have scrutinized almost every aspect of American public policy, foreign and domestic, and found it wanting. In one sense this is nothing new. Catholic theology has traditionally emphasized the responsibility of the Church to influence the political and social order. Catholic political philosophy has its origins in the view that Christianity is spiritually truncated whenever it is concerned exclusively with the internal ordering of the soul to the exclusion of the external ordering of the polity.

The authority of the American bishops to teach about both the soul and the polity, while subordinate to the universal Magisterium of the Catholic Church, is derived from their pastoral responsibilities as the appointed leaders of their respective dioceses. What is new about this invigorated social teaching are the principles that seem to animate its driving spirit. The bishops, collectively at least, have not merely challenged some of the most fundamental propositions and principles of the American political order; they seem to have done so by borrowing, sometimes selectively and sometimes wholesale, arguments drawn from the most radical ideologies of the political Left. The new politics have redrawn the older boundaries of friend and foe in the politics of Church and state. As a result, American Catholics are divided among themselves as never before in their history. The new social teachings of the American bishops have been aptly described as a "battle for the Amer-

ican Church."[1] And at the very center of this intellectual civil war is
the work of Michael Novak, one of the most original and prolific of
American Catholic writers.

What Michael Novak brings to the neoconservative movement is a
Catholic political philosophy, strongly rooted in Thomistic principles,
applied to a defense of the fundamental principles of the American
regime.[2] This orthodoxy has apparently put him and like-minded Catholic intellectuals on a collision course with significant elements of the
recent social teachings of the American bishops. In the opinion of
many neoconservatives, the new social teaching of the bishops has
produced a crisis of unprecedented proportions. For the first time in
our history the social teaching of the American Catholic Church appears
to be on a direct collision course with the political principles of the
American founding. Although this crisis is not yet evident to many
Catholic laity, Novak is convinced that the logic of the bishops' critiques
goes to the heart of the linkage between the right order of the soul
and the right order of the polity. In his opinion, the bishops' teaching,
like the political Left in general, seriously threatens to sever the linkage
of moral obligations beween American Catholics and their country. At
issue in his response to this newly formulated social teaching is whether
the good man, in the Catholic sense, and the good citizen, in the
American sense, are compatible in the same person. The fundamental
question is as old as Christianity itself, even as the particular setting
is as new as today.

Michael Novak and the American Catholic Heritage

In order to gain some perspective on Novak's quarrel with the
American bishops it will be useful at the outset to compare his thought
with that of John Courtney Murray, S.J. It is a comparison Novak
welcomes. He clearly sees himself as the heir to Murray's interpretation
of the American democratic experiment. What they share, in addition
to a common Catholic faith, is a commitment to merging the best in
traditional Catholic social teaching with the political principles of the
American polity. Both men's intellectual influence is based on their
unique ability to define the political dimension of religious issues.
Although the specific problems have changed dramatically, the fundamental problem of Christian man and the secular state has not changed
for some two thousand years. Its classic formulation by St. Augustine
was conceived as the question of the relationship between the City of
God, which is eternal, and the City of Man, which, like the United
States, is temporal and therefore finite. Where do these two cities

intersect and how? This is the heart of the question for Catholic political philosophy and the heart of the debate for Novak.[3]

That church doctrine and the principles of the American experiment are intertwined has always seemed obvious enough on the face of it. Church doctrine has always assumed that temporal affairs everywhere stand under the judgment of God and that the Church is the custodian of His revealed word. The Church is an intermediary institution between the two cities, representing man to God and God to man. The question has never been so much whether these two cities are related but how and where this meeting takes place. It is essential for the moral basis of any earthly city to understand how and where it comes under the judgment of the City of God. Such is the basis for the Christian understanding of how revelation complements political philosophy.

For John Courtney Murray this meeting of the two cities resulted in his qualified endorsement of what he called "the American proposition"—that is, the notion that the American political experiment is and must remain necessarily incomplete. It is qualified in the traditional sense that no mere political order could ever be mistaken for the City of God in historical time; the eschaton of history was a future event, not an immanent one. His view reflected the Church's traditional view of politics. It was shaped by an intellectually rich Thomistic approach to political philosophy that defined church-state relations in modern Catholic thought. Murray summarized this relationship with the observation that "the principles of Catholic faith and morality stand superior to, and in control of, the whole order of civil life."[4] The political side of the issue was never whether Catholicism could somehow be made compatible with American democracy, but whether American democracy could ever be made compatible with Catholicism. No meeting of the two cities could be expected to be perfect. Nor, by the very nature of the City of Man formed by man's sin, would such a meeting result in the perfection of earthly cities.

Although the differences between the City of God and the City of Man are absolute, traditional Catholic political philosophy was in tension but not necessarily at war with those states that could provide a measure of justice appropriate for the human condition. The City of Man is, after all, grounded in the nature of man as a social being. The state has its own natural place in the order of things; it is the image of man writ large and in its own way reflects man as created in the image of God. According to St. Thomas, the grace of God does not abolish this human nature, either in individuals or collectively, but rather perfects it. The political implications of this traditional theology suggest that human institutions, such as states, are not obliterated or negated by revelation. The state exists as part of the imperfect reality of ordinary human existence. Indeed, the imperfection itself is a constant reminder of the need for God in human affairs. The state, along with the multitude of human institutions preserved and protected by these ordinary political associations, has a rightful if subordinate place within a hierarchy of values. And for the Catholic citizen, the political community can lawfully command both his moral and physical support.

For Murray as well as Novak the American polity fits within a Thomistic conception of a morally defensible form of government—not the highest good, naturally, but it is a good nevertheless. The basis for this judgment is not a comparison of the American political order with the City of God; the basis is a comparison with other contemporary secular regimes, specifically the Fascist and Communist states that have been our most profound foes in the twentieth century. The political implication was that the duty of American Catholics as American citizens was not outwardly different from that of any other citizens. The Magisterium no doubt had more reservations about democracy than did many individual Catholic writers such as Murray, but by the latter half of the twentieth century the idea of democratic government gave every outward appearance of being protected by Catholic social teaching, thanks in large part to a string of influential Thomistic writers.[5] Thus, on the eve of Vatican II, Murray helped to reconcile church and state in America. The good man, in the Catholic sense, and the good citizen, in the American sense, were inclusive terms. Most American Catholics no doubt thought that the issue was settled once and for all.

But government in any form is a problematic notion for the Christian tradition generally and for Catholics in particular. Even if one accepts the idea that democracy is the best form of government in the City of Man, no one believes that God is a president or prime minister of His City. And if the Magisterium of the Catholic Church really is the repository for His word, there is bound to be some tension, to say the least, between the most just political democracy that must compromise on truth and a theology that must not make any such compromises.[6] The Church is built on a hierarchic basis that at least politically seems to be an anachronism in a democratic age. Church teaching, therefore, even if it deals only with social issues and not with faith and morals, is a powerful political instrument not easily reconciled to the principles of modern liberal democratic states. When used as an arm of secular ideologies, it can alternately become a mere instrument of the powers that be or an enemy of any particular democratic government as a matter of fundamental principle.

It is Novak's contention that for the majority of American bishops, Church social teaching has become a part of the Left's general assault on modern democracy. In the process the bishops, wittingly or not, have allowed themselves to be captured by intellectuals of a social science elite that is hostile to both liberal democracy and, ultimately, to the Catholic Church itself. Because American democracy is traditionally the standard by which other democratic experiments tend to be measured, any assault on American democracy is particularly ominous. The political debates are quickly transformed into the outward signs of a subtle theological debate over the word of God and who has authority to speak it.

Novak understands that capitalism and the teaching Magisterium have never been intellectual allies. But he also knows that socialism and Catholic Church doctrine have never been entirely compatible either. Many of the nineteenth-century secular battles against the Church took the form of socialist arguments. Nevertheless, it remains true that more Catholic writers who have sought to reconcile modern democracy with Church teaching have been more inclined to argue for democratic socialism than for democratic capitalism. Although the Church has never officially adopted either position, the dominant ethos of Catholic social teaching has been more comfortable with socialist than with capitalist economic assumptions.

The overriding problem Novak confronts in defending democratic capitalism in the United States is to argue convincingly that democracy and capitalism cannot be separated in practice, that democratic socialism, not democratic capitalism, is a contradiction in terms. Until this primary point is established, the other elements of arguments over social teaching cannot be adequately addressed. Most of the bishops seem to be genuinely if vaguely convinced that the advancement of democracy in politics requires the abolition of capitalist economics. If it can be shown that the abolition of capitalism also imperils democracy, the whole nature of the debate changes dramatically. This particular element in American Catholic thought is new, and how Novak has dealt with it has opened a new chapter in American Catholic political philosophy.

In one sense Novak's task is easier than the problems Murray confronted. Since Vatican II the Catholic Church has for the first time accepted the proposition that Protestants are indeed part of the community of Christians in communion with Christ. This makes it easier for Novak than for Murray to defend religious pluralism in American democracy because pluralism is one of the dominant traits of American economic life and political democracy.[7] But Novak faces difficulties Murray never dreamed of. The American political landscape of the post-Vietnam, post-Watergate era is unlike that of pre–Vatican II America. A Catholic interpretation of the American regime, even one defending traditional Church orthodoxy in the process, cannot simply duplicate Murray's arguments. The political heritage of Thomism in such writers as Jacques Maritain, Etienne Gilson, Yves Simon and Murray seems to have been forgotten or ignored by most bishops and never learned by the younger clergy. It is as if centuries of intellectual labor have disappeared down some odd memory hole. Whereas Murray could assume that the American bishops were generally supportive of his Thomistic approach to social analysis, Novak must operate on the assumption that they are hostile. And finally, if Novak is correct in his analysis of democratic capitalism, he is left with the uncomfortable conclusion that the bishops and their academic allies have abandoned traditional Catholic social teaching—a possibility that it is doubtful Murray ever entertained for a moment.

The Nature of the American Polity

Novak's defense of democratic capitalism must contend with a long trail of powerful critics, including the usual Marxists, socialists and assorted secular humanists as well as powerful elements within the Catholic Church itself. Capitalism is an idea that has not fared well with intellectuals in general, and Novak is well aware of this problem.[8] He has spent a considerable amount of time defending democratic capitalism by tracing the roots of a Christian defense of private property and market-based economics.[9] In this he has reintroduced to many American Catholics the ideas of an impressive collection of modern Catholic theologian-economists, such as Wilhelm von Ketteler and Heinrich Pesch, who grapple with the problems of capitalist economics and the modern liberal state. He has further reopened the debates over capitalism versus socialism with some of the most widely read Catholic authors of the past.[10] Withal he is convinced that democratic capitalism is defensible within a Thomistic framework.

It is true that Thomism has been, as its adherents have maintained, among the most powerful foes of modern totalitarianism. At one point immediately after World War II, a prominent Jewish philosopher could still argue that a Roman Catholic social science constructed on a foundation of Thomism was the most significant intellectual enemy of modern totalitarianism enhanced by the institutional power of the Catholic Church.[11] But it is even more true that Thomism has also been a sometimes foe of the modern liberal economic order for an even longer time. And in this instance it is well to remember that the

American experiment in republican government is the "new science" of liberal political economy par excellence.

The bishops' analysis of the American economy is set forth in their pastoral letter, *Economic Justice for All.*[12] Their fundamental criticism is that the American economy has failed to equitably distribute society's economic goods and services. The bishops attribute this failure to the excessive materialism inherent in capitalism. A market system of distribution, although neutral on the surface, is actually weighted in favor of the few and the rich. As a system, capitalism stands accused of being amoral at best and with more than a hint that it is probabaly immoral in its attachment to a market economy. The bishops' specific policy proposals need not concern us here. What is significant is that they assume that the present economic structure of American society must be fundamentally and radically altered in the name of Christian justice. Distribution of wealth, not its production, is their central moral concern. Furthermore, they seem implicitly aware that this amounts to a radical refounding of the American regime. They are less aware that this concurrently amounts to a philosophical critique of the original founding. In practice at least, the political economy of the new science of American politics is incompatible with the present teaching of the American bishops.

Novak's response to the bishops and his defense of the American regime are to be found in two primary works, *The Spirit of Democratic Capitalism* and *Freedom With Justice: Catholic Social Thought and Liberal Institutions.* In these and countless other writings, Novak provides a moral basis for a redefined democratic capitalism. According to that definition, democratic capitalism consists of three systems that cannot be separated in practice, although each may be dealt with separately as analytic abstractions. The bishops have noticed only the first part and by treating it as if it were the whole have missed the essential nature of democratic capitalism. First, as the bishops correctly note, democratic capitalism is dominated by a market economy in the distribution of goods and services. Second, democratic capitalism is governed by a political system respectful of the rights of the individual to life, liberty and the pursuit of happiness. Third, democratic capitalism is a system of cultural institutions motivated by ideals of liberty and justice for all. These last two components foster a moral ethos for democratic capitalism that is a necessary component of the American creed once defended by Murray, but with the important addition of the market economy.

What makes Novak's definition so important is that he gives a moral basis to capitalism decidedly lacking when it is defined by its critics. Novak's definition is not characterized by "greed," for example. But neither is "justice" one of its definable features. Political and market freedoms are means to ends, not ends themselves. Whether democratic capitalism is just will depend finally on input from the cultural sphere— in particular, government and church. Justice must be the end of every civil society that can be morally defended in terms of Catholic (or most other) political philosophy. When Novak asks, "Where does the justice of the regime come from?" the answer seems to be, "From the cultural institutions." If these cultural institutions do not supply justice, the purely market aspects of democratic capitalism can indeed become destructive of the common good. The ethics of the production of wealth require the same attention as does the distribution of wealth.

For a Thomist such as Novak one of the fundamental flaws of the bishops' critique of political economy is that it fails to make the essential distinction between divine justice and human justice. For St. Thomas, as for most natural law theorists, the typology of laws and the justice proper to each are of crucial importance. To criticize human economic and political behavior from the standpoint of an absolute morality, to criticize the City of Man because it is not the City of God, is not only utopian but dangerous as well. It radically breaks with the traditions of Catholic sociopolitical thought developed so carefully during the past century or so. Every society subject to such a test will fail, yet every successful society must have citizens who believe that they live in a society that promotes the common good. And every science of politics that aims at making moral distinctions must also be able to distinguish between vastly different systems and not treat all states as if they are morally equivalent. Catholic political philosophy cannot fall into the Hobbesian trap of collapsing every earthly city into a single type motivated by the pursuit of power.

The dangerous irony of the bishops' position is twofold. First, by subjecting the American state to such an impossible standard, they implicitly construct a Manichaean political typology that makes it impossible to differentiate between relatively just states and obvious tyrannies; all imperfect states, that is all actual states, tend to be unwittingly viewed in Hobbesian terms. The City of God may or may not embody political pluralism, but the City of Man certainly does. Second, when applied to generally free and just regimes, the bishops' criticisms undermine legitimacy when judged by such unrealistic standards. In this way, the good ironically becomes the enemy of the perfect. This utopian fallacy, Novak believes, follows from the all-too-common Christian notion that the City of God can be created here and now as an act of political will. The classic diagnosis of this political psychology, Novak points out, was "gnosticism," and he argues that there is an element of gnosticism in a large part of the critique of democratic capitalism.

The political strength of democratic capitalism is that it resists this gnostic temptation. It is a practical system as opposed to a purely theoretical one, but it is a practice that implies a powerful spiritual element. On this point Novak thinks that Max Weber was on the right track to look for the secret success of capitalism not in the economic modes of production, as did Marx, but in a new psychology regarding man's relationship to the surrounding world. The chief problem of economics was no longer distribution alone but also production. Absent production there would be nothing to distribute, and production depends on individual initiative, creativity, just laws, hard work, the protection of the fruits of labor in the form of private property, and above all, freedom to experiment with new ways of doing things. This last point tied market economics to a particular political system. It was also that aspect of capitalism least understood by its European critics and those Catholic intellectuals whose views have been shaped by romantic literary traditions. Catholic students of liberal economics, even the best of them, have tended to treat capitalism "as if it were a set of philosophic doctrines" rather than a practical system.[13] Capitalism is a system best measured by its practical successes.

Among the American Founders, especially James Madison, the political implications of a liberal economic order were well understood but, in Novak's opinion, inadequately articulated in the language of moral discourse. The principles were expounded in the language of "interests"—a word most moral philosophers have almost always found distasteful. But the proponents of this new science that combined a market economy with democracy were a "new breed: philosophers of practice."[14] Their accomplishments cannot be judged on the basis of a linguistic analysis divorced from an empirical study of the political communities they founded. Nor can their political communities be adequately studied through the intellectually flabby social science that Novak believes formed the basis of the bishops' study. It is here that a Thomistic political philosophy can make a contribution by filling in where the American founders of the new science were weakest—in articulating the justice of economic production and not merely of distribution.

Novak concedes that certain "bastard" forms of capitalism do seem to exist without democracy. But the very nature and logic of capitalism tend its political development toward democratic institutions. Some outside force, political or cultural, would have to intervene to thwart the pressures capitalism exerts in support of pluralistic democracy. Economic liberties without these political liberties are inherently unstable because economic growth will create an expanding class of citizens who naturally seek a voice in public as well as private life. If that voice is not heard, the resultant conflict between the economic and political spheres may destroy both; it will certainly destroy the economic order. Conversely, political liberty without an economic liberty that includes, for example, protection of private property, is not likely to protect the fruits of men's labor and basic human dignity. At some point in the evolution of these bastard systems, either free economic life or free political life will have to give way because both of these spheres of human activity complement and ultimately support each other. In Novak's view, the purpose of government in the Christian sense is betrayed if either political freedom or economic freedom is sacrificed on the altar of powerful political ideologies from either the political Left or the Right. The moral teaching from our common religious culture is the salt in this volatile mixture. If the salt is absent, any form of political economy can be corrupted.

The Problem of Community
in the Modern Liberal State

Nevertheless, after all is said in defense of the new science of the liberal state, there is a problem with democratic capitalism that will not go away despite Novak's arguments of its superiority to alternate forms. Not all of the opposition to democratic capitalism can be explained away as utopian or gnostic in origin. A perennial problem, especially for Catholic writers of all shades of political opinion, is the formation and maintenance of communities. For many of the bishops it may rank as *the* problem, a point of which Novak is well aware. Here a new question is posed: What type of political economy is most supportive of good communities? Even the most generous defenders of American freedom have sometimes questioned what American individualism and its market economy have done to the spirit of community in the polity as a whole.[15] Certainly this is one of the underlying themes of the bishop's pastoral letter on the economy, and it is a serious point that needs to be addressed.

On the question of community, Novak begins with a point made by Jacques Maritain, perhaps the most influential Catholic Thomist of the twentieth century, that the idea of community lies at the heart of Catholic sociopolitical teaching. Novak then develops some important twists of his own based on his understanding of market economic principles. Maritain made a sharper distinction between "community" and "political economy" than does Novak. Maritain described community as "a work of nature and more nearly related to the biological," whereas politics and economics are "the work of reason, and more nearly related to the intellectual and spiritual properties of man."[16] For Novak "community" is also a work of reason as well as biology, and economic interests can be a legitimate and moral basis of community. The economic principles of a democratic community may ultimately prove to be Novak's most lasting contribution to Catholic social thought. In particular, his linkage of the principles of market economics to a Thomistic political philosophy sets Novak apart from his most influential Thomistic predecessor.

The question of community in the American regime is scarcely a new one. It is a problem Alexis de Tocqueville noted, with some discomfort, early in the life of the republic. And it is a question raised often enough with respect to capitalism that we are entitled to wonder about the truth of the charge. For Novak the challenge arises because the American Founders were better statesmen than philosophers; they created a better system than they defended. So a central problem of his defense of democratic capitalism emerges as an effort to discover how this new science has actually built communities. In one sense it may be said that much of the statistical data assembled in *The Spirit of Democratic Capitalism* and *Freedom With Justice* aims at rescuing the practice of community-building in the American polity from friends and foes alike.

By his own account, Novak's transition from liberalism in the 1960s to neoconservatism in the 1970s hinged in part on this conception of community. Neither his personal nor his immigrant family experiences of community under American democratic capitalism matched the traditional criticisms of capitalism as destructive of those communities, much less the more radical New Left criticisms. His grandparents had fled one of the "organic" communities in Slovakia at the turn of the century—precisely the sort of community the critics of capitalism often find so appealing. They knew full well, and passed on as a legacy to their descendants, the knowledge that labor could be every bit as "alienated" in such a community as Marxists imagined in a capitalist system. These traditional peasant communities were what millions of Catholics had once fled. Indeed, the reality was that labor was less alienated under democratic capitalism than in these traditional communities so much praised by political romantics. The socialist dream of an organic community was just that, a "dream." But it was a romantic dream with hidden political consequences of which the bishops collectively seem unaware.

This concept of an organic community, Novak believes, if put into political practice, must result in a political tyranny, whether the particular ideology behind it is from the Left or the Right. Market economics provides the necessary corrective for this speculative utopia. Free markets have the further effect of helping to spawn new forms of community. Indeed, Novak goes so far as to argue that the modern business corporation as well as labor unions are new forms of community in the liberal state and serve the common good by the promotion of distributive justice.[17] These new communities must be empirically understood and not simply condemned because they have no precise counterpart in older political philosophy. As a simple fact, he observes, not all people have the same values or desire the same things, as is typically assumed in theories of the organic state. And this diversity of itself is neither immoral nor irrational; it is merely a reflection of the natural differences among men. The natural diversity of men is one of the protected ends of the new science of politics in America.

Novak emphasizes the elementary logic of free government, which, for example, was the logic of Madison in *The Federalist,* No. 10. If political order is directed by central authority, it cannot be free. If it is free, it cannot be directed. Yet a free polity that also embodies free markets can and, because men are naturally social, does oblige all of its members to be other-regarding, even in pursuit of their own interests. Such a system gives rise to a dynamic model of cooperative, orderly and peaceful behavior. It also produces conflict and occasional chaos. If not held together by a community spirit, such as patriotism, and a rule of law, such as the Constitution, it may indeed come to reflect the worst fears of its critics.

What happens as a consequence of this diversity is that free men then proceed to form new types of communities under the umbrella of free government. These communities are different than the historical experience of communities under previous forms of nondemocratic government. To paraphrase Madison, as long as men's opinions are fallible and they are free to exercise those opinions, an economic diversity reflected in the marketplace will be a natural result.[18] No imposition of rationality in the name of "substantive rationality" or "organic community" can escape a tendency toward coercion and the destruction of freedom.

The genius of the American political economy is its ability to promote the common good at the national level while it protects the integrity of the individual person. Economically this protection of the individual takes the form of protection of property rights. The primary purpose of protecting private property "is not so much to empower the person—God has done that—as to limit the powers of the state."[19] Private property is essential in the creation of the mediating social structures that protect the individual from the omnipresent state.[20] Man is, after all, a social animal and does not need any Hobbesian coercion to form artificial communities. Given political freedom, men will naturally form communities. But they will not be identical to the organic communities described in the traditional moral philosophy with which many Catholics have often identified.

But communities also require a core of common convictions, and if the diverse communities spawned by the American political-economic system are to endure, there must be some institutions(s) capable of transmitting those convictions. The American Constitution does not provide for such institutions in a formal sense—pluralism seems to preclude such an arrangement—but it does provide for their political protection. Properly understood, this is the role of Church social teaching. Americans are, as Novak puts it, "an astonishingly social people." Studies that emphasize only competitiveness or rugged individualism miss one of the most remarkable qualities of the American system by the exaggeration of this single aspect. By overlooking the degree of voluntary cooperation under market economies, many of the critics of democratic capitalism risk destroying the very principles and virtues of community they think they are advocating. The coercive implications of the bishops' approach to distributive economic justice threaten the foundations of free, democratic communities as surely as any foreign enemy does. The socialist vision of community, Novak admits, has its virtue in keeping alive the importance of authentic community life. But that vision must be translated into practice if it is to have something other than a theoretical life. It is in this arena that democratic capitalism wins over socialism as a matter of historical reality, if not abstract theory divorced from any empirical reference points.[21]

Democratic Capitalism and the American Bishops: What Is Really at Issue?

The implications of Novak's defense of democratic capitalism and the bishops' critique of it suggest that more is involved than a mere in-house quarrel among Catholics. Novak may be drawing the modern battle lines between Church and state in America over the perennial conflict between the City of God and the City of Man. If this is indeed the case, it is a conflict that will affect more than just Catholics and more than just Americans. To date, this conflict only implicitly raises questions about democratic citizenship in American Catholic thought. It is far from clear that all of the bishops and American clergy are themselves aware that this is what is involved, although many certainly are fully cognizant of where this may be leading—to a clash between the good Catholic and the good citizen. But when these debates are transposed onto the arena of foreign affairs, and especially onto any analysis of Third World countries, the implications quickly become explicit. How far can the American Catholic citizen go in defending the principles of the present American political economy, especially as that political economy confronts the Third World?

If Novak's arguments in defense of democratic capitalism are correct, it follows that the American political experience has universal significance. It represents a quantum improvement over alternate forms of political economies, such as democratic socialism, as well as over the older science of politics derived from Plato and Aristotle. Not only is the American polity defensible of itself in moral terms; it provides an object lesson for other nations struggling to get out of economic poverty and political tyranny. It is Novak's answer to both the political and economic dilemmas of the Third World.

But if the American bishops are correct in their criticism of American political economy—that it is built in principle on systemic greed, calculated inequities and a serious misallocation of wealth—there is little to recommend it for export. Wealth is, the bishops note, a source of political power in any system, and the maldistribution of wealth cannot produce democratic equality. They do not say that political freedom in America is an illusion, but they do hint that it masks a political oligarchy of sorts that controls public policy. And a political economy that can not be morally defended at home is scarcely one that can be imagined to have universal significance, except perhaps as a bad example. Indeed, the export of such a system would appear to be a kind of evil that the Church ought to condemn and help Third World countries, especially Catholic Latin America, resist. It therefore follows that the export of American capitalism is often interpreted as evidence of a malevolent or at best amoral system that is perhaps the ultimate cause of mass poverty in the Third World. According to this view, American economic imperialism prevents economic development among the less-developed countries.

Both Novak and the bishops have, quite naturally, looked to Rome and cited various papal encyclicals, documents from Vatican II and other Catholic sources in support of their own views. The response from Rome so far has not been entirely supportive of either position. One reason is that the question of exporting democratic capitalism to the Third World involves more than just a problem of politics or economics entwined with one another. It also includes a theological debate. It involves the Catholic Church in the emotionally charged issue of liberation theology, especially in Latin America. These problems are complicated because not everyone in the Catholic Church who has been critical of democratic capitalism is a supporter of liberation theology.[22]

The intellectual battle lines often change. Pope John Paul II is a case in point. He has been highly critical of liberation theology as a theological concept *and* has simultaneously expressed serious reservations about capitalism in principle. His *Laborem Exercens* specifically called for "the priority of labor over capital."[23] Although the Pope's notion that the good of labor and the ends of capital development somehow represent opposing economic principles may be challenged, there can be no doubt that it is a distinction he has drawn. If the Holy Father is wrong, Catholics of all shades of opinion would normally find it difficult to directly challenge him.

Novak is painfully aware of the Pope's reservations about capitalism. But Novak is also inclined to attribute the Pope's opposition to democratic capitalism not so much to his moral and theological teaching as to certain weaknesses inherent in how the Church as a whole has come to understand, or more accurately to misunderstand, the modern liberal state. This misunderstanding can be corrected, however, if an inquiry into the modern democratic state's political economy is based on a combination of moral principles *and* empirical data. Moral principles without empirical and historical reference points can too easily degenerate into ideology of the Left or Right, and data without moral wisdom are worthless. Novak is encouraged that the Pope's opposition to the theological underpinnings of liberation theology is the opening wedge of what he clearly hopes will be a later acceptance by the Pope of the principles of democratic capitalism.[24]

In Novak's opinion, the Catholic Church has never fully grasped conceptually either the inner dynamic of the capitalist moral spirit or how that dynamic has contributed toward making democracy a practical form of government. The problem of how the Catholic Church as a whole treats economic development in the Third World is a microcosm of the inadequacies of Catholic teaching about political economy in the modern world. It is not a theological problem entirely, although it can have consequences expressed as a theological problem, so much as it is a conceptual problem of practical political economics. As such, democratic capitalism is not in opposition to the City of God, but it does follow a certain logic of its own that is part of the moral order of the City of Man. It must be judged in the light of God's revealed word, but it is a practical system that ought not to be confused with the City of God itself.

This is where a traditional Catholic social teaching built around an unreflective Thomism and the New Left social science of the American bishops unexpectedly come together. A point both the American bishops and the Pope seem to share is the notion that the primary problem of poverty in the world is one of distribution: that the world is already

wealthy enough to solve any problems of economic scarcity and that
to the extent that such problems manifestly exist, the reason must be
a lack of will; that the market economies of the advanced nations of
the world are too selfish or too economically laissez faire to care about
the fate of the poor.

Novak disputes this reasoning. The amount of wealth in the world
is not sufficient to the task at hand. Fortunately, however, this is not
as serious a problem as it might otherwise be because the world's
wealth is not finite. Novak asserts, with impressive evidence in support
of his argument:

> The fundamental moral task is to produce more wealth. The secrets of
> how this may be done are well known. Every nation that follows the
> democratic-capitalist way enters, even within a generation, into the ranks
> of the . . . "developed" nations of the world. The surest recipe for
> remaining in poverty is to maintain a socialist economy. The empirical
> record for the last thirty years may be consulted for corroboration.[25]

Poverty in Third World countries is not due to their having been
plundered by the forces of market capitalism, Novak argues, but by
weaknesses in their own cultural-political institutions. Habits of thrift,
enterprise, initiative and political freedom have not been the most
distinguishing characteristics of Third World cultures. Yet these features
constitute the necessary preconditions for any political development.
These virtues make democracy possible and help to create the spirit
of democratic capitalism. Such virtues, Novak believes, provide the
only way out of poverty and dependency.

What the social teaching of the Church must do if it is serious about
Third World poverty is teach the moral virtues that support democratic
capitalism and stop blaming outside forces. Liberation theology is not
a solution for economic development in Latin America but rather a
false utopia that exacerbates the problem.[26] Liberation theology is
utopian in that it identifies evil as a product of "systems" rather than
as an individual disposition toward God. It supposes that the City of
God can be built on earth by a truer, more "authentic" Christianity.
As a form of utopianism it is precisely the expression of gnosticism
that Christianity in general and Catholic doctrine in particular warn
against. "The pursuit of utopia is the primal madness of the race,"
Novak writes. "It is, if one may humbly say so, the original sin. The
pursuit of 'if only,' the pursuit of a better world through chemistry,
the pursuit of the kingdom of God upon the earth . . . who brings
God into history kills God."[27]

The production of wealth is, as Novak says repeatedly, *the* moral imperative of our time. The reason we find poverty morally unacceptable is because we have for the first time in human history a conception that it is not the inevitable fate of most men. And the origin of this conception is not Christianity per se, but Adam Smith. The problem with Catholic social teaching on economics is that it was formulated at a time when the economic pie was thought to be fixed and any increase in wealth by one class or group could only be affected at the expense of some other class or group. In political terms this implied either civil war within the state or wars between states over the acquisition of wealth. To prevent just this sort of conflict, the overriding moral issue of Catholic political philosophy easily and understandably focused on the distribution of fixed wealth. The social teaching of the Catholic Church refined the morality of distribution around a Thomistic theology that was integral to how the Church taught citizenship in the City of Man. The discovery that wealth was not fixed proved to be not only an economic revolution but a political one as well.

The Catholic conception of citizenship in the modern liberal state, essentially a democratic polity, requires that the Church come to terms with the morality of how and why wealth is produced. Thanks in large part to Murray, the Church has already come to terms with democracy and religious pluralism. But in Novak's opinion, the Church has not yet fully come to terms with all of the implications of a democratic political economy that aims at freedom and justice simultaneously. This means, among other things, the acceptance of a greater degree of pluralism than traditional Church social teaching before Murray and Vatican II generally admitted. Too much Church social teaching, even on the part of the most radicalized bishops, is still tied to the notion of the organic state—the idea that right reason will lead everyone to the same moral and political conclusions, not only as a matter of abstract theory but of political practice as well. This teaching is a vision of the state in which the tensions between the City of God and the City of Man are somehow dissolved. In such a state the tensions between the good Christian and the good citizen would necessarily cease to have any meaning.

To be sure, there are unresolved problems with Novak's argument. How traditional Thomism meshes with Adam Smith may be more problematic than Novak hints at in his works on the subject so far. Furthermore, even if one accepts the notion that modern capitalism and the modern liberal, democratic state are linked by an umbilical cord of mutual support, it does not necessarily follow that liberal democracy is the best polity. Democracy itself needs more of a defense than Novak has undertaken, despite his awareness of the problematic character of all forms of government. But this would miss the point of his argument altogether. More is involved here than economics or even economics combined with politics. His ultimate concern is how to be a good Christian, and this means rescuing Catholic social teaching from those who would trivialize its message.

Paradoxical as it seems to many of Novak's critics, the distinction between the City of God and the City of Man is essential to the moral integrity of each or at least to our proper understanding of the moral judgments appropriate to each. The notion that one can only be a good Christian if one works to overthrow "sinful social structures" means as a matter of practice that one can only be a good Christian in opposition to all historical reality because all historical states are under the judgment of the City of God. When combined with the notion that social structures can somehow be sinful apart from the men who are the authors of these structures, "Christianity becomes a social theory," not a doctrine of salvation. "Where religious life atrophies, political passions often become surrogates for religious passion. Worldly visions invested with religious passion become ersatz religion."[28]

In any analysis of Novak's work it is important to recall two essential points. First, he does not maintain that either democracy or capitalism represents the City of God. "Both are matters of the temporal order, which changes, and not of the transcendent order in which we place our faith."[29] Second, he does not identify democratic capitalism simply with markets; markets have existed in one form or another almost everywhere since the dawn of recorded history and no doubt before such records. Latin America has markets, but no Latin American state can be considered a capitalist state by any reasonable definition of the term. Novak's democratic capitalism is marked first and foremost by its "spirit," and that spirit is understood by him to be a reflection of the moral qualities in man as God created him. The confounding of eternal faith with a political utopianism is the great theological heresy of our time. The virtue of democratic capitalism is that it is not utopian, it does not promise political salvation, but it does promise greater wealth. What we do with that wealth is a separate moral question. For Novak the moral problem is, as it has always been, and with all of the ambiguities implicit in its original formulation, a problem of rendering unto Caesar the things that are Caesar's and rendering unto God the things that are God's.

Notes

1. George A. Kelley, *The Battle for the American Church* (Garden City, N.Y.: Doubleday, 1979).

2. Michael Novak, *Moral Clarity in the Nuclear Age* (New York: Thomas Nelson, 1983).

3. For classical statements of this problem in Catholic thought, see Heinrich A. Rommen, *The State in Catholic Thought: A Treatise in Political Philosophy* (New York: B. Herder Book Co., 1945); and Jacques Maritain, *Man and the State* (Chicago: University of Chicago Press, 1951).

4. John Courtney Murray, S.J., *We Hold These Truths: Catholic Reflections on the American Proposition* (New York: Sheed and Ward, 1960), p. ix.

5. On this point see the excellent piece by Paul E. Sigmund, "The Catholic Tradition and Modern Democracy," *The Review of Politics* 49, no. 4 (Fall 1987).

6. The most uncompromising and intellectually rigorous statement of this position can be found in Joseph Cardinal Ratzinger with Vittorio Messori, *The Ratzinger Report* (San Francisco: Ignatius Press, 1985), esp. Chap. 3.

7. See William Weston, "Michael Novak's Pluralist Religion," *This World* (Fall 1987), pp. 14–26. Weston is quite critical of Novak on this score for having abandoned what he regards as the more consistent arguments of Murray. It is a thoughtful article. But also see the combative reply by Novak in the same issue, "Three Porcupines of Pluralism," pp. 27–51.

8. See Michael Novak, ed., *Capitalism and Socialism: A Theological Inquiry* (Washington, D.C.: American Enterprise Institute, 1979).

9. See, in particular, Novak's introduction to Alejandro A. Chafuen, *Christians for Freedom: Late-Scholastic Economics* (San Francisco: Ignatius Press, 1986).

10. See Novak's introductions to reissues of G. K. Chesterton, *The Collected Works of G. K. Chesterton,* vol. 5 (San Francisco: Ignatius Press, 1987), and Amintore Fanfani, *Catholicism, Protestantism and Capitalism* (Notre Dame, Ind.: University of Notre Dame Press, 1984).

11. Leo Strauss, *Natural Right in History* (Chicago: University of Chicago Press, 1953), p. 2.

12. The teaching is set forth in *Economic Justice for All: Pastoral Letter on Catholic Social Teaching and the U.S. Economy* (Washington, D.C.: U.S. Catholic Conference, 1986). For a good background review of the post–Vatican II social teaching of the American bishops, see J. Brian Benstad, *The Pursuit of a Just Social Order: Policy Statements of the U.S. Catholic Bishops* (Washington, D.C.: Ethics and Public Policy Center, 1982).

13. Michael Novak, *Freedom with Justice: Catholic Social Thought and Liberal Institutions* (New York: Harper & Row, 1984), p. 67.

14. Michael Novak, *The Spirit of Democratic Capitalism* (New York: Simon and Schuster, 1982), p. 19.

15. Yves R. Simon, *Freedom and Community,* Charles P. O'Donnell (New York: Fordham University Press, 1968). For Novak the various works by Jacques Maritain on this subject are of pivotal importance.

16. Jacques Maritain, *Man and the State* (Chicago: University of Chicago Press, 1951), p. 2.

17. Michael Novak, *Toward a Theology of the Corporation* (Washington, D.C.: American Enterprise Institute, 1981), p. 23.

18. Novak, *Freedom with Justice,* pp. 116–117.

19. Michael Novak, "Democracy and Human Rights," in Peter L. Berger and Michael Novak, *Speaking to the Third World: Essays on Democracy and Development* (Washington, D.C.: American Enterprise Institute, 1985), p. 35.

20. For a more complete discussion of the role of mediating structures and community building, see Michael Novak, ed., *Democracy and Mediating Structures: A Theological Inquiry* (Washington, D.C.: American Enterprise Institute, 1980).

21. Michael Novak, ed., *Capitalism and Socialism: A Theological Inquiry* (Washington, D.C.: American Enterprise Institute, 1979), pp. 109–123.

22. For example, see the diverse collection of articles on this point assembled by James V. Schall, S.J., ed., *Liberation Theology in Latin America* (San Francisco: Ignatius Press, 1982).

23. "Laborem Exercens," in Michael Walsh and Brian Davies, eds., *Proclaiming Justice and Peace: Documents from John XXIII to John Paul II* (Mystic, Conn.: Twenty-third Publications, 1984), p. 287. Aside from the Pope's own pronouncements, one of the best discussions of Pope John Paul II's thought is James V. Schall, S.J., *The Church, the State and Society in the Thought of John Paul II* (Chicago: Franciscan Herald Press, 1982).

24. See Michael Novak, "Liberation Theology and the Pope," in Quentin L. Quade, ed., *The Pope and Revolution: John Paul II Confronts Liberation Theology* (Washington, D.C.: Ethics and Public Policy Center, 1982).

25. Michael Novak, "The Politics of John Paul II," *Commentary* 68, no. 6 (December 1979): 60.

26. Michael Novak, *Will It Liberate? Questions About Liberation Theology* (New York: Paulist Press, 1986). Novak's views on liberation theology are specifically taken to task in Phillip Berryman, *Liberation Theology: The Essential Facts About the Revolutionary Movement in Latin America and Beyond* (New York: Pantheon Books, 1987), esp. pp. 179–200.

27. Michael Novak, *A Book of Elements: Reflections on Middle-Class Days* (New York: Herder and Herder, 1972), pp. 26–27.

28. Michael Novak, *Confession of a Catholic* (New York: Harper & Row, 1983), p. 188.

29. Ibid., p. 204.

PART FOUR

Foreign Affairs

To this point, we have seen that American conservative opinion leaders differ fundamentally in their views on many domestic, economic and social issues. The area of greatest convergence in conservative opinion today may be foreign affairs. Of course there are important differences among these thinkers over foreign trade, investment and international law. But they come together in their support of anti-Communist foreign poilcies. While many traditionalist conservatives and neoconservatives argue about big government and the welfare state, they agree that U.S. foreign policies must emphasize anticommunism.

Earlier chapters on George F. Will, William F. Buckley, Jr., Irving Kristol, Norman Podhoretz and Jeane Kirkpatrick raised the nature of the foreign policy debate in conservative circles. The following chapters analyze and assess the ideas of two more conservative thinkers who are influential in the foreign policy realm: Edward Luttwak and Richard Pipes.

Robert A. Strong's chapter on Edward Luttwak illuminates the paradox of a conservative strategic thinker who has been one of the most serious critics of the foreign and defense policies of conservative administrations. As Strong demonstrates, Luttwak has thought seriously about such complicated issues as arms control and détente and has developed policy views more sophisticated than the views of many prominent conservative foreign policy advisers.

John Eastby's chapter on Richard Pipes makes clear the conflict in the conservative movement between foreign policy conservatives and corporate interests seeking free trade with international allies and adversaries alike. Eastby points out that according to Pipes, improved relations between the West and the Soviet Union are unlikely. Eastby examines critically Pipe's analysis of the nature of the Soviet threat.

12

Edward Luttwak
and Strategy
in the 1980s

Robert A. Strong

Paradox, Edward Luttwak argues, is at the heart of all strategic thinking.[1] What appears to be a logical and efficient military maneuver or a sensible weapon design is often disastrously misguided if it is easily anticipated or countered by a clever opponent. Thus, successful armies do not travel well-paved roads in broad daylight on the shortest path to the enemy border; they move through difficult terrain, often at night, so that they can attack at an unexpected time and from an unexpected direction. Standardized and inexpensive vehicles make sense for a postal service that encounters very little armed resistance from the recipients of mail; but fighting forces need a variety of different and expensive transportation and weapon delivery systems that will greatly complicate the problems for an enemy on the field of battle. What makes sense in the world of domestic policy in which efficiency properly reigns can be dangerously inappropriate for the world of international conflict in which paradox is always present.

Paradox can also be found in Luttwak's own political commentaries on the central strategic issues of the 1980s. An ardent supporter of many of the foreign and defense policies adopted during the Reagan presidency, Edward Luttwak also ranks among the administration's most serious and thoughtful critics. Reviewing his writings on strategic issues in the last decade opens a world of paradoxes and provides a provocative analysis of some of the major military and foreign policy debates of the Reagan era.

The Critique of Détente and Arms Control

The foreign policy priorities of the Reagan Administration were set, in large part, by opposition to détente and arms control. Whether détente was adopted by Republican or Democratic presidents, Ronald Reagan was dependably against it. His reasons were frequently repeated in the speeches he gave during his 1976 and 1980 presidential campaigns. Détente had led the United States to place its trust in Soviet leaders who were, in fact, the untrustworthy rulers of what would later be called an "evil empire." The Soviets used détente to distract Western attention from their growing military power and the expansion of their influence in Angola, the horn of Africa, Southeast Asia and, most significantly at the end of the 1970s, Afghanistan. They negotiated arms control agreements that gave preferences to their large and growing strategic forces and then failed to keep the agreements they signed. The resulting shift in the superpower strategic balance and the emerging vulnerabilty of American land-based missile systems meant that the time was rapidly approaching when the United States could be threatened by a disarming Soviet preemptive nuclear attack. Even if no such attack ever took place, the possibility that it could occur would seriously weaken the ability of the United States to function in an international crisis or in the day-to-day competition with the Soviet Union for power in the world at large.

The most serious problem with détente was that it blinded the American people to what was going on around them. Lulled into complacency by the apparent virtues of improved relations with the East, Americans neglected their military strength and lost the resolve to use the force that remained at their disposal. Edward Luttwak supported much in this line of argument but did so with far more sophistication than did Ronald Reagan or his principal foreign policy advisers. Where the conservative politicians of the late 1970s and early 1980s found obvious faults with détente and arms control, Luttwak saw complicated paradoxes.

Edward Luttwak was an opponent of arms control long before that became a fashionable position. One of his early public policy studies was a review of the strategic balance at the time of the Strategic Arms Limitation Talks (SALT I) that ended with words of warning about superpower arms agreements.[2] Two years later his evaluation of the strategic nuclear balance included a critique of mutual assured destruction, which was supposed to be the foundation of the first SALT treaties.[3] In 1972, the United States was well ahead of the Soviet Union by any comprehensive measure of strategic power, and SALT I, which involved a temporary freeze on the number of strategic launchers each side could have, did not weaken the ability of the United States to maintain a theoretical deterrent.

But the first SALT agreement had a problem. The Soviet Union was permitted to maintain larger numbers of missiles than was the United States. Soviet missiles were admittedly inferior to those in the American arsenal, but public perceptions of the military balance never fully grasped this fact. Professional analysts such as Luttwak understood the real strategic relationship, but in the paradoxical world of strategy, reality mattered less than perception. The fact that the American public suspected Soviet superiority under the terms of SALT I (and were led to do so by Senator Henry Jackson and later by presidential candidate Ronald Reagan) would, in Luttwak's view, have significant consequences for the political strength of the North Atlantic Treaty Organization (NATO) alliance and the ability of the Soviet Union to engage in an activist foreign policy in the Third World. SALT I was therefore a mixed bargain—it did no direct harm to the essential military strength of the United States, but it left us vulnerable to public fears of growing Soviet power. SALT II would be much worse. By the time the second SALT agreement was signed, seven years after the first, Luttwak had assumed a leading role among the influential critics of arms control negotiations with the Soviet Union.

His 1978 article in *Commentary,* "Why Arms Control Has Failed,"[4] nevertheless gives some credit to the theory behind arms control negotiations. It should, after all, be possible for two imaginary nations to reach an agreement to save money and reduce the risk of war, particularly the risk of nuclear war. All other things being equal, it would clearly be in the interest of any two countries to take this course of action. The problem is that there are more than two nations in the world and arms control negotiations do not take place between imaginary entities. In the real world, SALT, according to Luttwak, had adverse effects on the NATO alliance because it weakened the credibility of the American nuclear guarantee to Europe. Moreover, the United States and the Soviet Union have distinct histories and negotiating styles that do not make them equal partners in arms negotiations. The Soviet Union, Luttwak argues, is particularly effective in winning concessions from the United States because its negotiators are notoriously cautious and patient. They wait for the United States to put forward negotiating positions and then choose to accept the features in those positions that are to their liking. As a result, the SALT negotiating process becomes the accumulation of mostly American concessions until a time is reached when both sides decide to sign an agreement.

Up to this point Luttwak's criticisms of the SALT process are relatively conventional, based on the same kinds of arguments and evidence put forward by many conservative politicians and the leading members of the Committee on the Present Danger. Luttwak goes further, however, and points out some of the paradoxical outcomes that accompany arms control arrangements. Treaties to restrict the deployment of one type of weapon may merely distort weapons development decisions so that both sides begin to build systems outside the restrictions they have just accepted. Cruise missiles and Backfire bombers are commonly cited as examples of this phenomenon. On a grander scale, this redirection of resources can have much more serious consequences. The entire SALT process may be defective, in Luttwak's view, because the United States has a natural advantage in the kinds of highly technical and capital-intensive weapon systems that SALT attempted to regulate; whereas the Soviet Union has obvious advantages in manpower and continental warfare. Reducing strategic arms may end up giving the Soviets an opportunity to redirect their resources into the categories of military spending in which they can be expected to excel.[5] Arms control agreements, even if they are reasonably fair, and are perceived to be reasonably fair, may produce unintended consequences that make their overall value dubious. In the paradoxical world of strategy, laudable attempts to control arms can end up making the world a less safe place in which to live.

Opposition to détente and arms control constituted the negative side of defense and foreign policy in the early Reagan years; the positive side was military spending. Luttwak was a vocal critic of the low level of defense expenditures in the 1970s, the so-called decade of neglect, and no doubt welcomed the changes in budget priorities that Reagan introduced. But Luttwak's principal concern was never the level of defense spending approved by American political institutions. For Luttwak the quality of defense decisionmaking that accompanied whatever resources were made available to the military establishment was much more important. A label he uses for the 1970s, "America's unstrategical decade,"[6] conveys the nature of the neglect he most regretted. Writing in 1978, Luttwak observed that "if one excludes a few pages in the Annual Report of the Secretary of Defense (in its better years), and a handful of writings by Brodie, Osgood, Kissinger, and a few others which now date back two decades or more, there is no strategy."[7] The test for the Reagan Administration, in Luttwak's view, was not whether it could increase defense spending, but whether it could introduce serious strategic planning where it had previously been absent. To a significant degree, the Reagan Administration failed that test.

The Critique of the Pentagon Buildup

The increased defense spending of the Reagan years bought very little in the way of new strategic armaments, and even less in added military manpower and meaningful conventional strength. In *The Pentagon and the Art of War,* Luttwak gives his account of what went wrong with the resource-rich Department of Defense of the early 1980s. Pointing out that the Reagan Administration did not, in fact, raise spending on strategic weapons much above average postwar levels (expenditures for strategic systems in the final years of the Carter Administration were unusually low, thereby making the Reagan increases a return to normalcy[8]), Luttwak argues that the much criticized Reagan refueling of the arms race did not take place. What did happen was some modest modernization of strategic forces that had been in planning since the Nixon Administration; an appropriate increase in spending on spare parts, munitions, and other supplies that had reached dangerously low levels in the 1970s; a dramatic increase in naval forces; a slight increase in tactical air power; and orders for new equipment for an army that, in Luttwak's opinion, remained undermanned and overstaffed with senior officers and Pentagon officials.[9] The general argument in *The Pentagon and Art of War* is that an overly bureaucratized military establishment, with officers trained as managers rather than as soldiers, failed to learn the lessons of Vietnam, neglected the study of military history, focused attention on the building of weapons rather than the development of strategy, and substituted careerism for genuine leadership. The invasion of Grenada, in Luttwak's view, involved a repetition of all the problems that the United States encountered in Vietnam with the single difference that the scale of operations was small enough to produce a farce instead of a tragedy.[10]

The usual conservative critique of Vietnam is that Washington leaders failed to fully use American military resources and that a resurgence of naive moralism hampered the ability of the nation to take the harsh actions that would have been necessary to bring the war to a successful conclusion. In the aftermath of the war, the American people and their leaders ignored pressing defense requirements and lost the will to make any effective use of force in international relations. The Reagan Administration presumably brought the post-Vietnam era to an end when it restored full funding to the Pentagon and sent the fleet to restore freedom to Grenada. Luttwak takes a different view.

Without excusing American political leaders or public opinion in the Vietnam era, he makes the case that deeper institutional and cultural forces were at play in the American failure in Southeast Asia. The organization of American military power throughout the Vietnam

War was fundamentally flawed. Our forces were top-heavy with officers who served in overstaffed headquarters commands, saw little combat, and knew little about the day-to-day conduct of the war. The three services competed for roles and missions in the region without ever effectively coordinating their activities. A general materialist bias led American military leaders to believe that a guerrilla war could be won by increasing the tonnage of bombs, improving the accuracy of artillery shells, and engaging in a "gross overuse of firepower" that became "the most visible symptom of the inability of the American military institution to formulate a coherent strategy."[11] The war produced endless Pentagon statistics, "combat" command experience for officers seeking promotion, but no lasting strategic lessons. The Caspar Weinberger version of the Vietnam legacy—that the military should carry out only popular operations supported by the Congress and the American people—is for Luttwak a dangerously narrow conclusion that is largely disproved by the inability of American armed forces to accomplish several of the reasonably popular objectives that presented themselves in the late 1970s and early 1980s.

The botched Iranian rescue mission at the end of the Carter presidency and the comically overdone invasion of Grenada in Reagan's first term, along with several ill-fated operations in the Middle East, are offered by Luttwak as case studies of typical Pentagon failures. All of the cases he reviews demonstrate the inefficiencies of interservice rivalries, the interference of distant commanders, and the bureaucratization of military planning. The worst part of these operations is that their weaknesses go largely unnoticed. "The most disheartening aspect of the entire Grenada episode was the ease with which the performance of the armed forces was accepted as satisfactory, even praiseworthy."[12]

For Luttwak, improving American strategy must begin with institutional reform of the military. His specific reform proposals involve efforts to break down service rivalries currently inhibiting the effective command of forces, planning of operations, and presentation of professional military advice to political leaders. He advocates the creation of a new cadre of "national defense officers" who will be released from all service connections and commitments during the final years of their careers and only then given command of genuinely joint military organizations.[13]

Luttwak's version of military reform is perhaps more remarkable for what it leaves out than for what it proposes. In a decade of growing public concern about military contracting and the efficient expenditure of Pentagon dollars, Luttwak was able to write an article entitled "Why We Need More 'Waste, Fraud & Mismanagement' in the Pentagon."[14] His point in the article is that our concerns for waste and corruption provide further evidence of our materialist bias and our natural tendency to apply conventional government thinking to the paradoxical world of international conflict in which efficiency is of little concern. If we are building the wrong weapons, what difference does it make whether we build them cheaply? And if we have the wrong plans for war and the wrong command structure to carry out those plans, what difference does it make that our senior military officers will be able to find well-paying jobs on the other side of the famous revolving door? Luttwak would gladly push most senior American officers through those doors. Wasteful spending is not nearly as serious a problem as is unstrategical thinking.

Luttwak's attacks on the Pentagon in the early 1980s are perhaps more harsh that one would expect from a commentator generally sympathetic to the military and from a consultant who has worked for the Department of Defense. It is perhaps the kind of honest criticism that only a friend might offer. It is also prompted by a fear that our major enemy suffers from fewer drawbacks in the current competition for world power. Paradoxically, Luttwak's evaluation of the Soviet danger is based on his awareness of the USSR's many weaknesses.

The Soviet Union is the last of the great nineteenth-century empires, which by a combination of brute force and ideology has been able to suppress the otherwise irrepressible force of twentieth-century nationalism. The ability of the Soviet Union to continue an imperial policy that no other major power was able to sustain after this century's two world wars is remarkable. This is particularly true in a period when the promises of economic development and well-being central to the Communist ideology are increasingly seen to be false. The long-term economic and nationalist problems facing the Soviet Union are precisely the conditions that make it so dangerous in the 1990s.

According to Luttwak, at the same time that the Soviet Union was challenging the historical trends of our time, it was overcoming the limitations of its own military history and traditions. The classic Russian strategy has been to absorb invasions within vast and inhospitable continental territories and then defeat the exhausted remnants of the invading army that is always overwhelmed by the size of the prize it attempted to take. By a "pattern of defensive-offensive warfare" the Russians and the Soviets "created the greatest empire on earth."[15] But in recent decades the Soviets have stepped away from their traditional military style. They have built a vast offensive military machine and used it in limited and elegant resupply and coup d'état operations in Africa and Afghanistan. They have largely abandoned mass movements of the Left, sometimes supported in the past for ideological sympathy rather than strategic gain, and increasingly cast their lot with terrorist and guerrilla nationalist forces. The Soviets are building new types of weapons and adopting new tactics and strategies at a time when the United States is doing none of these things or doing none of them well. The temporary gains that may become available to the Soviet Union in the near future are made more dangerous when they are combined with the long-term sources of Soviet economic and social weakness. The West may be facing a Soviet Union under the influence of a "fatal conjunction of regime pessimism and military confidence."[16]

All of this was written before Mikhail Gorbachev's rise to power and the Soviet withdrawal from Afghanistan, but Luttwak's long-range view of the Soviet threat may not be fundamentally changed by these events. In his early 1980s analysis of the Soviet situation he predicted that no massive economic reform of Soviet society could ever be implemented without threatening the interests, and perhaps the survival, of a large body of middle-ranking officials.[17] Gorbachev has not yet solved this problem and is regularly reported to be in trouble with various elements of the Communist bureaucratic-political order. Even if he is not overthrown for attempting to push his reforms too far, Gorbachev may himself be drawn to the temptations of imperialism in an era of declining domestic progress and continued military strength.

Luttwak's lament that the United States lacks a coherent grand strategy while the Soviet Union possesses a highly dangerous one is perhaps overdone. In his most recent book, he gives his favorite subject—strategy—its most thorough treatment and describes it as such a complicated and multilayered phenomenon that it may not be possible for any nation or administration to have a coherent strategy.[18] Democracies like the United States may be at some marginal disadvantage in this regard, but the paradoxes of strategic logic must be nearly as hard for imperial Communists to master.

Conclusion

The 1980s have ended with a series of remarkably dramatic and paradoxical shifts in superpower relations. Ronald Reagan came to Washington preaching American weakness after a decade of U.S. failure to respond to a massive Soviet buildup. He had little use for arms control, saw some validity in the possibility of limited nuclear war, and had people in his administration who talked loosely about fighting and winning a nuclear war with the Soviet Union. All of this brought forth a widespread public reaction in the form of a European peace movement, an American nuclear freeze campaign, and a series of criticisms from sectors of society—doctors and Catholic Bishops—who usually play no role in strategic policy.

Reagan stood up to the nuclear protesters and proceeded with the deployment of Cruise and Pershing II missiles in Europe; but he also gave in to these same protesters. After 1983 he repeatedly said that a nuclear war could not be won and should not be fought. In March of that year he gave his famous Star Wars speech and called for the development of new technologies that would protect us from the horrors of nuclear war. To a surprising extent the arguments for a strategic defense initiative were similar to those that fueled the nuclear protest movement. Accidents might happen, miscalculations might occur, and crisis situations might get out of hand. Moreover, strategic defense helped to address the moral critiques of the nuclear age that had given the freeze movement and the bishop's letter much of their popular appeal. Defensive systems would protect the American people without resort to the morally uncomfortable threats of retaliatory annihilation.

By the end of the Reagan Administration détente had been resumed in everything but name. Regular meetings were being scheduled between Soviet and American political leaders with all the fanfare of the Nixon-era summits. Exchange programs to increase cultural understanding between East and West were fully reinstated. Arms control negotiations were back at the top of the agenda in Soviet-U.S. relations; and the first treaty eliminating a whole category of offensive arms was signed by both superpowers amid mixed reactions from our European allies. Exaggerated expectations for the prospects of further arms control and for the capabilities of futuristic strategic defenses even led Reagan in Reykjavik to seriously consider the possibility of a world without any nuclear weapons at all.[19] Paradoxes indeed.

Of all the conservative commentators, Edward Luttwak is perhaps least likely to take the Reagan Administration to task for its apparent inconsistencies and sell out to the arms control community. More than most, Luttwak would have an appreciation for the paradoxical shifts and slides in the nonlinear logic of international politics. More than any, he would see in the future of both the Soviet Union and the United States opportunities for new and grander strategic errors.

Notes

1. Edward Luttwak, *Strategy* (Cambridge, Mass.: Belknap, Harvard University Press, 1987), pp. 3–17.

2. Edward Luttwak, "The Strategic Balance 1972" (New York: Library Press, 1972).

3. Edward Luttwak, "The U.S.-U.S.S.R. Nuclear Weapons Balance," *The Washington Papers,* 2, no. 13 (1974).

4. The article appeared in the January issue of *Commentary* and was reprinted as Chapter 9 in Edward Luttwak, *Strategy and Politics* (New Brunswick, Conn.: Transaction Books, 1980).

5. Luttwak, *Strategy and Politics,* p. 104.

6. Edward Luttwak, *On the Meaning of Victory* (New York: Simon and Schuster, 1986), p. 246.

7. Luttwak, *Strategy and Politics,* p. 92.

8. Edward Luttwak, *The Pentagon and the Art of War* (New York: Simon and Schuster, 1984), pp. 234–236.

9. Ibid., p. 258.

10. Ibid., pp. 23–67.

11. Ibid., p. 38.

12. Ibid., p. 57.

13. Ibid., p. 272.

14. The article originally appeared in the February 1982 edition of *Comentary* and is reprinted in *On the Meaning of Victory,* pp. 85–115. A chapter with a similar title is included in Luttwak, *The Pentagon and the Art of War,* pp. 130–156.

15. Edward Luttwak, *The Grand Strategy of the Soviet Union* (New York: St. Martin's Press, 1983), p. 18.

16. Ibid., p. 116.

17. Ibid., p. 38.

18. Luttwak, *Strategy,* pp. 231–235.

19. This is an idea Luttwak has recently considered himself. See Edward Luttwak, "An Emerging Postnuclear Era?" *The Washington Quarterly* (Winter 1988): 5–15.

13

Richard Pipes: Conservatives and the Russian Empire

John Eastby

A national security community exists in the United States.* This community is a loosely knit and ill-defined group made up of academics, private citizens, corporate leaders with an avocation for foreign affairs, and government officials responsible for making foreign policy. The expertise of these foreign and defense policy analysts makes it possible for them to cross over from one sector to another. While this elite group is relatively small, it is far from homogenous in its views on foreign policy. The range of political opinions taken by members of this association mirrors or, more often, establishes the opinions of the general public. The community is also divided into areas of expertise because it is impossible for one person to master all issues that make up the substance of foreign policy.

Richard Pipes is one of these experts. Pipes is primarily a historian of Russia, whose many books include *The Formation of the Soviet Union, Europe Since 1815, Russia Under the Old Regime, U.S.-Soviet Relations in the Era of Détente, Survival Is Not Enough,* and a two-volume biography of Peter Struve.[1] Pipes was an adviser on Soviet affairs to the National Security Council during the first year of the Reagan Administration. He served in various capacities as a consultant on the Soviet Union to executive agencies and to congressional com-

*The Center for International Studies at the University of Missouri–St. Louis provided research and writing facilities for this chapter. The university is not responsible for the conclusions presented here.

mittees. He was a major figure in the Committee on the Present Danger, a group that warned of the growth of Soviet power and called for the buildup of U.S. defense capabilities.[2]

Pipe's most notable publication is *Russia Under the Old Regime.* In it he argues that Russia's political development established a "proto-totalitarian" regime that made its society ripe for the Soviet-style totalitarianism instituted under Marxism-Leninism. As history, Pipes's thesis has received serious consideration but hardly unanimous support. As policy analysis, Pipes's argument has been accepted by important conservative members of the foreign policy community. Indeed, the notion that Russia's traditional foreign policy objectives have been easily fused to the Marxist goal of world domination has become the dominant opinion among conservatives.[3] Drawing on Pipes's arguments, some conservatives, although not Pipes himself, seem drawn to the idea that U.S.-Soviet relations can be treated as the traditional geopolitical rivalry that inevitably occurs between great powers.

Pipes's theme is revisited in his recent book, *Survival Is Not Enough,* in which he examines world diplomacy from the perspective of both the United States and the Soviet Union. Pipes's intention is "to alter the nature of the discussion on East-West relations and the means of preventing nuclear war by shifting attention from internal American concerns and disagreements to Soviet realities."[4] The book is divided into three parts. The first presents a theoretical-historical discussion of the nature of the Soviet Union. The second details the Soviet economy and the political crisis that became evident in the late Brezhnev years. The third section attempts to outline the elements of a prudent U.S. policy toward the Soviets.

Pipes contends that the policy debate in America is dominated by doves, on the one hand, and by military hawks, on the other. For him, the doves' argument is feasible but undesirable, whereas the hawks' position is desirable but not feasible. Doves, represented by liberal Democrats, peace activists and some in the business community, do not adequately understand the dangers of détente with the Soviet Union. Détente is dangerous because it does not attempt to change the fundamentally aggressive nature of the Soviet state. Therefore, only the symptoms of U.S.-Soviet hostilities are treated, not the disease itself.

Hawks most often propose containment of the Soviet empire, and this is a worthy goal according to Pipes, if such a policy could be effectively enforced. But containment as it has been practiced in the post–World War II era is no longer possible because it depended on the geographical contiguity of the Soviet empire. The present worldwide Soviet alliance network undermines the practicality of the hawk policy.[5]

Pipes's alternative to the dove-hawk debate involves the formulation of a counterstrategy to the Soviet Union's grand designs. Although military containment may no longer be feasible, Pipes contends that it is possible to coordinate a military, political and economic plan designed to accentuate the existing contradictions within Soviet society. Moreover, he claims that this can be done without creating the impression within the Soviet leadership that a military response is advantageous.[6]

At the time *Survival Is Not Enough* was published the Brezhnev succession had not been settled. Therefore, it is unclear how Mikhail Gorbachev's *perestroika* and *glasnost'* may have altered Pipes's attitude toward the Soviet Union. Yet we can infer from other of Pipes's writings two criteria by which he judges whether the difficult task of true reform has actually begun. In the domestic sphere his standard is the government's treatment of the many diverse nationalities that make up the Soviet Union. To the extent that these people are freed, the leadership will have exhibited its commitment to change. For Pipes this tranformation need not entail the abandonment of Marxism or the collapse of the Party, but it does entail the development of a more democratic socialism not administered solely by Great Russians. To measure up to Pipes's standard in foreign policy, the Soviet Union would need to abandon its role in fomenting regional strife and thereby reduce the pressure it has placed on the non-Communist world.[7] In Pipes's estimation, these two developments cannot occur independently.

Pipes's account of the Soviet Union has been enormously influential. Therefore, my purpose is to decribe and analyze that thesis. In what follows, I examine two basic themes: first, Pipe's view of the relationship between Marxism and Russian history and second, his presentation of the threat posed by the Soviet Union to the United States and the West. Because Pipes contends that the threat is caused in part by the relationship betwen Marx's principles and Russian historical development and in part by Western naïveté, a brief critique of his argument will conclude the discussion.

As noted earlier, Pipes considers Marxism-Leninism and Russian national character to have been mutually adaptable and synthetic. Yet an alternative perspective, best represented by the Russian writer Aleksandr Solzhenitsyn, holds that it is dangerous to trace the origins of Soviet misbehavior to a defective Russian national character. According to Solzhenitsyn, Pipes's view obscures the role that Marxist ideology has played in dictating the actions of Soviet leaders. Furthermore, Pipes's failure to appreciate the power of ideas in his treatment of Russia can be generalized to his understanding of Western society as well. In the conclusion I will suggest the limitations of Pipes's approach.

A Soviet or Russian "Threat"?

Pipes fears that Americans tend to treat the Soviet Union as though it were essentially the same in character as the United States. To his mind, however, the Soviet Union, because of its different evolution, is barely comparable to nations of the West. The Soviet Union became a great power in a manner and with expectations and modes of behavior greatly dissimilar to those of America. While Pipes acknowledges that all people are alike in that they wish to live and reproduce, he reasons that the effects of geography and history on culture creates subspecies of human beings that are, for practical purposes, quite different from each other. The West and the Soviet Union are representatives of such subspeciation.

Pipes contends that if one carefully examines the factors that produce the different behaviors and perceptions exhibited by nations, certain foreign policy constants come to light. These basic cultural yearnings are more reliable guides to an understanding of a nation's foreign policy than are analyses based on short-term responses to events, balance-of-power theory, or carrot-and-stick psychology. For example, Pipes holds that the political life of the Soviet Union after the death of Joseph Stalin was dominated by people whose origins can be traced to the lower class, the group least exposed to Western ideals. An awareness of the value of private property, law and individual rights was absent from their social consciousness. Exposed to little else in their private lives but hardship, such people inevitably seek expansion and control at the international level when they exercise political power. According to Pipes the Russian people were fertile soil on which the worst aspects inherent in Marxist ideology grew. Theirs was a particularly cunning, ruthless and hostile formulation of socialist thought. "In its present form, the Communist system of the Soviet Union and its dependencies is the product of two factors: the Russian political tradition and the ideology of Marxism-Leninism. Neither of these factors, taken by themselves, can explain the structure and behavior of Communist regimes."[8]

In many ways this statement is common-sensical. The behavior of a nation is determined by the ideals that it holds dear and by the character of the people that make it up. This general truth explains why the American, French and Iranian revolutions resulted in such different consequences. What is left begging in Pipes's initial formulation, however, is the question of which is more important, the fundamental principles or the history of a people. Put in other terms, when we fear the Soviet Union, should we distrust the Russians, the Communists or the Russian Communists?

Pipes does not provide a satisfactory answer, although he does indicate that the Soviet Union would be much easier to get along with if it moved away from the Communist system of a centrally planned economy and a one-party state. He seems to propose that ideology is predominant when he says that "as long as the present system prevails in the Soviet Union, war will remain an ever-present danger."[9] Nevertheless, he also maintains that the Russian character is particularly adaptable to communism and that Communist ideology accentuates negative tendencies that already existed in Russia. According to Pipes Russian communism is conditioned by three factors:

1. Russian feudalism had no tradition of the aristocracy restraining the monarchy. In fact, Russian unity was built on the conquest of neighboring princes.
2. Russia was a "classical patrimonial regime" with no regard for the protection of private property. Private property was introduced only toward the end of the eighteenth century.
3. Orthodox Christianity isolated Russia from the spiritual ideas of the West and gave it a feeling of "national-religious uniqueness."[10]

The consequences of these conditioning factors are:

1. Until the end of the eighteenth century, Russia was "unfamiliar with the distinction between political authority and the rights of private ownership." As this distinction is so fundamental to the West, its absence in Russia "accounts for some of the greatest differences between the behavior of Russian and Western governments."
2. "The lack of a feudal tradition" that limited Russian princes resulted in that nation having no "concept of law as a force superior to human will, binding alike on rulers and subjects."
3. Whether serf or gentry, all subjects of Russian rulers were bondsmen.[11]

Thus, political culture in Russia has always been deficient in its respect for "private property, law, and human rights."[12] Pipes insists that a nation's political culture will determine how it puts philosophic doctrines into practice. "Revolutionary governments may attempt by means of decrees to reshape . . . culture to their liking, but in the end they are invariably defeated: the fate of revolutions everywhere indicates that instead of traditions changing to suit revolutions, revolutions sooner or later accommodate themselves to traditions. The fate of Marxism in Russia provides an excellent illustration of this rule."[13]

Pipes contends that this axiom also can be seen in the Third World Marxist countries of Asia, Africa and Latin America, which although "receptive to European ideas, lack European traditions and as a result have turned Marxism into a justification for repressive forms of government.[14]

It was V. I. Lenin, Pipes insists, who intellectually and practically stripped Marxism and socialism of the liberal and democratic elements that had characterized these doctrines in the West. The cultural impact of Russia on Marxism was to make it authoritarian and nondemocratic. The West merely adapted socialism to its long-standing democratic heritage in a tame and decent manner. Thus, Marxism as such is not dangerous to liberalism; it becomes dangerous only when it is adopted by illiberal cultures. Pipes elaborates:

> The historian is struck by the ease with which Lenin and his lieutenants slipped into the role so recently vacated by the imperial sovereign. Lenin arrogated to himself not merely the powers of the constitutional monarchy of Nicholas II, nor even the semi-patrimonial authority of nineteenth century emperors, but those of patrimonial autocracy in all its seventeenth century splendor. The violence of 1917–1920 resulted in the wholesale destruction of the upper and middle classes, which happened to have been the principal Westernized groups in Russia. The disappearance of that relatively thin Westernized layer permitted the unregenerated Muscovite Russia, which had survived intact underneath the veneer of European influences, to float to the surface. Nationalizing in the name of socialism, the means of production in land and industry had the effect of once again placing all resources of the country at the disposal of the government; as in medieval Muscovy, sovereignty and ownership came to be fused. The introduction of the principle of compulsory labor for the state, the sole employer, rebonded the entire population of the country in the service of the state. Laws and courts were swept aside to be replaced by summary justice.[15]

But how did this nationalist autocracy take hold among Lenin and the Bolsheviks, who were internationalist in orientation? Pipes explains that when successful Marxist revolutions failed to occur in Europe, Lenin and his followers were left the task of governing the new Soviet state in a hostile world. Because the Bolshevik party was relatively small, the administration of many state affairs and much of the leadership of the armed forces had to be put in the hands of imperial bureaucrats and officers. These officials brought with them the old habits, says Pipes, and the "fusion of traditional Russian autocracy and Marxism, adapted to Russian conditions and mentalities, produced a regime that was quite outside the experience of the West. . . . It pushed to the forefront in Russia those elements that had remained unaffected by Western culture. . . . The Revolution threw Russia back to its pre-Western origins, to patrimonialism, to lawlessness, to human bondage, to the sense of uniqueness and isolation."[16]

If Pipes is correct in arguing that communism is but a continuation of Russian tsarism as practiced prior to the Westernizing reforms of Peter the Great, the main challenge to the security of the West is not Marxist ideology but the Russian people themselves. Pipes stresses this point by insisting that the post-Stalin elite is not in any sense grounded in the ideals of the West. Indeed, the effect of the Stalinist purges was to eliminate the Leninist dependence on imperial bureaucrats, as well as most Leninists, and to replace them with a new elite drawn from "an amorphous petty bourgeoise." According to Pipes this change made matters worse because the traditional attitude of the peasantry was one of "resentment, conservatism, anti-intellectualism, and xenophobia." In contrast to the gentry, the new elite was barely exposed to Western culture, and what exposure it did have was not viewed in a positive light.[17]

There are several points in his writings in which Pipes indicates that the United States can hope to conduct normal relations with the Soviet Union if it alters its political system in decisive respects. Yet, the way in which Pipes constructs his argument leaves the impression that the crude and suspicious nature of the Russian people makes the Soviet Union a dangerous adversary. If true, no improvement of the Soviet system that would make it more tolerable to the West is imaginable.[18] Presumably, even if significant reforms were introduced, the peasant origins of the Party leadership would still effectively leave the Soviet Union a suspicious and aggressive state. It is inconceivable that the entire state bureaucracy would relinquish its power as a means of inaugurating better relations with the West. It is possible that in order to improve the domestic economy the leadership might be forced to abandon Marxist ideology, which up to now has provided a justification for the elite's privileged position. But this would still leave those with the same peasant psychology in charge of making policy. Thus, on the basis of Pipes's formulation, even if domestic politics improved and Marxist ideology were discarded, it is unlikely that the West's difficulties with the Soviet Union would cease.

In Pipes's opinion international communism gives Soviet rulers a powerful stimulus and tool by which to pursue policies that any Russian state would be inclined to follow. Therefore, the West is faced with a particularly strident example of traditional Russian behavior. Nevertheless, Pipes argues that only a transformation of the internal politics of the Soviet state will make the Soviet Union a good global neighbor. But how does he account for this seeming contradiction?

Is There a Soviet Threat?

For Pipes the real problem facing the West is not that Russians are governed by a distasteful regime but that the internal dynamics of their political system requires an imperialist foreign policy. The cause of Soviet expansionism is an oligarchy concerned both with the "need to justify its authority" and "the desire to enhance this authority."[19] Conveniently, the principles that the elite invokes to justify its policies derive from a universal ideology that calls for the extension of communism throughout the world. Russia's traditional yearning for expansion and Marx's ideal of global revolution have combined to make any area outside Soviet control fair game for its interventionist policies.

The origins of Soviet expansionism can be traced to the Russian Revolution. When the worldwide revolution predicted by Karl Marx did not take place, the new leaders of the Soviet state were suddenly responsible not merely for dispossessing the old ruling class in Russia but for defending and expanding the global interests of the working class. Whereas Marx had expected the state (whose only function was to maintain by force the property relations of the ruling class) to wither away, no such event took place in the Soviet Union. Pipes explains:

> The communist state should by now have withered away completely. But, of course, the immense parasitic corps of the Party and state functionaries that had ensconced itself in power and privilege since the Revolution, has not the slightest interest in the state's disappearance. The state is the source of its livelihood; for the *nomenklatura* it provides a style of life that is not inferior to that of the Western middle class in a country where the vast majority of citizens subsists on a Third World standard. It needs to justify its power and privileges, and this justification it can find only in keeping alive the specter of the "bourgeoisie" and arguing that while the "bourgeoisie" has indeed been liquidated in Communist societies, it still survives and continues to threaten the socialist community, this time from the outside. Since the triumph of Communism in Russia, class war, which had once been internal, has been transferred onto the international arena. . . . In other words, the *nomenklatura* requires the foreign class enemy to legitimize its authority; without him, and without the threat that he allegedly poses, it has no excuse left for holding on to power. For this reason, international tension and the specter of war, in the form of an "imperialist" attack on the Soviet Union, are vital to the interest of the Communist elite. . . .

The best way to demonstrate the need for a powerful Communist state and military establishment is constantly to expand the Communist realm. . . . It has been noted by many observers that the Soviet aggrandizement and acts of repression abroad (e.g., against Czechoslovakia and Poland) enjoy popularity with the mass of Soviet citizens; it confirms to them that their own lot, with which, as a whole, they are not very happy, will also be that of the rest of mankind, that those foreigners who boast of freedom and prosperity will not be allowed to do so for long.[20]

Pipes draws the picture of an elite that does not simply pursue the national interest of the Soviet state but rather follows a policy designed to perpetuate its own oligarchic privileges. The means of keeping power is not peace, but conquest. As little else is given to the populace, foreign adventure becomes its staple—leaving the rulers to dine on a fuller repast. In formal terms, the long-term aim of the Soviet leadership is to overthrow capitalism and to replace it with a socialist society. But the real intent of the oligarchy is to satisfy the imperial ambition of the masses and thereby ensure the continuation of its own predominant position.[21]

Pipes sees the activities of the Soviet government as a "kind of imperialism," one that "calls for a protracted, patient, and prudent but unremitting *war of political attrition.* Its purpose is to undermine the authority of hostile governments and the will of their citizens to resist, while maintaining their own base solid, impregnable, and in a permanent state of mobilization."[22] The Soviet rulers do not desire to incorporate the entire world directly into Soviet territorial boundaries, Pipes reasons, but they do intend to establish a global hegemony. (And the United States is the most important obstacle to the achievement of that goal.[23]) Furthermore, the triumph of hegemony does not require that a rival state be thoroughly destroyed. "In modern times," Pipes explains, "successful imperialism demands a combination of means— diplomatic, psychological, ideological and economic, as well as military—for the purpose of eroding the opponent's ability and will to resist."[24] The attempt to mix these means into a victorious foreign policy constitutes the Soviet grand strategy.

The Soviet grand strategy is an attempt to undermine the political will of the opponent through a well-orchestrated program that: exploits "the 'contradictions' in the enemy's camp"; plays on the fears of the population, particularly on the fear of nuclear war; redefines the political vocabulary; bends "the rules of international conduct"; seeks to divide and conquer by preventing or destroying alliances directed against the Soviet Union; and limits the enemy's access to raw materials.[25]

In Pipes's view the Soviets consider war to be an extension of politics through other means. They prefer to use the military as a means of intimidation, but they will resort to force if the correct circumstances arise. They even believe that it is possible for them to win a nuclear war, as their military preparations indicate. Only in their propaganda do they demonstrate a disposition toward peace. But, according to Pipes, their propaganda is deceptive. Their argument runs as follows: "(1) nuclear war would destroy life on earth; (2) since life on earth is the highest good, anything is preferable to nuclear war; (3) nuclear war can be avoided only if the interests of the Soviet Union and its Bloc are respected; (4) the interests of the Soviet Union and its Bloc are determined by the Soviet government; (5) any challenge to the wishes of the Soviet government, therefore, threatens nuclear war and extinction of life on this planet."[26]

Pipes argues that the Soviets have been able to paralyze the West but maintain their own freedom of action. They have done this through a skillful combination of propaganda and assertiveness. On the one hand, they appeal to the yearning for peace found within Western public opinion, and on the other, they play on the West's fear of nuclear war. They promote the idea that they are more willing to use force (including nuclear weapons) to gain their political objectives than are Western nations. At the same time, they use propaganda to cast Western military forces as the true enemy of world peace. Pipes concludes that the psychological advantage the Soviets have gained by the use of this strategy makes that nation a most serious threat to the interests of the West.

Reconsideration

Is Pipes correct? Are the Russian people so defective in character that their country will always remain a menace to the peace-loving peoples of the world unless it adopts Western democratic practices? Does the defense of the West require that its citizens develop a distaste for the very soul of the Russian nation?

There is an alternative to Pipes's position. It is most forcefully presented by Aleksandr Solzhenitsyn in a 1980 *Foreign Affairs* article. Using the works of Pipes as an example, Solzhenitsyn criticizes both the methods and conclusions of Western scholarship as applied to Russia's past. He argues that Western academics have tended to mindlessly accept the assertions of Soviet propagandists. And the Soviets have had an interest in discrediting the old regime, for then their own failures would not seem so bad. Specifically, he argues that Pipes's *Russia Under the Old Regime* distorts the development of Russian culture and civilization (the land, after all, that produced Aleksandr Pushkin, Fyodor Dostoevsky, Leo Tolstoy, and Boris Pasternak, to name but a few of Russia's writers) and leaves the impression that totalitarianism was inevitable.[27] Pipes incorrectly blames Russia, not Marxism, for the ill fate that swept over Solzhenitsyn's native soil.[28]

Solzhenitsyn goes so far as to label Pipes's anti-Russian prejudice "racism." Solzhenitsyn also presents a more theoretical attack on Pipes's position. He points out that far from glorifying Russian traditions, the Soviet state since 1917 has done all it could to destroy every remnant of Russian cultural identity and replace it with a socialist society. The leadership has ignored the good of the Russian nation and its people in order to apply the ideology of Marx, a doctrine originating in the West and not derived from Russian patrimonialism. Indeed, communism developed out of a movement in Western thought that began with Thomas Hobbes's call for greater political equality and culminated in Marx's assertion that any differences in social rank were illegitimate. That this ideology settled in Russian soil was Russia's great misfortune.[29]

According to Solzhenitsyn, the rise of a totalitarian state in the Soviet Union was not the consequence of Marxism-Leninism perfecting pre-Petrine patrimonial "proto-totalitarianism." Nor is the source of Soviet aggressiveness the need of the Russian people to see others as badly off as themselves. On the contrary, the cruelty of the Soviet state at home and its imperialism in foreign affairs arise out of a narrowly defined adherence to the tenets of Marxism-Leninism on the part of the ruling Communist Party.

If Solzhenitsyn's argument is correct, the practical effect of Pipes's analysis is to lead American citizens and foreign policymakers to perceive the wrong enemy. Whereas Americans should be concerned with opposing the doctrines of Marx and Lenin, instead they come to regard the Russian people as their foe. But, Solzhenitsyn claims, the Russian people, too, are victims, exhausted after seventy years of Communist rule.

Some might object that Russian tsarism was often cruel and the society closed, but that objection misses the point. Solzhenitsyn would have us judge the Soviet Union from the standpoint of its animating principle. From that perspective it is little wonder that he objects to Pipes's willingness to see tsarist Russia as a sort of proto-totalitarian regime, for the legitimating principle of tsarism was Orthodox Christianity. In this sense Pipes's failure to analyze the spiritual content of a people's life might be a major defect of his work.

This is not the place for an extended discussion of the impact of first principles on the character of a regime. We may note, however, that all political communities are required to use similar methods of governance—some fair and some foul. Yet in the end, the first or organizing principles of a nation will dictate which among the available political methods are more likely to be selected by those in power when they seek to formulate and implement policy. Thus, it is a weakness of Pipes's work that he is unwilling to differentiate between a form of government devoted to the health of the soul and one intent on perpetuating class warfare (based on an analysis of human nature that denies the possibility of the soul). For example, if the Soviet oligarchy became more moderate and even went so far as to encourage development of the soul, Pipes's stated position would still cause him to be critical, for the leadership would not have transformed Russia into a Western, liberal state.

Moreover Pipes's analysis does little to help us understand the reforms undertaken by Gorbachev. One can say that Gorbachev was born a Russian and became a Marxist-Leninist. In bringing about change in the Soviet Union, he has not metamorphosed into another nationality. He has, however, been forced to jettison the economic principles conceived by Marx and the governmental structure initiated by Lenin.

As the world increasingly turns from the Soviet model because it does not satisfy material desires in an adequate manner, it might be worthwhile to remember that there are other reasons for rejecting Marxism. Pipes argues that the political effect of Marxism in the West was positive. It did not lead to totalitarianism as it did in the Soviet Union and other underdeveloped countries, because in the West, with its emphasis on the rule of law and its concern for private property, Marxism was practiced against a backdrop that took human rights as its highest value.[30] Yet it seems odd that a historian would ignore the dissolution of civil existence in Germany, once thought to be the most cultured nation in Europe, between the pincers of communism and the national communitarian doctrine of Nazism. It also seems odd that in arriving at his conclusion, Pipes would ignore the precarious tenure of liberal governments throughout most of the European continent for the better part of this century.

Pipes is not merely a historian; he is also an advocate. He wishes to overcome the naïveté and weakness of the West by arming it with a distrust for things Russian. But how effective will this antipathy really be? It seems unlikely that national animosities can withstand the sight of smiling Russian faces on TV. Indeed, whenever Westerners have had interpersonal contacts with average Russians, the former hardly have cast the latter as power-hungry ogres. Rather than inspiriting the West, Pipes's doctrine might actually undermine Western resolve. For if the Russian people can be shown, as many peace groups presently argue, to be "just like everybody else," the West will have lost its pretext for self-defense.

Pipes's desire to fortify the West makes him a supporter of a strong defense. He realizes that for a people to defend its way of life adequately, its foreign policy must be based on a value more substantial than the protection of mere life, for it is unreasonable for citizens to risk sacrificing their lives in order to preserve their lives. He reasons that the principle in the West that elicits sacrifice is its devotion to human rights, as guarded by the rule of law and supported by a respect for private property. Yet it is possible that these very rights may lead people to be unduly concerned with materialism and the mere preservation of life.[31] Of course, the rights protected by the West do not deny people the opportunity to act civic-mindedly or to perfect their souls. Yet the enormous freedom accorded to people in the West makes precarious such activities as sacrificing for the common good and renders in continual danger of closure such activities as seeking to elevate the soul. Certainly one cannot expect vigilant protection of Western ideals if the public is persuaded that first principles do not matter and that all human motivation derives from national character and the hope of material satisfaction.

Finally, we must ask whether the conservative argument that Pipes presents can succeed. If one looks at the coalition put together during the Reagan years, one sees social conservatives, foreign policy conservatives and economic conservatives. Because these factions within conservatism have different ends, there are inherent contradictions in the alliance. Most of the differences between social and economic conservatives are likely to be fought out over domestic issues. The foreign policy conservatives have serious misgivings about the attitudes of their economic brethren. As I noted earlier, Pipes considers a number of American business interests to be naively dovish in regard to détente. He and many other foreign policy conservatives decry the tendency of the business community to pursue profit by trading with the Soviet Union without regard for the harm done to the national interest. What Pipes fails to acknowledge is the consistency in the economic conservatives' desire to reach an accommodation with the Soviet Union. The values that Pipes attributes to the West as its greatest achievement— law, property and human rights—are themselves grounded in a materialist interpretation (originated by Thomas Hobbes) of the conditions of happiness. At the root of the West's justification for law, property and human rights is an understanding that the end or purpose of each is the preservation of life and the desire to make that life comfortable. In this particular circumstance, Pipes sees and dislikes the weakness of Western liberal politics, but he is unable to point to its cause.

Perhaps a criticism of the Soviet Union that cannot rise above ethnicity and historical practices to include first principles is also not adequate to understand other issues that face the contemporary world.

Notes

1. Richard Pipes, *The Formation of the Soviet Union: Communism and Nationalism, 1917–1923,* rev. ed. (Cambridge, Mass.: Harvard University Press, 1964); *Europe Since 1815* (New York: Harper & Row, 1964); *Russia Under the Old Regime* (New York: Charles Scribner's Sons, 1974); *U.S.-Soviet Relations in the Era of Détente* (Boulder, Colo.: Westview Press, 1981); *Survival Is Not Enough* (New York: Simon and Schuster, 1984); *Struve, Liberal and Left* (Cambridge, Mass.: Harvard University Press, 1970); and *Struve, Liberal and Right, 1905–1944* (Cambridge, Mass.: Harvard University Press, 1980).

2. See Jonathan Alter, "Reagan's Dr. Strangelove," *The Washington Monthly,* 13, no. 4 (June 1981): 10–17.

3. See, for example, Colin S. Gray, *Maritime Strategy, Geopolitics and the Defense of the West* (Washington, D.C.: National Strategy Information Center, 1986), p. 41 and note.

4. Pipes, *Survival,* p. 14.

5. Ibid., pp. 218–222, 278.

6. Ibid., pp. 222–224 ff.

7. Richard Pipes, "The *Glasnost* Test," *The New Republic,* February 2, 1987, pp. 16–17.

8. Ibid., p. 17. Most references are to *Survival Is Not Enough.* A corresponding reference to *Russia Under the Old Regime* is not added unless necessary. Pipes writes that his characterization of the Soviet Union in *Survival* is but a condensation of his thesis in *Russia Under the Old Regime.*

9. Pipes, *Survival,* p. 280.

10. Ibid., p. 18.

11. Ibid., p. 19.

12. Ibid.

13. Ibid., p. 20.

14. Ibid., p. 21.

15. Ibid., p. 23.

16. Ibid., p. 24.

17. Pipes, *U.S.-Soviet Relations,* pp. 4–5.

18. Pipes, *Survival,* pp. 204–207; also Pipes, *Russia,* p. 141.

19. Pipes, *Survival,* p. 43.

20. Ibid., pp. 42–43.

21. Ibid,. p. 41.

22. Ibid., p. 53.

23. Ibid., p. 50.

24. Ibid., p. 51.

25. Ibid., p. 53.

26. Ibid., p. 67. Also see Richard Pipes, "Why the Soviet Union Thinks It Could Fight and Win a Nuclear War," *Commentary* 64, no. 1 (July 1977): 21–34.

27. Aleksandr Solzhenitsyn, "Misconceptions About Russia Are a Threat to America," *Foreign Affairs* 58 no. 3 (Spring 1980). Reprinted as *The Mortal Danger* (New York: Harper & Row, 1980).

28. See Pipes's critical review of Solzhenitsyn's Harvard Commencement Address, "Solzhenitsyn and the Russian Intellectual Tradition: Some Critical Remarks," *Encounter* 52, no. 6 (June 1979): 52–56.

29. Aleksandr Solzhenitsyn, *A World Split Apart* (New York: Harper & Row, 1978), p. 33; *Letter to Soviet Leaders,* (New York: Harper & Row, 1974), pp. 55–66; "Correspondence," *Foreign Affairs* 59, no. 1 (Fall 1980): 196–210; and *From Under the Rubble* (Chicago: Regnery-Gateway, 1981). For a thoughtful discussion of Solzhenitsyn, see James F. Pontuso, "Crisis of a World Split Apart: Solzhenitsyn on the West," *The Political Science Reviewer* 16 (Fall 1986): 185–236; "Solzhenitsyn on Marx: The Problem of Love of One's Own," *Teaching Political Science: Politics in Perspective,* 13, no. 3 (Spring 1986): 108–119; and "On Solzhenitsyn's Stalin," *Survey* 29, no. 2 (Summer 1985): 46–69.

30. Pipes, *Survival,* p. 21.

31. See Solzhenitsyn, *A World Split Apart,* pp. 55–56.

PART FIVE

Constitutional Interpretation

Conservatives have experienced considerable success in influencing federal court appointments since the Reagan era began. True, President Reagan did not shift the composition of the Supreme Court with his three appointments. But Reagan appointed more than one-half of all federal court justices. The Reagan Justice Department implemented an ideological screening test for appointments to the courts. This test ensured that court appointees would adhere to the administration's conservative agenda.

Since 1981 conservative constitutional thinkers have gained enhanced stature. The following chapters examine the constitutional philosophies of an unusual duo—James Jackson Kilpatrick and Chief Justice William H. Rehnquist. The former is a polemicist, a popularizer of conservative constitutional doctrines; the latter, like any Supreme Court justice should be, is a reflective constitutionalist divorced from the world of direct opinion leadership. Nonetheless, both men in very different ways are opinion leaders on constitutional issues. Kilpatrick's position as a national columnist and television commentator dictates that he influence currents of thought in the country. Rehnquist influences constitutional interpretation for years to come with his Court opinions.

Edward S. Twardy critically examines James Jackson Kilpatrick's views on federalism, individual rights and constitutional change. Gary L. McDowell assesses Chief Justice William H. Rehnquist's "jurisprudence of common sense." McDowell finds Rehnquist, a true constitutionalist, to be the kind of jurist that the American constitutional framers expected.

14

James Jackson Kilpatrick: Southern Conservative

Edward S. Twardy

For more than four decades James Jackson Kilpatrick has elevated the character and intensity of national debate between liberals and conservatives. His cogent analysis of the country's halting efforts to reconcile its past with dramatic economic and social change has earned him membership in a respected circle of national opinion leaders. In a time when our country traversed perhaps the second most convulsive period of its history, Kilpatrick's twentieth-century voice of southern conservatism has been an especially potent force in the development of the contemporary version of a traditional American philosophy. Frequently adamant, often elegant and nearly always tightly reasoned, Kilpatrick's opinions consistently have been presented in the manner of one who fully enjoys "the free and unrestrained combat of ideas."

Representing what, for many, was seen as a losing cause—the preservation of traditional southern social structure—Kilpatrick nonetheless provided an evolving American conservative movement with a framework of priorities that transcended the instant battle over desegregation. With uncommon common sense he defined the ground rules by which the South would attempt to resist the tide of liberal intrusion. But, more importantly, he rose above his own specific battle to reestablish the line between state and individual and, decades before their adoption, issued clarion appeals for key tenets of contemporary conservative policy. His was often the singular southern voice decrying the hysteria of McCarthyism or urging that the nation acknowledge reality and formally recognize Red China. In at least these instances, Kilpatrick urged that the nation's leaders recognize the country's real long-range objectives in the post–World War II era.[1]

Evidence of Kilpatrick's contribution to the modern American conservative movement is to be found by examining his messages through the prism of several issues critical to the polarization of contemporary conservative thinking. These include the emergence of an activist Supreme Court generally—but specifically the school desegregation struggle; the growth of government generally—but specifically its collision with the individual's rights; and the inevitability of change generally—but specifically how these changes affect modern conservatism. The raw material for this examination can be found in hundreds of editorials, many articles, several books and numerous televised discussions in various formats. Yet even these many sources do not provide sufficient grist to begin to appreciate Kilpatrick's point of view. That requires a bit more knowledge about the man.

Kilpatrick's Background

Kilpatrick began his journalistic career in 1941 when he took a job as a reporter for the *Richmond News Leader* in the staid and comfortable capital city of the Commonwealth of Virginia. Living in Virginia has meant a great deal to Kilpatrick from the very first, and it is important to understand that fact in order to appreciate both the wisdom and bias of his conservatism. He has known and loved the entire South, and across countless editorials and the pages of at least five books one catches glimpses fondly recalled of a childhood in Oklahoma and Louisiana; of travels through city, hamlet and farm; of a sturdy affection for quiet loveliness and a sense of certainty about the order of natural things.

Further, Kilpatrick seems always to have been in touch with the essence of his conservatism; even his first news stories recognize the difference between a metaphysical abstraction and the rule of law. He believes in the rights of the individual and in the rightness of law as well as in the spirit of both in a free society. His understanding of an individual's contributions to, and responsibility for, the spirit of the law underlies his conservatism. Thus, he believes in freedom and justice—that is, in individual freedom to succeed or fail and in the essential justice of enjoying the freedom to try. His belief in justice has tempered his pen and added wisdom and stature to his defense of tradition.

Kilpatrick's Defense of Southern Tradition

Defending the traditional South to the rest of the country was a task Kilpatrick thoroughly enjoyed. He had been in the process of defining the essence of the South to his Virginia neighbors long before his promotion, in 1949, to chief editorial writer for the *Richmond News Leader.* His defense was a labor of love. Points were made, politicians chastened or encouraged, foolishness ridiculed with all the unspoken understanding of someone offering advice to his family. There was no need in the day-to-day travail to refer to the family's memories of "sacred stories"; everyone knew them.

The rest of the nation was another matter. Throughout his appeal to this larger audience Kilpatrick attempted to teach what the South, his South—the traditional South—was all about. The messages were about "an amalgam of the smiles, hopes, fears of the Southerner's life, a mosaic of countless fleeting impressions and experiences."[2] He was seeking, of course, to build an understanding of the South's resistance to school desegregation.

In so doing, however, Kilpatrick painted, with far more eloquence than most, a sketch of the intangible values that unite many modern conservatives. Among these are a strong sense of community and family, a deeply rooted respect for property, an affection for the deliberate pace of an agrarian society, a profound respect for divine power, and an almost universal dedication to strong local government based in part on an instinctive suspicion of all government. "We do not *like* authority, especially needless, lint-picking, petty authority, and a broody pessimism constantly evokes the apprehension that government, if given half a chance, will put a fast one over on the people."[3]

Local government is visible and immediately accountable. City managers, county supervisors and even state officials were unlikely to resort to mysterious incantations of sociological statistics to justify changes in policy. They were members of the family.

Not so the distant federal government, and alas, even more alarming to Kilpatrick, not so the federal courts. The cause for his alarm became increasingly clear in the early 1950s: The courts were beyond virtually all accountability to an injured minority—in this case, the South. Thus, after an "erring" President Dwight Eisenhower appointed Earl Warren to the highest bench, and whereupon the latter presided over a series of cases that in one swoop upended one hundred sixty years of tradition and social structure, the South and James Jackson Kilpatrick were outraged.

After defending Earl Warren's right to honor an invitation, extended early in 1954, to address the faculty and "very important friends" of the College of William and Mary (on the occasion of that institution's 175th anniversary), Kilpatrick spoke for a unified family of southern aristocrats and common folk alike in an editorial entitled "From the Not Very Important People." With cold rage he informed the visiting

Chief Justice that: "you and your associates have dishonored the Constitution, as we have known and cherished it; you have substituted the vague precepts of "psychology" for the plain mandates of law and precedent; you have trampled upon the clear rights of the States when it was your duty to preserve them; you would impose upon the South a form of tyranny the Not Very Important People deeply, strongly resent. And they are a proud people, these ordinary men and women; they do not choose to be coerced."[4]

Yet in the conclusion of that editorial, Kilpatrick revealed another tenet of modern conservatism, a value that has characterized his position throughout his career: respect for the law. He set a standard, in that early autumn tinder box of southern discontent, for the South's response to the unanimous opinion in *Brown* v. *Board of Education*[5]: "We will resist this judgment of the Court; we will resist it quietly, honorably, lawfully, but we will resist it with the strength of a tradition that has resisted tyranny before."[6] But this respect for the law and the legal process would, for Kilpatrick, be on shaky ground if the Court were to continue relying on social science for the justification of its rulings.

To rally the country to the side of the traditional South he took on the Court in an attack from two fronts. The first was a classic defense of states rights. Drawing on the intellectual arsenal of champions long retired from the fight, Kilpatrick fashioned a brilliant, if one-sided, argument for relief from the Warren Court's folly.[7] His second was a gambit meant to upbraid the Court for its use of sociological research on which to ground Constitutional decisions and then to counter the statistics with bushel baskets of his own. Of course, neither approach met with much success, and an author wiser for the effort but resigned to the futility of the South's initial resistance remarked, in 1962, about his new vantage point, "I wrote one book about the South a few years ago, when Virginia was still in the thick of it, and I was on a horse and the pen was a lance. The sidelines offer a better perspective."[8]

From the position of a scholarly observer Kilpatrick continues to make a contribution to the evolution of the conservative movement. Not that Kilpatrick does not enjoy a good fight. In fact, he respects, perhaps as much as any ideal, a tightly reasoned "discussion" of principle. Bemoaning (before the advent of televised counterpoint confrontation) the state of contemporary debate, he allowed that "among the more melancholy aspects of the genteel world we live in is the slow decline in the enjoyment that men once found in the combat of ideas, free and unrestrained."[9] That he relishes such encounters is no mystery to those who have read his columns during the past four decades or watched him skewer on a point of law some poor, ill-prepared liberal, stranded before the television camera.

The Growth of Government Versus Individual Rights

Kilpatrick began to rally conservatives in response to an immediate threat to his way of life. In this respect he honors the tradition of conservatism. During the several years in which he waged his struggle to turn back the tide of court-mandated civil rights measures, Kilpatrick began to hit with increasing frequency upon the point on which some of his earliest news stories seemed to hang. It is a point threaded throughout most contemporary conservative doctrine: the rights of the individual in modern society. In fact, his contribution to the doctrine can clearly be seen by examining his views on the topic across several salient issues of our time. To do so, let us begin on familiar ground— Kilpatrick's case for segregation in southern schools—then move on briefly to the issue of press censorship and finally arrive at the highly flammable and very current right to life controversy.

From the beginning of his struggle to establish an acceptable foundation for the South's resistance to integration, Kilpatrick focused on the expanding role of the Supreme Court in the changing fabric of the democracy. He pilloried the Warren Court for the adoption of an unchecked activism that threatened to sweep away the intention of the Constitution with "the caprice, or the sociology, of a majority of the Court."[10] According to his analysis, the principal beneficiary of the Court-imposed federal encroachment was the Court itself; the net direct loss was felt by the individual who lost the right to associate with whomever he chose. Characterizing the nation's conservatives as those who "believe in limited government and in individual responsibility," Kilpatrick commanded that the hour was at hand to risk sacrifices in order to reclaim a fundamental, natural right.[11]

This theme of individual responsibility was no stranger to the countless threads of logic and opinion that had spun out of Kilpatrick's typewriter. In his books of that era, he drew upon the South's abiding mythology to establish one element of the individual southerner's value system that was consistent with the conservative philosophy writ large: the legend of southern gentlemen as "men of ease, and grace, and elegance, and high birth; men who lived by a code of honor, and died beneath the dueling oaks; men who gambled with skill, and loved with passion; men who fought with a royal disdain for risk."[12] Thus, individual responsibility should be read by all Americans as it had always been understood in southern myth; it meant being honorable, self-reliant and ready to fight for freedom. That was, and still is, how Kilpatrick read the concept.

He identified two significant threats to this essential American characteristic. The first, obviously the result of a quest for "equality," was the erosion of constitutional protections of individual liberty; the second, in direct inverse proportion, was the growth of the distant federal government. "The proliferation of the bureaucracy and the steady corruption of the Constitution, under the guise of shaping its provisions to make them more adaptable to the twentieth century, seem to me both symptoms and causes of other national problems . . . [and] have contributed materially to a weakening of personal responsibility and to a growing contempt for law."[13]

Of course Kilpatrick speaks here not just of the type of change but of the pace of change and its impact on the rugged and unique American in a free society. On the one hand, the changes have led to the growing impotency of the individual: "It is the loss of privacy, the loss of self, the loss of variety; and the virus manifests itself in giant corporations and giant unions, in automated mills and prefabricated parts, in Zip Codes and symbols and a Social Security number for the baby."[14] On the other hand, the rapidity of change has diluted the individual's certainty in the law, a certainty that an unchanging constitutional interpretation had provided.

There is an element, however, in this shower of sparks, that Kilpatrick soon recognized as extending beyond his immediate aim of preventing forced integration. His unshakable belief in common sense justice had always led him to apply the rights of the individual to all men, black and white.[15] He had, in 1960, in a book about obscenity and censorship, transferred that declaration of individual right to a larger canvas: "The one great, precious factor that distinguishes a free society from a totalitarian society is the absence of unwarranted governmental restraint upon the free man. Within the broadest possible limits the free man may work as he pleases, live as he pleases, come and go as he pleases, think, read, write, vote, and worship as he pleases. His liberties, of course, are not absolute . . . but . . . extend to the point at which Citizen A causes some serious loss, risk, or inconvenience to Citizen B."[16]

There was no inconsistency in this view and Kilpatrick's continued resistance to school desegregation in the South. He had established that individual freedom was never absolute. Common sense would have it no other way. In the view of the southern conservative, the forced association of children of different races in public schools was certain to undermine the foundation of traditional society. That condition, it was argued, would clearly cause serious loss, risk and inconvenience to Citizen B.

There is no defense for the inflammatory racism that infected Kilpatrick's diatribes against public school desegregation. It is shallow stuff. In his books on the issues of states' rights and school segregation he dredged up statistics designed to show inalienable differences between white and Negro on nearly every index.[17] The crux of his position is useful for present purposes only insofar as it illuminates another element of his conservative credo: inequality of men.

For Kilpatrick the notion that all men were created equal did not translate into anything more than a metaphysical truth. His lifelong observation revealed no other equality. He saw and could document inequality of intelligence, morals and character everywhere in the nation. One could not legislate away the God-given differences in people. The result of efforts to do so, he reasoned, were producing grave consequences for the nation and not just in schools. In an article encouraging a conservative candidate for president, Kilpatrick urged Barry Goldwater to come to grips with the reasons for an erosion of national productivity, growth and traditional pride in the quality of American workmanship. He suggested that "one profound reason for this [settling for mediocrity in the quality of American workmanship] lies in the superficial doctrines of equality . . . the national lunacy that all men ought to be regarded, quite literally, as equal. There is not one word of truth in the notion; it is demonstrably false, as Louis taught Braddock."[18] Kilpatrick saw, as the Founders did two centuries ago, that equality existed only in liberty; the southern conservative saw clearly that there was no liberty in court-mandated racial equality.

Yet during the turbulence of the mid-1960s, liberty was increasingly construed by people outside the South to mean the right to have an opportunity. Here Kilpatrick reveals a telling aspect of southern conservative resistance to desegregated public schools. For he, too, prior to the court mandates, seems always to have recognized the right of all Americans to have access to opportunity. In 1950, for example, in the absence of professional schools for blacks that were equal in all respects to such units at long established, and still segregated, white universities, he urged the admission of *qualified* Negro graduate students—admission even to the law school at Thomas Jefferson's University of Virginia. The justice of that position was understood even in Richmond. It was when the actions of the federal government intruded into the lives of children not yet fully inculcated with the traditional values of their community that Kilpatrick drew his line. But what of children not yet born?

On this explosive issue Kilpatrick is forced by his sense of consistency to apply the conservative principle "to preserve the individual's right to be left alone"[19] to an arena in which not all conservatives wish to be counted. In 1979, in response to a ringing call for Americans to unite on the right to life issue to form a seamless "one-issue" electorate, Kilpatrick refused to join ranks.[20] He chose not to do so for two reasons. First, it seemed patently silly to him to vote to cast out elected officials with whom one agrees on virtually every issue save one. In that regard he is doubtless joined by many other conservatives. Second, in explaining his position on the instant case, he joined ranks with the supporters of *Roe* v. *Wade*[21] in many aspects of the debate. The rationale for his principled stance is vintage Kilpatrick: "I had supposed it to be a fundamental principle of conservatism to challenge *every* doubtful intrusion of the state upon the freedom of the individual. The more serious the intrusion, the more it must be resisted. Only the most compelling interests of society can justify a major invasion by the government of a person's right to be left alone. . . . If these are not fundamental principles of conservatism, I have wasted thirty years in the contemplation of that philosophy."[22] He protested, obviously, the suggestion that government intrude upon a woman's rights and was content to let stand the Court's test of fetal viability as the line for establishing individuality. In this signal example Kilpatrick demonstrates the depth of his unchanging philosophy and thus the essence of his contribution to the conservative ideal. Yet he is not immune to change.

Conservative Change

Throughout his ardent battle to defeat federally mandated civil rights measures, Kilpatrick sought to establish the position that the Constitution should not be subject to constant reinterpretation. The meanings of the framers and of those who won the original struggles over the scope of amendments were set in unchanging brilliance like the crystals in a geode. Opening the record of debate reveals them sparkling.

Yet by 1962, Kilpatrick recognized the inevitability of change, even in his beloved culture. Speaking more to the family than the rest of the world, he sought wryly to ease the strain by explaining, "Instead of casting away all our old prejudices, as Burke once remarked cheerfully of English Conservatives, 'we cherish them to a very considerable degree, and, to take more shame to ourselves, we cherish them because they are prejudices; the longer they have lasted, and the more generally they have prevailed the more we cherish them.'"[23] His wise counsel to those who would resist blindly all change was simply to realize that the South was already changing. He began to explain, and understand, about change: "A wise and enlightened conservatism does not resist all change; it resists what it views as impulsive change, or change simply for the sake of change."[24]

What then does the future hold for southern values? And what of the future of modern conservatism? Here Kilpatrick has not changed at all. In 1966, he anticipated the philosophy's emergence as the rising force in American politics. "In a nation that is beginning to ache for a return to law and order, for a renewed respect for property rights, and for a greater measure of personal freedom, the time for these ideas moves steadily toward the striking hour."[25] But setting aside the arguments from ancient champions, he stepped away from strident calls for strict construction and warnings against the pernicious effect of judicial activism. Without abandoning his course, Kilpatrick swung to another tack.

Both the cause of cultural preservation and his continued career as a journalist had deepened his study of the Court. As he learned more, that element of common sense that cannot often ignore reality took hold. He saw that the philosophy of the justices on the bench was part of the engine of democracy. He began to urge conservative political leaders to apply their screen to the High Court selection process. What was needed on the bench were individuals of conservative philosophy who shared the comfortable set of values that nurtured individual responsibility and honored those committed to the southern tradition of cultural husbandry. Reliance solely on the wisdom of justices considering historic Court decisions was not sufficient to maintain constitutional protections. Conservatives must take the steps necessary to reclaim a majority on the Supreme Court.[26] "The 'intent of the Framers' cannot be determined by computer analysis or by divine revelation. It can only be determined by mortal men; reading history, pondering precedents. . . . [Yet] the Constitution is only abstractly a document of the ages. It is more accurately a document as fresh as this morning's paper, edited by five judges who hold its meaning in their hands."[27] The "flaw" that he had discovered in the Constitution during his reflex rejection of the Warren Court's civil rights activism was not fatal after all.[28] In fact, he recognized that it could prove to be an extraordinary means of checking "impulsive change."

Simply another common sense conclusion? Perhaps. Yet Kilpatrick has often recognized what many other conservatives have not yet seen. At base, his contributions to modern conservatism occur not because his vision is broader or deeper; they continue because he has an uncommon ability to understand fully and explain with great clarity what he sees. Frequently, he has identified long-range objectives that are ultimately accepted by both liberal and conservative as being in the country's best interest. Ironically, it was his inability to see at first the value of racial integration to American culture that thrust him into national visibility and led to his success.

Conclusion

Southern conservatism seems to be far more complex than a "traditional conservative" opined some decades ago.[29] It is more than a tradition of distaste for change based upon an agrarian desire for tranquility and a love of local rights. Tradition, while important to the southern philosophy, ensures primarily the structure of faith, not its content. Philosophic content for southern conservatism is homegrown each generation from the rich loam of personal relationships with family and neighbors, town and country, church and school. Some elements of this culture erode quickly without close attention. Much of it can endure a lot of wind and rain. James Jackson Kilpatrick understands that about the South, and he understands people, which may help explain why he leads opinion.

Notes

1. See, for example, "Foreign Policy" (editorial), *Richmond News Leader,* July 1, 1950, p. 3.

2. James Jackson Kilpatrick, *The Sovereign States: Notes of a Citizen of Virginia* (Chicago: Henry Regnery, 1957), p. 258.

3. James Jackson Kilpatrick, *The Southern Case for School Segregation* (New York: Crowell Collier Press, 1962), p. 29. In addition to his own observations, Kilpatrick quoted, with fondness, the work of W. J. Cash, especially his *The Mind of the South.* For example: "Cash had described as 'the ruling element' of Southern tradition, this 'intense distrust of, and, indeed, downright aversion to, any actual exercise of authority beyond the barest minimum essential to the existence of the social organism.'"

4. Editorial, *Richmond News Leader,* September 25, 1954, p. 10. In attempting to quell coarse public outcry against Warren's appearance, Kilpatrick noted that it did not matter that the invitation had been extended two months before the fateful *Brown* v. *Board* decision had been handed down on May 17, 1954. Southern hospitality and decorum mandated that the Chief Justice be treated with the dignity befitting his office.

5. *Brown et al.* v. *Board of Education of Topeka et al.,* 347 U.S. 483 (1954).

6. Editorial, *Richmond News Leader,* September 25, 1954, p. 10.

7. Kilpatrick, *The Sovereign States;* and Kilpatrick, *The Southern Case,* esp. pp. 213–220.

8. Kilpatrick, *The Southern Case,* p. 8.

9. Kilpatrick, *The Sovereign States,* p. ix.

10. Ibid., p. 95.

11. Ibid., p. 306.

12. Kilpatrick, *The Southern Case,* p. 32.

13. James Jackson Kilpatrick, "What a Southern Conservative Thinks," *Saturday Review,* April 25, 1964, p. 18.

14. Ibid., p. 16.

15. In editorials throughout his tenure with the *Richmond News Leader,* Kilpatrick urged consistently that Negroes, the term then used for African Americans, be treated equally by government. See, for example, the editorials relating to a denial of beach access to Negroes by the city of Colonial Beach, Virginia, in which he berated the town fathers for refusing to provide blacks access equal to that provided the white community, July–August 1950, especially Editorial, *Richmond News Leader,* August 7, 1950, p. 10.

16. James Jackson Kilpatrick, *The Smut Peddlers* (Garden City, N.Y.: Doubleday, 1960), p. 217.

17. See, especially, Kilpatrick, *The Sovereign States;* and Kilpatrick, *The Southern Case.*

18. Kilpatrick, "What a Southern Conservative Thinks," p. 18.

19. James Jackson Kilpatrick, "The New Right: What Does it Seek?" *Saturday Review,* October 8, 1966, p. 125.

20. James Jackson Kilpatrick, "A Comment," *National Review,* May 25, 1979, pp. 678–680. Kilpatrick responds to the opinion of Grover Rees III, "The True Confessions of One One-Issue Voter," published in the same issue, pp. 669–672, 678.

21. *Roe* v. *Wade,* 410 U.S. 113 (1973).

22. Kilpatrick, "A Comment," p. 679.

23. Kilpatrick, *The Southern Case,* p. 38.

24. Ibid.

25. Kilpatrick, "The New Right," p. 125.

26. For a useful summary of Kilpatrick's assessment of an activist Court in general and the Warren Court specifically, see James Jackson Kilpatrick, "A Very Different Constitution," *National Review,* August 12, 1969, pp. 794–800.

27. James Jackson Kilpatrick, "The High Court: Where Now?" *National Review,* November 19, 1971, p. 1291.

28. One example of this "discovery" can be found as Kilpatrick draws upon James Madison: "What Madison here recognized and what he later was to overlook is that the Constitution has one major flaw: The Constitution had established an ingenious system of checks and balances by which every conceivable source of oppression, *with a single exception,* may effectively be held in bounds." That single exception is the Supreme Court of the United States (*Sovereign States,* p. 91).

29. Russell Kirk, *The Conservative Mind: From Burke to Santayana,* 2nd ed. (Chicago: Henry Regnery, 1954).

15

Language and the Limits of Judging: Chief Justice Rehnquist's Jurisprudence of Common Sense

Gary L. McDowell

Words move, music moves
Only in time; but that which is only living
Can only die. Words, after speech, reach
Into the silence.
                                        —T. S. Eliot[1]

Since he ascended the highest bench in 1971, William Hubbs Rehnquist has been derided as the lone champion of an archaic notion of states' rights; condemned as a conservative whose ideology is so inflexible that it corrupts his judicial craftsmanship; chastised as an advocate of reliance on the Founders' intentions—at least when it suits his political purposes; and, most recently, indicted as a mindless legal positivist who foolishly believes one can simultaneously advocate legal positivism and adherence to original intention as the foundation of constitutional interpretation. It would be hard to think of another justice whose juridical corpus has ever been more subjected to conflicting views and interpretations than has that of Chief Justice Rehnquist.[2]

But the fact is that Rehnquist is a devoted believer in original intention and in a sort of legal positivism—which one might call Madisonian positivism—whose jurisprudence is actually deeper and more philosophically rooted than his critics are willing to admit. No simpleminded advocate of states' rights, Rehnquist's jurisprudential roots are to be found in a traditional understanding of federalism and an appreciation for the processes and prospects of popular, representative democracy. In short, Rehnquist is the sort of justice the Constitution anticipates in Article III; indeed, he is the embodiment of the sort of jurist anticipated in the debates in the Constitutional Convention and especially in *The Federalist*. For he is, at bottom, a constitutionalist.

Rehnquist's Constitutionalism

Rehnquist's jurisprudence springs from his understanding of the history and political theory of the Constitution's founding. His point of departure is that "the Constitution was, not merely in theory but in fact as well, a fundamental charter that had emanated from the people." It was a document "designed to enable the popularly elected branches of the government, but not the judicial branch, to keep the country abreast of the times." Like Alexander Hamilton in *The Federalist*, No. 78, Rehnquist sees the Constitution as more than a mere list of strictures; it embraces a coherent theory of politics. The theory of politics it embodies is one that sees the Constitution, as Hamilton said, as the expression of the "intentions of the people"; and that theory of popular sovereignty does not allow the agents of the people—neither executive, legislative, or judicial—to supplant those original intentions with contemporary notions of their own.[3]

The foundation of original-intention jurisprudence is the idea of popular sovereignty and the belief that the written Constitution is the concrete expression of the consent of the governed, the only legitimate source of political authority. As Rehnquist has put it, popular sovereignty "must be taken as a first premise in any attempt to define the source of authority exercised by a government or to define any theory of political obligation which gives moral sanction to the actions of a government based on the rule of the majority." The result of this confidence in popular sovereignty demands a restrained view of the judicial power of interpretation; the Court can wield no power greater than that which is granted to it by the express terms of the Constitution. For judges to expand their role and impart new meaning to the Constitution is to deny the most basic premise of popular consent as it is expressed in a written Constitution of clear and common language.[4]

The framers, Rehnquist has observed, "inscribed the principles that control today. Any deviation from their intentions frustrates the permanence of that charter and will only lead to . . . unprincipled decisionmaking."[5] As he put it in *Nevada* v. *Hall*:

> Any document—particularly a constitution—is built on certain postulates or assumptions; it draws on shared experiences and common understanding. On a certain level, that observation is obvious. Concepts such as

"State" and "Bill of Attainder" are not defined in the Constitution and demand external referents. But on a more subtle plane, when the Constitution is ambiguous or silent on a particular issue, [the Supreme Court] has often relied on notions of a constitutional plan—the implicit ordering of relationships within the federal system necessary to make the Constitution a workable governing charter and to give each provision within that document the full effect intended by the Framers. The tacit postulates yielded by that ordering are as much enshrined in the fabric of the document as its express provisions, because without them the Constitution is denied force and often meaning.[6]

To discern those tacit postulates, that original intention, is not always easy: "The Framers were not simple-minded. The Constitution is animated by an array of intentions." But to say that discerning that original intention is difficult—or even impossible in some few cases—is in no way a justification for judges to dispense with the effort, arduous although it be, and plunge into the risky business of attempting to be the "voice and conscience of contemporary society." For that, there is no constitutional warrant, not even if, as Hamilton said in *The Federalist,* the consensus of the people on a certain point should be known without a doubt. "A mere change in public opinion," Rehnquist has written in agreement, "since the adoption of the Constitution, if unaccompanied by a constitutional amendment, should not change the meaning of the Constitution." As Walter Berns has put it, the point of judicial power is not to keep the Constitution in tune with the times but to keep the times in tune with the Constitution.[7]

Deriving from Rehnquist's view that the Constitution is the expression of the consent of the governed is his belief that what the governed originally consented to must still control; and what the governed originally consented to (and what we still consent to absent formal amendment) is a decentralized republic where the states and localities are expected to provide the primary forums for political activity. It is there, in the rough-and-tumble give and take of politics that people come to know freedom; in that process the moral judgments of the people are expressed and translated into law.[8]

Some have recently criticized Chief Justice Rehnquist for his alleged legal positivism, his failure to appreciate the moral dimension of our constitutionalism, and his willingness to defer to the legislative power even in cases in which the claims raised by the litigant appear to have the force of moral right behind them.[9] The result, so the critics argue, is an amoral constitutionalism that is at odds with the true intentions of those who wrote, proposed and ratified the Constitution. But the fact is that Rehnquist is not the proponent of an amoral politics; he simply rejects the notion that the moral content of our political life is to issue from the judiciary. Indeed, as he has put it, "a government or a society ought to be measured primarily by . . . the extent to which [it] succeeds in vindicating the moral judgment of its members." But community morality must find its expression in democratic deliberation within representative institutions, not in judicial decree.[10]

The primary confusion among his critics stems from a famous article in the *Texas Law Review* over a decade ago on "The Notion of a Living Constitution." In this article, Rehnquist went on at length about the political problems of moral judgments:

> If . . . a society adopts a constitution and incorporates in that constitution safeguards for individual liberty, these safeguards . . . take on a generalized moral rightness or goodness. They assume a general social acceptance neither because of any intrinsic worth nor because of any unique origins in someone's idea of natural justice but instead simply because they have been incorporated in a constitution by the people. Within the limits of our Constitution, the representatives of the people . . . enact laws. The laws emerge after a typical political struggle in which various individual value judgments are debated and likewise take on a form of moral goodness because they have been enacted into positive law. It is the fact of their enactment that gives them whatever moral claim they have on us as a society, however, and not any independent virtue they may have in any particular citizen's own scale of values. . . .
>
> Beyond the Constitution and the laws in our society, there is simply no basis other than the individual conscience of the citizen that may serve as a platform for the launching of moral judgments. . . . Many of us necessarily feel strongly and deeply about our own moral judgments, but they remain only personal moral judgments until in some way given the sanction of law.[11]

This is not as objectionable as Rehnquist's critics portray it. Indeed, it is a position that has a good deal in common with a view held by Thomas Jefferson. During the years of Federalist control of the new government and the adoption of the despised Alien and Sedition Acts, the Republicans were confronted with a similar question. The Federalists argued that the Constitution was not limited to its text but, as a matter of law, embraced the entire common law tradition. Federalist Harrison Gray Otis argued that Article III of the Constitution "granted the federal courts common law jurisdiction over criminal cases, including sedition." He went beyond mere implication and claimed that Article III explicitly conferred such jurisdiction on the federal courts by providing that the judicial power should extend to "all cases arising under the Constitution." As this clearly meant something other than statutes, Otis concluded that "cases arising under the Constitution" were in fact cases arising under the common law, "the legal discretion which had been exercised in England since time immemorial."[12]

Jefferson and his party were outraged. To assume that the common law had been incorporated into the Constitution, Jefferson held, was not only a dangerous assumption; it was logically flawed. The law of the United States could not precede in time the establishment of the United States; the law became law only after there were "organs" established for declaring that law. Therefore, "the common law did not become, ipso facto, law on the new association; it could only become so by a positive adoption, & so far only as they were authorized to adopt." To preserve liberty, the Jeffersonians thought, it was necessary to preserve the Constitution inviolate. The common law arguments of the Federalists would stretch the Constitution into something the framers never intended, injecting into it all the uncertainties of English forms of jurisprudence and its unwritten constitution. In such a circumstance, the law would depend not on the stable and fixed provisions of the Constitution but only upon the fluctuating and uncertain opinions of judges.[13]

Moral judgments, common law rights, natural rights and natural law might all have great weight in political affairs; but under a written constitution of limited and enumerated powers they do not provide a basis for the exercise of power more extensive than is clearly provided. As Jefferson and Madison viewed the common law, so Rehnquist views contemporary moral judgments as a source of authority in constitutional adjudication.

But this is not to say that Rehnquist is somehow a proponent of an amoral politics. It is not a question of *whether* a polity will act on moral judgments but only a question of *where* those moral judgments are to be given vent. To believe, as many of his critics do, that it is legitimate for judges to give vent to them by importing their best moral judgments into their decisions is to believe the judiciary is somehow more above political reproach for bad decisions than history suggests. The modern advocates of a moral jurisprudence who argue that judges are and must be seen as the "voice and conscience of contemporary society" press upon the public a view that is "genuinely corrosive of the fundamental values of our democratic society."[14]

This is surely an important place for moral discourse in the political system created by the Constitution. Indeed, moral judgments are essential to a properly functioning government that claims to be popular in its foundation and operation. Individual moral judgments, Rehnquist has pointed out, afford a springboard for action in society. . . . They are without doubt the most common and most powerful wellsprings for action when one believes that questions of right and wrong are involved. Representative government is predicated upon the idea that one who feels deeply upon a question as a matter of conscience will seek out others of like view or will attempt to persuade others who do not initially share that view. When adherents to the belief become sufficiently numerous, he will have the necessary armaments required in a democratic society to press his views upon the elected representatives of the people and to have them embodied into positive law. . . .

It should not be easy for any one individual or group of individuals to impose their value judgments upon their fellow citizens who may disagree with those judgments. Indeed, it should not be easier just because the individual in question is a judge.[15]

Rehnquist's view is basically that of James Madison in *The Federalist,* No. 10. It is a belief in the system that is designed to draw unto itself all the opinions, passions and interests of the people and to refine and enlarge those opinions, passions and interests through a scheme of successive filtration; through deliberation a consensus is reached that reflects adequately the general public good as defined and refined by the multiplicity of interests that is the extended commercial republic. This is not to say that every decision of the majority is right or acceptable; there are the auxiliary precautions of the Constitution's interior contrivances to check that. But it is to say that there is no legitimate way the judicial branch can supplant the view of the people for one the judge likes better. As Rehnquist has said, "If we'd not . . . contain the courts in some way from negating a law that, although unwise in the eyes of some, is nonetheless rendered unconstitutional only by a considerable stretch of judicial imagination, we risk . . . 'Judicial Supremacy.'" The point is not that the majority will always reason right, that every law will be the embodiment of justice, or that "the policies resulting from the democratic process are better; only that judicial 'government by injunction' is, in the long run worse."[16]

The Constitutionalism of Common Sense

The philosophic assumptions underlying Chief Justice Rehnquist's jurisprudence merit a bit more explication. As a judge, Rehnquist does not always thoroughly explore the foundations of his own position; deciding concrete cases and controversies does not always require excursions into the philosophic and historical bases of a judge's views of the nature and limits of his power. Yet it is clear that Rehnquist is part of a larger and older tradition in constitutional thinking that rests on the assumption, as Hamilton once put it, that the "rules of legal interpretation are rules of *common sense,* adopted by the courts in the construction of the laws."[17]

For much of our history—certainly in the eighteenth and throughout the nineteenth and into the twentieth centuries—it was common sense to embrace the proposition that the Constitution as our fundamental law is a document with a discoverable meaning, one found in the words of the text as illuminated by the intentions of those who framed, proposed and ratified that text. This commonsense approach did not involve specific results in cases or controversies; rather, it was a mode of analysis that took the written Constitution seriously. This was the mainstream of legal and constitutional thinking from 1789 into the middle part of this century. It is this tradition to which Rehnquist turns in his constitutional jurisprudence.

James Madison and Alexander Hamilton, Thomas Jefferson and Edmund Randolph, John Marshall and Joseph Story, Felix Frankfurter and Robert Jackson, were among the greatest of our statesmen, lawyers and judges who took this approach to the Constitution and who understood that all branches of our government stood under it. And this view of the Constitution and its limiting character was assumed by judges, if not explicitly argued for, during most of our judicial history. In constitutional cases, judges began by seeking to discern the original meaning of the text. In other words, they *assumed* its fundamental intelligibility. They understood the Constitution as law binding judges no less than anyone else.

James Madison expressed the consensus on this matter almost two centuries ago. "If the sense in which the Constitution was accepted and ratified by the nation," he wrote, "be not the guide in expounding it, there can be no security for a consistent and stable government, more than for a faithful exercise of its powers."[18] This was the common sense of what legal interpretation was all about. Finding the sense or meaning of the Constitution as it was accepted and ratified by the nation, as Madison said, required serious consideration of the words in their general and popular usage. Beyond the obvious meaning, the words had to be read in the context in which they were written; attention had to be paid to their intended effects and consequences, to the spirit or reason of the law. This mode of analysis that looked to the intention of the lawgiver as expressed in the words of the law was widely accepted. It was, in short, so common as to be second nature.

So it was that Chief Justice John Marshall, writing in 1819 under the fitting pseudonym "Friend of the Constitution" in a defense of his controversial opinion in *McCulloch* v. *Maryland,*[19] stated that "the most complete evidence [is] that *intention* is the most sacred rule of interpretation."[20] In this Marshall was merely reiterating the understanding voiced at least as long ago as 1615 by Sir Edward Coke that "in acts of Parliament which are to be construed according to the intent and meaning of the makers of them, the original intent and meaning is to be observed."[21] As the example of Marshall makes clear, when the Americans parted from England, they did not abandon this bit of juridical wisdom.

As the early Americans moved from colonies to nation and framed and ratified the Constitution, they continued to understand that the text, as illuminated by intention, was the only legitimate means of interpretation. This is not to suggest that constitutional interpretation was or should be easy or simple. Neither is it to say that everyone in Madison's or any other time came to the same conclusions. Interpretation can be and often is a difficult intellectual task, and conscientious Americans have reached different, even contrary conclusions about the meaning of certain provisions. Hamilton and Jefferson, for example, differed on the constitutionality of a National Bank. So did Marshall and President Andrew Jackson. But the fact that two people conclude differently after a serious interpretive effort does not mean that there is no correct interpretation or that one interpretation cannot be deemed better than others. Most assuredly, it does not mean that the effort to construe the Constitution according to the sense in which it was ratified and accepted by the nation should be abandoned.

Some interpretations are straightforward—there can be no religious test for office. Some are less so. Others are difficult; some provisions are ambiguous. But it was understood from the beginning of our tradition of a written constitution binding on us all that we must take it seriously by conscientiously seeking the original intention. As one of the first justices of the Supreme Court, James Wilson (who, by the way, signed both the Declaration of Independence and the Constitution) said, "The first and governing maxim in the interpretation of [law] . . . is to discover the meaning of those who made it."[22] A much later, twentieth-century justice, the famous Oliver Wendell Holmes, Jr., put it much the same way. A constitutional amendment, he wrote, should be read in a "sense most obvious to the common understanding at the time of its adoption."[23]

This commonsense approach to interpretation constituted the received *tradition* of our commitment to the idea of the rule of law. It was not deemed quaint or archaic to suggest the Constitution was law limiting all governmental power, including judicial power. Indeed, to have argued otherwise would have been considered bizarre. But during the past thirty years or so a radically new view of the Constitution has appeared. This new and radical approach holds that the Constitution's original meaning either cannot be discerned or, if discerned, cannot—more accurately, should not—be applied today. The general belief is that "judicial decisions should be gauged by their results and not by . . . their coincidence with a set of allegedly consistent doctrinal principles."[24] This new jurisprudence argues that judges act properly when they seek to infuse the Constitution with new meanings derived from their perceptions of contemporary morality. It is only a matter of allowing judges to pour fresh ideological wine into the old constitutional bottle.

The major source of this new jurisprudence has been the law schools. In recent decades we have seen, as Judge Robert Bork has put it, a "torrent of constitutional theorizing . . . pouring from America's law schools."[25] Consider this new approach to the Constitution as expressed by three leading scholars. Ronald Dworkin, for example, has argued that

> courts . . . should work out principles of legality, equality, and the rest, revise those principles from time to time in light of what seems to the Court as fresh moral insight, and judge the acts of Congress, the states, and the president accordingly.[26]

Laurence Tribe has suggested that

> the Constitution is an intentionally incomplete, often deliberately indeterminate structure for the participatory evolution of political ideals and governmental practices. . . . The structural norms through which a substantive value is best preserved may be expected to vary over time and from one setting to the next.[27]

The last of this trio, Philip Bobbitt, has said that

> constitutional decisionmaking has . . . an expressive function. . . . The Constitution is our Mona Lisa, our Eiffel Tower, our Marseillaise. . . . [I]f we accept the expressive function of the Court, then it sometimes be in advance of and even in contrast to, the largely inchoate notions of the people generally.[28]

However poetic these formulations, to view the Constitution as infinitely mutable and to place such a soft wax in the judges' hands are to deny the document's substance and lasting power. Ultimately, this new jurisprudence denigrates the Constitution's status as law.

It is hard to imagine Madison or Hamilton, Jefferson or Marshall discoursing about the Constitution as our Mona Lisa and referring to the "inchoate notions of the people." For they believed—and with considerable evidence—that they had crafted a document that would well serve the ordinary and free people who would live under it. There are today, as Chief Justice Rehnquist has noted, "currents of ferment in the legal world that seek to revise or even overthrow traditional notions of judicial interpretation."[29] Not only is the modern theorizing at odds with our past, both with the intentions of the Founders and with the legal tradition that came to be built upon it; it is at odds with that sturdy foundation of common sense upon which our entire constitutional and legal edifice rests.

It is precisely this new fashion of radical imprecision, of meandering moralizing in the law that Chief Justice Rehnquist stands against. His jurisprudence is an effort to retain—perhaps more accurately to resurrect—the older and more prudent tradition of the Founders' belief in language as the source of limitation on government through the mechanism of the written law.

Language, Law and Limited Government

There is a stunning simplicity to Rehnquist's understanding of how judges ought to go about their business; in a legal world increasingly muddled by theoretical jargon, his commonsense approach is startling. But in its very simplicity lies its power. At the most basic level, Rehnquist approaches judicial interpretation at the level of the purpose of language. Judicial interpretation means nothing more complicated than construing such things as contracts, statutes, rules or constitutional provisions, "all of which are embodied in written words." As a result, he has noted,

> it is essential for those engaged in judicial interpretation to realize that the underpinnings of our legal system depend upon the assumption that such words have an objective meaning—one set of words, that is, has a different meaning from another set. This is not to say that the meaning of a particular set of words will be crystal clear to each judge who is called upon to interpret it, but only that those judges, familiar with ordinary English usage, will be able to agree that the words at their broadest embrace only so much, and necessarily exclude matter beyond that.[30]

The idea of "objective meaning" lies at the core of Rehnquist's theory of judging, which views the act of judging as limited by the text and intention of the written law. This is especially critical in an age given to thinking that interpretation of law need not differ from the interpretation of literature, poetry, or scripture. In Rehnquist's view, there is a latitude in the latter not allowed in the former because in law, the written word is "used for a particular purpose—to obtain the consent or agreement of someone beside the author of the words to a particular proposition thought to be embodied in the words." The "entire legal system is built on the principle that written words generally do have a meaning which will be apparent to the parties consenting to be bound by them."[31]

Disagreement over meaning does not disprove the possibility of an "objective meaning" waiting to be given judicial expression through interpretation. Without the assumption that the words of the law have "an objective content" the "whole notion of popular government in representative democracy would really be quite meaningless." Further, even though the Constitution may be seen as resting at a higher level of generality than ordinary law, that generality does not eclipse the objectivity of the meaning of the words used in the Constitution. If one assumes that the words contained in the Constitution have no objective meaning,

> then the whole idea of a constitutional republic is a "tale told by an idiot, full of sound and fury, but signifying nothing." If the words embodied in a particular clause do not have some objective meaning, including some matter and excluding other matter, then the close votes on the floor of the convention and in the ratifying conventions . . . really amount to nothing.[32]

To Rehnquist's way of thinking, such an assumption would be more than erroneous; it would be absurd.

For Rehnquist, the belief in a discoverable "objective meaning" must be the basic principle, the simple faith, a jurist brings to the act of judging. Whereas subjectivity may be not only permissible but encouraged in literary interpretation, it is to be avoided in legal and constitutional interpretation because given the political premises of the law and the theory of limited government, such subjectivity is simply illegitimate. It is precisely the notion of objective meaning, judicially discerned, that legitimates the power of judicial review in the first place. As Rehnquist has said:

> Judicial interpretation . . . involves the determination of what particular sets of words mean, and in that sense may be thought to be a subspecies of interpretation along with literary criticism and other kinds of interpretation of words. But the poet, the dramatist, the director, the reader are all free to import their own meaning to words in a way that judges

are not. If in reading a poem or staging a play I wish to totally depart
from the normal meaning of the words and derive from them a highly
unusual meaning, I may do myself a disservice but I harm no one else.
But if as a judge I deliberately choose to import completely idiosyncratic
meaning to the words of a statute or of a constitutional provision I am
dealing with words whose ordinary meaning other people have probably
relied on in giving their consent that a bill in question become a law,
or that a constitutional amendment be ratified. The difference seems to
me fairly obvious. It is like the difference between cheating at solitaire
and cheating at bridge.[33]

Conclusion

The idea of the consent of the governed—that law embodies consent—is the heart of Chief Justice Rehnquist's belief in the limits of
judging. Because the Constitution and the laws embody the intentions
of those who wrote and ratified them, judges are *morally* obligated to
defer to those intentions by the principle of popular government; similarly, they are *constitutionally* obligated to defer to those intentions by
the principle of limited government secured by the written law.

Rehnquist is no longer the lone voice on the Supreme Court. With
the advent of the other Reagan appointees—but especially of Antonin
Scalia—there is a rising chorus now being heard in praise of judicial
restraint. While such a view is still derided as conservative by those
fond of the judicial policymaking of the last quarter century, it is not
simply so; it is surely not so in the ideological sense. Ultimately, judicial
restraint and its antecedent beliefs in original intention and the "objective meaning" of legal language are matters neither of liberalism nor
of conservatism: they are matters of constitutionalism. And no one has
given clearer expression to that understanding of constitutionalism
during the past two decades than has William Rehnquist.

Notes

I am indebted to Eric Jaso for his good services in assisting with the
research for this article.

1. T. S. Eliot, "Burnt Norton," *T. S. Eliot: The Complete Poems & Plays,
1909–1950* (New York: Harcourt Brace Jovanovich, 1980), p. 121. Reprinted
by permission of the publisher.

2. See, for example, Owen Fiss and Charles Krauthammer, "The Rehnquist
Court: A Return to the Antebellum Constitution," *The New Republic,* March
10, 1982, pp. 14–21; David L. Shapiro, "Mr. Justice Rehnquist: A Preliminary
View," *Harvard Law Review* 90 (1976): 293; Thomas Kleven, "The Constitutional Philosophy of William H. Rehnquist," *Vermont Law Review* 8 (1983):

1; John Denvir, "Justice Rehnquist and Constitutional Interpretation," *Hastings Law Journal* 34 (1983): 1011; Robert C. Lind, Jr., "Justice Rehnquist: First Amendment Speech in the Labor Context," *Hastings Constitutional Law Quarterly* 8 (1983): 93; and, for the most bizarre account, Harry V. Jaffa, "What Were the Original Intentions of the Framers of the Constitution of the United States?" *University of Puget Sound Law Review* 10 (1987): 351.

3. William H. Rehnquist, "The Notion of a Living Constitution," *Texas Law Review* 54 (1976): 693, 697, 699. See *The Federalist,* No. 78, ed. J. Cooke (Middletown: Wesleyan University Press, 1961).

4. William H. Rehnquist, "Government by Cliche," *Missouri Law Review* 45 (1980): 379, 384.

5. *Wallace* v. *Jaffree,* 105 S.Ct. 2479, 2520 (1985), dissenting opinion.

6. *Nevada* v. *Hall,* 440 U.S. 410, 433 (1978), dissenting opinion.

7. *Garcia* v. *San Antonio Metropolitan Transit Authority,* 105 S.Ct. 1005, 1034 (1985), dissenting opinion; and Rehnquist, "The Notion of a Living Constitution," pp. 695, 706, 696. See also Hamilton's remarks in *The Federalist,* No. 78, pp. 527–528.

8. For an extended discussion of this point, see Gary L. McDowell, "Federalism and Civic Virtue: The Anti-Federalists and the Constitution," in Robert A. Goldwin and William A. Schambra, eds., *How Federal Is the Constitution?* (Washington, D.C.: American Enterprise Institute, 1987), pp. 122–144.

9. See Jaffa, "What Were the Original Intentions?" and Leonard Levy, *Original Intent and the Framers' Constitution* (New York: Macmillan, 1988).

10. William H. Rehnquist, "Isaac Parker, Bill Sikes, and the Rule of Law," *University of Arkansas at Little Rock Law Journal* 6 (1983): 485, 499.

11. Rehnquist, "The Notion of a Living Constitution," p. 704.

12. As quoted in Gary L. McDowell, *Equity and the Constitution* (Chicago: University of Chicago Press, 1982), pp. 56–57.

13. Ibid., pp. 51–69.

14. Rehnquist, "The Notion of a Living Constitution," p. 706.

15. Ibid., p. 705.

16. William H. Rehnquist, "Point-Counterpoint: The Evolution of American Political Philosophy," *Vanderbilt Law Review* 34 (1981): 249, 263. See Nancy Maveety, "The Populist of the Adversary Society: The Jurisprudence of Justice Rehnquist" (unpublished ms.), p. 43.

17. *The Federalist,* No. 83, p. 559.

18. James Madison to Henry Lee, *The Writings of James Madison,* ed. G. Hunt (Philadelphia: Lippincott, 1900–1910), vol. 9, p. 191.

19. *McCulloch* v. *Maryland,* 17 U.S. 316 (1812).

20. G. Gunther, ed., *John Marshall's Defense of McCulloch v. Maryland* (Stanford, Calif.: Stanford University Press, 1969), p. 167.

21. *Magdalen College Case,* 11 Co. Rep. 66, 73, 77 Eng. Rep. 1235, 1245 (K.B.1615). For a superb general account of these issues, see Raoul Berger, "Some Reflections on Interpretivism," *The George Washington Law Review* 55 (1986): 1.

22. *The Works of James Wilson,* ed. R. McCloskey (Cambridge, Mass.: Harvard University Press, 1967), vol. 1, p. 75.

23. *Eisner* v. *Macomber,* 252 U.S. 189, 220 (1920), dissenting opinion.

24. Arthur S. Miller and Ronald F. Howell, "The Myth of Neutrality in Constitutional Adjudication," *The University of Chicago Law Review* 27 (1960): 661, 690–691.

25. Robert H. Bork, Foreword to Gary L. McDowell, *The Constitution and Contemporary Constitutional Theory* (Cumberland, Va.: Center for Judicial Studies, 1985), p. v.

26. Ronald Dworkin, *Taking Rights Seriously* (Cambridge, Mass.: Harvard University Press, 1976), p. 137.

27. Laurence Tribe, *American Constitutional Law* (Mineola, N.Y.: Foundation Press, 1978), p. iii.

28. Philip Bobbitt, *Constitutional Fate* (New York: Oxford University Press, 1982), pp. 185, 211.

29. William Rehnquist, "The Nature of Judicial Interpretation" (Speech delivered at the American Studies Center Conference on The Judicial Interpretation of the Constitution, Washington, D.C., June 12, 1987), p. 1.

30. Ibid., p. 2.

31. Ibid., pp. 3, 4.

32. Ibid., pp. 6–8.

33. Ibid., p. 10.

About the Contributors

Mark J. Rozell is assistant professor of political science at Mary Washington College, Fredericksburg, Virginia. He is author of *The Press and the Carter Presidency* (1989). Rozell has published articles in *Political Science Quarterly, Journal of Law and Politics, Modern Age* and several other journals.

James F. Pontuso is assistant professor of political science at Hampden-Sydney College, Hampden-Sydney, Virginia. He has contributed articles to such journals as *Modern Age, The Political Science Reviewer* and *Survey.* Pontuso is the author of a forthcoming book on Aleksandr Solzhenitsyn's political thought.

John Wesley Young is assistant professor of political science and history at Andrews University, Berrien Springs, Michigan. From 1980 to 1985 he served as an editorial assistant on the staff of *The Papers of George Washington.* Young is currently writing a book on Orwell's Newspeak and its Nazi and Communist antecedents.

David E. Marion is chair of the Department of Political Science at Hampden-Sydney College. His teaching and research have covered the fields of public administration, public policy and constitutional law. His essays and articles have appeared in a number of scholarly journals and books including *The Review of Politics, Administration and Society, Presidential Studies Quarterly* and *The Constitutional Polity.* He presently serves on the Speakers Bureau of the National Commission on the Bicentennial.

Roger M. Barrus is associate professor of political science at Hampden-Sydney College. He is writing a book on Mormonism and the limits of religious tolerance.

Jeffrey J. Poelvoorde is assistant professor of political science at Converse College, Spartanburg, South Carolina. He has published articles in refereed journals in the fields of American politics and political theory. He has taught political science at Dickinson College, Carleton College and the College of William and Mary.

A. Craig Waggaman is assistant professor of political science at Radford University, Radford, Virginia. His teaching and research cover the fields of international affairs, Latin American politics and political thought.

Sidney A. Pearson, Jr., is professor of political science at Radford University. He is author of *Arthur Koestler* (1978) and editor of *The Constitutional Polity: Essays on the Founding Principles of American Politics* (1983). Pearson is editing the public and private papers of Arthur J. Goldberg. He is also writing with Goldberg a constitutional law casebook for undergraduate studies.

Robert A. Strong is chair of the Politics Department at Washington and Lee University. He has held teaching positions at the University College of Wales and Tulane University. In 1988–1989 he was an American Political Science Association Congressional Fellow. He is the author of *Bureaucracy and Statesmanship: Henry Kissinger and the Making of American Foreign Policy* (1986) as well as numerous articles on foreign affairs, arms control and the presidency.

John Eastby is assistant professor of political science at St. Cloud State University, St. Cloud, Minnesota. He is author of *Functionalism and Interdependence* (1986). Eastby's current research focuses on international organizations and the European Economic Community.

Edward S. Twardy is associate dean for academic affairs and associate professor, Division of Continuing Education, University of Virginia. Formerly a professor in the Department of Public Administration at the University of Nebraska, his current research emphasizes organizational theory and public management.

Gary L. McDowell is vice president for legal and public affairs at the National Legal Center for the Public Interest in Washington, D.C. From 1985 to 1987 he was associate director of public affairs at the U.S. Department of Justice where he served as chief speech writer to Attorney-General Edwin Meese III. His most recent book is *Curbing the Courts: The Constitution and the Limits of Judicial Power* (1988). This chapter was prepared while the author was a Bradley Resident Scholar at the Center for Judicial Studies and a fellow at the Woodrow Wilson International Center for Scholars at the Smithsonian Institution.

Index